AGENTS AND MERCHANTS

JACK M. SOSIN

Agents
and Merchants

*British Colonial Policy and
the Origins of the American Revolution,
1763–1775*

UNIVERSITY OF NEBRASKA PRESS

LINCOLN   1965

Publishers on the Plains

UNP

Contents

List of Illustrations

Key to Abbreviations

Add. MSS.	Additional Manuscripts, British Museum, London
C.O.	Colonial Office, Public Record Office, London
H.M.C.	Royal Historical Manuscripts Commission
P.A.C.	Public Archives of Canada, Ottawa
P.R.O.	Public Record Office, London
S.C.H. & G.M.	*South Carolina Historical and Genealogical Magazine*
S.P.	State Papers, Public Record Office, London
T.	Treasury, Public Record Office, London

Introduction

BRITISH colonial policy in the decade preceding the American Revolution has long attracted historians, for in a few crucial years an empire which had endured, prospered, and expanded for almost two centuries was lost to England. Seeking to understand this momentous development, scholars have asked why in the years following the Peace of Paris did succeeding British ministers adopt those ill-fated measures destined to disrupt the Old Empire. By what process did they arrive at these programs? To what extent, if any, did they consider the interests of the North American colonists for whom they legislated? In answering these questions, historians have given divergent and often contradictory explanations. This might be expected insofar as the variety of the past lends itself to many interpretations, and answers to some historical questions may be contingent upon the assumptions, background, and interests of the individual scholar. But interpretations of British policy leading to the American Revolution have varied much beyond the legitimate limits allowed by variety of outlook and research techniques.

The amount of research on imperial policy for the period 1763 to 1775 has not been commensurate with the historical interest in the subject. With so much of the relevant evidence close at hand, British scholars hitherto have not devoted much attention to the problem.[1]

1. Bernard Donoughue's *British Politics And The American Revolution. The Path to War, 1773–1775* (London, 1964) came to hand as this work went to the printer. It seems to substantiate many of the conclusions expressed in the final chapters of this book.

Introduction

Perhaps they have deferred to their colleagues across the Atlantic. But American historians of the Revolution, emphasizing primarily the colonial reaction to imperial measures, too frequently have been satisfied with a cursory examination of statutes, reports, tracts, and unreliable Parliamentary declamation. Supposition, innuendo, and speculation have replaced systematic research in the archives. In supporting the arguments of the patriot protagonists of the Revolution, some recent historians have not made an effort to discover what English administrators were attempting and why.[2] Neither have they demonstrated an appreciation of the work of those historians of the imperial school who have made the effort. Yet even Osgood, Beer, Gipson, and Andrews for the most part did not carry their intensive investigations beyond 1765.[3]

Colonial historians often discuss imperial policy in terms of mercantilism, a structured pattern of governmental activity wherein narrow economic interest underlying British measures ignored the needs of a mature colonial society. This technique, imposing an artificial simplification on a complex administrative system, also has resulted in confusion and disagreement among scholars. John C. Miller claimed that the imperial government did not follow the welfare of all subjects but simply the economic interests of British merchants and manufacturers, who, pursuing their own interests at the expense of the colonists, determined imperial legislation. British laws restraining the provincial economy demonstrated that "a handful of English capitalists carried more weight at Westminster than the welfare of millions of Americans." Claude H. Van Tyne, sharing this view, added another charge. Ministers at Whitehall, concerned only with British profits and acting on information only indirectly acquired from America, were oblivious to the needs of the colonists across the Atlantic. Van Tyne did concede, however, that British merchants, realizing in the last critical months before the outbreak of the Revolution that their profits were endangered,

2. See the comment of the late Professor Richard Pares in his review of Robert E. Brown, *Middle-Class Democracy and the Revolution in Massachusetts, 1691–1780* (Ithaca, N.Y., 1956) in *English Historical Review*, LXXXII (1957), 122.

3. At the time of writing, Lawrence Henry Gipson has yet to complete his multi-volume work *The British Empire Before the American Revolution* (10 vols. to date, Caldwell, Idaho, and New York, 1936—).

sought to ease the burden on the colonists. But the government, controlled by "the great families, the landowners, the squires, bent on realizing an imperial idea fated to stir rebellion in America," ignored their last-minute pleas. These views were characteristic not only of American scholars. John A. Doyle, an English historian, condemned almost all British statesmen of the period for approaching colonial questions wholly insensible to the importance of understanding, "still more of conciliating, colonial sentiment." [4]

Disagreement by historians on the extent to which imperial administrators considered the needs of the colonists is further reflected in divergent opinions on the institution of the colonial agency, a rudimentary imperial lobby in London. While scholars have studied the activities of this group—mainly from an institutional view[5]—one writer denied its influence in imperial administration,

4. John C. Miller, *Origins of the American Revolution* (Boston, 1943), pp. 18, 23; Claude H. Van Tyne, *England & America. Rivals in the American Revolution* (Cambridge and New York, 1927), pp. 31, 40, 58; and John A. Doyle, "The Quarrel with Great Britain, 1761–1776," in A. W. Ward, G. W. Prothero, and Stanley Leathes (eds.), *The Cambridge Modern History* (13 vols., London, 1902–1912), VII, 147.

5. Alfred Owen Aldridge, "Benjamin Franklin as Georgia Agent," *Georgia Review*, VI (1952), 161–173; Marguerite Appleton, "The Agents of the New England Colonies in the Revolutionary Period," *New England Quarterly*, VI (1933), 381–387; Beverley W. Bond, Jr., "The Colonial Agent as A Popular Representative," *Political Science Quarterly*, XXXV (1920), 372–392; James W. Barnwell, "Hon. Charles Garth, M.P., The Last Colonial Agent of South Carolina in England, and Some of his Work," *S.C.H. & G.M.*, XXVI (1925), 67–92; James J. Burns, *The Colonial Agents of New England* (Washington, D.C., 1935); Samuel James Ervin, Jr., "The Provincial Agents of North Carolina," *The James Sprunt Studies in History and Political Science*, Vol. XVI, No. ii, 63–77; Malcolm Freiberg, "William Bollan, Agent of Massachusetts," *More Books: The Bulletin of the Boston Public Library*, 6th Ser., XXXIII (1948), 43–53, 90–100, 135–145, 168–182, 212–220; Ross J. S. Hoffman (ed.), *Edmund Burke, New York Agent, with his letters to the New York Assembly and intimate correspondence with Charles O'Hara 1761–1776* (Philadelphia, 1956); Edward P. Lilly, *The Colonial Agents of New York and New Jersey* (Washington, D.C., 1936); Ella Lonn, *The Colonial Agents of the Southern Colonies* (Chapel Hill, 1945); Lewis B. Namier, "Charles Garth, Agent for South Carolina," *English Historical Review*, LIV (1939), 632–652; Lillian M. Penson, *The Colonial Agents of the British West Indies: a study in colonial administration mainly in the eighteenth century* (London, 1924); Calvin Stebbin, "Edmund Burke, his Services as Agent to the Province of New York," American Antiquarian Society *Proceedings*, new Ser., IX (1893), 89–101; Edwin P. Tanner, "Colonial Agencies in England during the

maintaining that in a conflict of interest the British merchant emerged triumphant over the spokesmen of the colonists in England, the provincial agents. Contrasting sharply with this emphatic declaration is the equally positive assertion of Lawrence Henry Gipson: so great was the influence of the agents that the government at Whitehall made no major decision affecting the colonies without carefully considering their arguments and advice.[6] Lewis B. Namier suggested a middle position between these two opposing views, although he too perceived an economic motive in British policy and did not distinguish between the goals of the Rockingham Whigs and their associates on the one hand, and Lord North and his supporters on the other. Sir Lewis seemed certain that to the Whigs too, "trade was the soul of Empire. . . ."[7] Consequently the opinions of merchants did carry weight at Whitehall, but when their interests seemed to vary with those of the colonies, the provincial agents solicited the support of the English mercantile community and, by employing a policy of persuasion, obtained practical adjustments. By the pre-Revolutionary decade, agents and merchants cooperated, and between this rudimentary lobby or concert and specific administrations a "system of reasonable and friendly 'give and take'" existed.[8]

While Namier and Gipson minimized the conflicts between agents and merchants, other writers denied the exclusive economic orientation of British colonial policy and the assumption that the material interests of England and her colonies were incompatible. On the contrary, so closely integrated were the economies of the mother country and the provinces, argued Oliver M. Dickerson, that the

Eighteenth Century," *Political Science Quarterly*, XVI (1901), 24–49; Norman B. Wilkinson, "The Colonial Voice in London," *The Historian*, II (1940), 22–36; Mabel Pauline Wolff, *The Colonial Agency of Pennsylvania, 1712–1757* (Philadelphia, 1933); and John Joseph Zimmerman, "Benjamin Franklin: A Study of Pennsylvania Politics and the Colonial Agency, 1755–1775" (Ph.D. dissertation, University of Michigan, 1956).

6. Winfred T. Root, "The American Revolution Considered," in "The American Revolution: A Symposium," *Canadian Historical Review*, XXIII (1942), 21; and Gipson, *The British Empire Before the American Revolution*, I, 19.

7. Lewis B. Namier, *England in the Age of the American Revolution* (London, 1930), p. 45.

8. Namier, "Charles Garth, Agent for South Carolina," pp. 637–638.

English were financially committed to and dependent upon continued colonial prosperity. Charles McLean Andrews even maintained that British commercial legislation after 1763 aimed primarily not to advance the interests of British merchants, but rather to conserve and increase imperial revenue as well as other considerations, such as the needs of the state, legislative authority, and executive prerogative. Despite the variety of aims, imperial administrators operating within an inflexible system adhered rigidly to political and commercial principles.[9]

Clearly historians disagree over the motives behind imperial policy, the relationship between colonial and British interests, and to what extent imperial statesmen concerned themselves with the views and wishes of the American colonials.

The diversity of interpretation stems perhaps not only from insufficient research and oversimplification but also from the intellectual and psychological needs of scholars as distinct from those of practical men of affairs. Seeking to make their interpretations "meaningful," historians may have considered British measures as part of "policy" in the sense of a deliberate comprehensive plan. But this type of rationalizing is, as George Unwin warned some years ago, "more often an illusion of the scholarly mind than a fact of history."[10] May this not be the case with some interpretations of British policy?

Imperial measures were not necessarily specific manifestations of theoretical doctrines such as mercantilism, although officials often couch their reports in its language. Frequently, beneath formal reports and Parliamentary rhetoric, ordinary administrative and political forces operated. The relatively few men who exercised political power in Georgian England were not intellectuals or scholars with the need to operate from involved theories. They were primarily administrators who arrived at particular solutions for specific problems as these arose. It was not ideologies or institutions that figured critically in policy decisions, but the political capabilities

---

9. Oliver M. Dickerson, *The Navigation Acts and the American Revolution* (Philadelphia, 1951), p. 163; Charles McLean Andrews, *The Colonial Period of American History* (4 vols., New Haven, 1934–1938), IV, 269n1, 426, 299.

10. George Unwin, *Studies in Economic History: The Collected Papers of George Unwin*, ed. Richard H. Tawney (London, 1927), pp. 184.

and experience of ministers and the nature of the problems they faced. Experienced, politically strong administrations made their decisions at professional boards. Questions of highest policy lay with the cabinet, or a high-ranking inner circle within government. During inept, inexperienced, or politically divided administrations decisions were made either by individual ministers or outside regular governmental levels at informal sessions with private interest groups. The present work is an attempt to utilize this framework.

This study moreover is an attempt to contribute to a further understanding of British policy by evaluating the role that colonial agents and British merchants played in imperial administration. Gipson's biography of Jared Ingersoll, sometime agent for Connecticut, and the brief, provocative treatment by Sir Lewis Namier of the agents and merchants Charles Garth, John Thomlinson, Jr., and Anthony Bacon [11] during the Grenville administration aroused the author's interest in the problem. Specifically, he has attempted to analyze the influence of the agents and merchants, and the limitations imposed on them by the vicissitudes of colonial politics and the rise of the Revolutionary movement in America. Rather than dealing with all of the activities of the agents and merchants, particularly those of a local or parochial nature, the author has concentrated on those issues relevant to the development of the Revolution and, as the committee of correspondence of South Carolina put it, where the general interest and liberties of America were concerned.

In the dozen or so years preceding the American Revolution there existed in London a rudimentary lobby, not a fully developed organization in the modern sense, but a concert of men who acted together usually to achieve specific legislative or administrative acts. Although motivated for different reasons, these agents and merchants did join to play a highly significant role in the administrative process of the British Empire. In general they worked together, not at cross purposes, for the aims of the merchants and of the agents

11. Lawrence Henry Gipson, *Jared Ingersoll: A study of American loyalism in relation to British colonial government* (New Haven, 1920); Chapter IV, "The House of Commons and America," in Namier, *England in the Age of the American Revolution*, pp. 285–327; and Namier, "Charles Garth, Agent for South Carolina," pp. 632–652.

were the same, although in supporting the colonists British merchants may have been furthering their own economic interests. But to the merchants the well-being of the mother country also meant the well-being of the North American provinces, and vice versa. Indeed, some merchants, Barlow Trecothick, Dennys DeBerdt, and John Thomlinson, Jr., who were also agents, recognized this. They saw no conflict between their two roles. The interests of the two groups were generally identical, and British administrators, more concerned with the realities of governmental administration than with ideological abstractions, consulted these men familiar with conditions in America.

On almost any particular question relating to the North American colonies—paper money, trade, revenue, or the Mutiny Acts, for example—the agents and merchants presented the views of the provincials and were able to win concessions or important modification of impending legislation by suggesting practical alternatives and avoiding the crucial issue of British sovereignty. But in the closing years of the pre-Revolutionary decade, several factors operated against the lobby. The pressure of the merchants was effective only when supported by the various ministries. Moreover, apathy and political factionalism, under the guise of constitutional principle, in some provincial assemblies curtailed the effectiveness of the agents. Disputes among the various branches of the colonial governments further limited, if not precluded, the choice of agents in other colonies. But most important was the identification of some agents with the growing revolutionary movement in America. As the number of agents decreased those few who remained, such as Benjamin Franklin and Arthur Lee, became identified in the minds of the British ministers with a colonial party challenging the authority of the British government and enunciating a doctrine denying the sovereignty of the mother country. The challenge to British sovereignty proved decisive in frustrating the efforts of the agents and merchants.

The author hopes that in a particular sense this study is objective —that it follows the evidence. It is biased in that it is primarily an attempt to understand *British* administration and policy, and treats the colonial viewpoint only incidentally as it affected decisions made in London. Naturally, British policy and the colonial reaction are related. What is important, however, in understanding the American viewpoint and the ensuing Revolution is not what was necessarily true about British measures, but what the Whig patriots believed to be true. Yet historians must do more than merely accept and register colonial protests of British misrule. They must discover how, why, and by what means a significant element of American society came to believe that British rule threatened essential liberties. The agents and merchants in London were their prime source of information, and while the Whig leaders may have been aroused by false impressions from their correspondents in the imperial capital, patriot hostility to British rule after 1763 also stemmed from tensions in colonial society and from the relations between those who held and those who aspired to political power.[12]

12. Scholars might do well to consider Sir Lewis Namier's suggestion that history is made by men who do things both infinitely smaller and infinitely greater than they know. Historians of the American Revolution might also profitably consider the provocative thesis of Bernard A. Bailyn, who points out that in the rebellion of 1689 which overthrew the Dominion of New England under Sir Edmund Andros, it was neither ideology, religious belief, abstract political principles, nor party loyalty, but political power that separated the rival politicians. He further suggests that a divergence between political and social leadership at the upper echelon created by great economic and social fluidity resulted in permanent conflict in the colonies. Men who had risen to social and economic prominence sought concomitant political power denied them by a previously established group, and in the name of legislative rights attacked those associated with imperial or proprietary authority. Bernard Bailyn, "Politics and Social Structure in Virginia," in James Morton Smith (ed.), *Seventeenth-Century America: Essays in Colonial History* (Chapel Hill, 1959), pp. 90–115; and Bailyn, "Communications and Trade: The Atlantic in the Seventeenth Century," *Journal of Economic History*, XIII (1953), 378–397.

AGENTS AND MERCHANTS

CHAPTER I

Merchants, Agents, and
Practical Issues

I

ALTHOUGH the American Revolution ruptured the political ties between Great Britain and America, it demonstrated the viability of the commercial empire uniting the English communities of the Atlantic. Within a few years after the United States had won their independence, Anglo-American commerce had returned to century-old channels of trade. British merchants, then as before, played a vital role in the economies of both societies by mobilizing credit and marketing the produce of America and manufactured goods of Britain.

By the middle of the eighteenth century there resided in England some 2900 eminent merchants. Since commercial activities had not as yet become specialized, they performed general economic services rather than specific commercial tasks. The merchants came predominately from the middle elements in British society—a group generally sympathetic with American ideas during the Revolution[1] —and particularly from retail trade, a socially inferior group. They did not, however, constitute a mercantile patrician class, for the fluidity of English society did not preclude movement from one

1. Vincent T. Harlow, *The Founding of the Second British Empire, 1763–1793* (London, 1952), p. 151.

stratum to another. Since no institutional barriers prevented a man from engaging in trade, the merchants came from diverse origins and entered the business world by many paths. Consequently the composition of the mercantile community constantly changed. Important distinctions within this amorphous community nonetheless did exist, differences between the merchants of London and those of the outports[2] or the interior manufacturing towns. Indeed the metropolitan merchant and his smaller counterpart in the provinces, differing in ideas and interests, were often opposed on economic matters.

Even in London significant differences existed, particularly basic political antagonisms between the great merchant financiers and the smaller traders. The "City" of London in a restricted sense consisted of a small number of persons, closely connected with whatever government happened to be in power and concerned primarily with the machinery for creating and mobilizing credit. The great figures in this circle were no longer concerned purely with commercial activities, but with capital and credit primarily for overseas trade and public finance. In a broader sense the "City" included the "middling" men, small merchants, tradesmen, and master craftsmen. And if the financial interest supported government, the more numerous group almost always opposed it. Leaders of Parliamentary factions could appeal to them and the country gentry against an administration by invoking outworn prejudices and sentiments.

The leaders of the commercial and trading group of London, for their part, were particularly adept at organizing extra-Parliamentary pressure. Politicians such as Chatham, Shelburne, and Rockingham—consistent supporters of the American colonists— cultivated the metropolitan merchants in their struggles with government. Shelburne and Chatham relied on William Beckford, a West India planter, merchant, and onetime Lord Mayor of London. In the City of London the chief supporter of the Rockingham faction

2. In the generation or two preceding the American Revolution there possibly existed a tendency for various outports to specialize in trade, Liverpool in the slave trade, and Glasgow in the Chesapeake tobacco trade. Jacob M. Price, "The Rise of Glasgow in the Chesapeake Tobacco Trade, 1707–1775," *William and Mary Quarterly*, 3rd Ser., XI (1954), 190.

was Barlow Trecothick, the most influential of all the London merchants trading to America. The Whigs were also connected with William Baker, son of Alderman Sir William Baker, an important merchant in the colonial trade, friend and adherent of the Duke of Newcastle, and one of his chief advisers on American affairs.[3]

Business and politics in England during the eighteenth century rested largely on personal relations. Ties of amity, marriage, and blood also connected the Atlantic trading community of Great Britain, the West Indies, and the North American colonies. Many English merchants spent some time in the colonies establishing and cementing contacts. American residents were common to many Scottish firms engaged in the Glasgow-Chesapeake tobacco trade. Later in matters of trade they often relied on the judgment of their overseas correspondents. Frequently religious beliefs tied men in transatlantic economic ventures. The Quaker merchants of Philadelphia dealt almost exclusively with such coreligionists in England as David Barclay,[4] whose son in 1774 succeeded Barlow Trecothick as spokesman for the merchants supporting America.

Many businesses were in reality Anglo-American family concerns. Customarily one brother engaged in business in England and another in the colonies. Thomas and John Bromfield are one example. Stephen Apthorp headed the family firm in Bristol while his brother Thomas ran the business in Massachusetts. Henry Cruger was prominent in New York mercantile circles while his son established himself in England and represented Bristol in the Parliament elected in 1774. Charles Crokatt, a London merchant largely concerned in the rice trade, trafficked with America, especially South Carolina, where his brother resided for some time and acted as agent for the province.[5] One noteworthy transatlantic house was that of DeBerdt,

3. Walter E. Minchinton, "The Merchants in England in the Eighteenth Century," *Explorations in Entrepreneurial History*, X (1957), 62, 65, 67, 68; Lucy S. Sutherland, "The City of London in Eighteenth-Century Politics," in Richard Pares and A. J. P. Taylor (eds.), *Essays Presented to Sir Lewis Namier* (London, 1956), pp. 49–51, 54, 57, 67–69.

4. Frederick B. Tolles, *Meeting House and Counting House: The Quaker Merchants of Colonial Philadelphia, 1682–1763* (Chapel Hill, 1948), pp. 90–91; Price, "Rise of Glasgow in the Chesapeake Tobacco Trade," p. 193.

5. Kenneth Wiggins Porter, *The Jacksons and the Lees. Two Generations of Massachusetts Merchants, 1765–1844* (2 vols., Cambridge, Mass., 1937), I, 178. On the

3

Burkett and Sayre. Dennys DeBerdt, at one time agent for the Massachusetts House of Representatives, was the senior partner while Stephen Sayre of New Jersey and New York was the junior member of the firm. Another agent-merchant was Barlow Trecothick, a Londoner who for a time settled in Boston and then married the daughter of Charles Apthorp, a prominent Bay Colony merchant. When Trecothick returned to England and a successful career in trade and politics, Charles Apthorp became the American representative for the London firm of Thomlinson and Trecothick. His son, migrating to England, later entered the business.[6]

Americans often moved to England and singly tried their fortunes as merchants in the mother country. The Virginian William Lee rose to be alderman in City politics. Thomas Adams, another Virginian, also resided for some time in London as a merchant. John Huske, a native of New Hampshire, spent the last twenty years of his life in Great Britain, sat in Parliament, and gained a reputation as an expert on American affairs.

The Great War for the Empire (1755–1763) brought British and American merchants even closer together. The government usually awarded contracts for provisions and remittance of pay for the troops in America to English merchants with business connections in the colonies. These men then appointed their American associates to act as their agents. One firm with victualling contracts, Baker, Kilby, and Baker, employed the New York house of Delancey and Watts. Sir William Baker, the senior partner, was a Member of Parliament with pro-American sentiments. His son, with the same name, in 1771 married the granddaughter of William Penn. Christopher Kilby of the firm of Kilby and Bernard was a native of Boston and served as colonial agent for Massachusetts from 1741 to 1748. Another victualling contract went to the brothers James and

---

Crokatt family see Lewis B. Namier, *The Structure of Politics at the Accession of George III* (2 vols., London, 1929), II, 396. William L. Sachse, *The Colonial American in Britain* (Madison, Wisc., 1956), p. 97, describes James Crokatt as "long a prominent Charleston merchant" who established himself in London commercial circles. In this case it seems difficult to tell if Crokatt was English or American.

6. Porter, *The Jacksons and the Lees*, I, 192; Sachse, *Colonial American in Britain*, p. 126; Alfred B. Beaven, *The Aldermen of the City of London* (2 vols., London, 1908–1913), I, 325; and Theodore D. Jervey, "Barlow Trecothick," *S.C.H. & G.M.*, XXXII (1931), 157.

Merchants, Agents, and Practical Issues

George Colebrooke, who with Arnold Nesbitt worked in partnership with Moses Franks of London. Franks had relations in the mercantile communities of New York and Philadelphia. The Colebrookes, Nesbitt, the Thomlinsons, and John and Osgood Hanbury used as commercial agents the correspondents of the Boston house of John Thomlinson and Charles Apthorp. Thomlinson and his son were colonial agents for New Hampshire. The elder Charles Apthorp, a prominent Boston merchant, was a commercial agent in the provinces for the English firm of Thomlinson and Hanbury, later reorganized as Thomlinson and Trecothick.[7]

Personal, family, and business connections extended not only to England and the mainland colonies, but also to the West Indies. Traditionally historians have viewed the economy of the islands as distinct from, and incompatible with, that of North America, and have emphasized the existence of the West India "interest" in the House of Commons as an extensive block voting for the special economic requirements of the islands to the detriment of the continental colonies. It is essential to realize, however, that the economies of the two colonial blocks were complementary, for the islands depended on the mainland as a market for their molasses and as the chief source of foodstuffs, livestock, and lumber. Nor was the West Indian lobby as powerful as is sometimes thought. The zenith of the island influence only coincided with the development of a very definite organization. Although this reached an appreciable stage in the decade of the 1760's, in its final form the West India committee—a powerful influence on British policy—appeared only after the American Revolution.[8] Many merchants sitting in the House of Commons traded both to the West Indies and to North America. In the House of Commons elected in 1761 there were fifty members whose families held property and office in the islands, or resided there.[9] Yet office holding or material interest did not mean that a "West Indian"

7. Virginia D. Harrington, *The New York Merchants on the Eve of the Revolution* (New York, 1952), pp. 218, 292, 293.

8. Lillian M. Penson, "The London West India Interest in the Eighteenth Century," *English Historical Review*, XXXVI (1921), 391; Lillian M. Penson, *The Colonial Agents of the British West Indies: A study in colonial administration mainly in the eighteenth century* (London, 1924), p. 196.

9. Namier, *Structure of Politics*, I, 210–211; Lewis B. Namier, *England in the Age of the American Revolution* (London, 1930), pp. 273, 277. Sir Lewis Namier

would necessarily vote in Parliament for the islands against the economic benefit of the North American colonies. Barlow Treco-thick, the absentee owner of a plantation in Jamaica, agent for New Hampshire, and a merchant trading to North America, consistently supported the continental colonies. Alderman William Beckford, another Jamaica planter, and Richard Oliver of Antigua, both West Indian merchants and members of Parliament, also aligned them-selves with the American cause during the controversy with the mother country.[10]

If we use the standard of economic interest and blood relations, then an American interest existed in England and a West Indian interest existed in America. In the half century before the Declara-tion of Independence, West Indians and Pennsylvanians jointly owned some eighty-two vessels built at Philadelphia. Merchants from the continental and island colonies often formed partnerships. Con-tinuous commercial relations forged other ties. West Indians held estates on the mainland and North Americans owned property in the islands. Aaron Lopez, a merchant of Rhode Island, owned a planta-tion on Antigua while Thomas Benson of Jamaica held property in Philadelphia. The Middletons, Bulls, and Colletons of South Caro-lina were plantation owners in Barbados and Jamaica. Many North American families intermarried with the West Indians, and some of these personal connections survived the Revolution. The Redwoods of Rhode Island, the Livingstons of New York, and the Dickinsons of Pennsylvania retained their West Indian property and the de-scendants of other Island families such as the Searles, Silvesters, and Morrises resided on the mainland.[11]

As evidenced by this brief survey, the bonds of blood, common culture, and economic interest as well as political institutions linked the Atlantic communities of the first British Empire.

---

and John Brooke, *The History of Parliament: The House of Commons 1754–1790* (3 vols., New York, 1964), I, 156–157.

10. On them see Sutherland, "The City of London in Eighteenth-Century Politics," pp. 65, 68n.

11. Richard Pares, *Yankees and Creoles: The Trade Between North America and the West Indies before the American Revolution* (Cambridge, Mass., 1956), pp. 2–3, 8; and Agnes M. Whitson, "The Outlook of the Continental American Colonies on the British West Indies, 1760–1775," *Political Science Quarterly*, XL (1930), 62–63.

II

The administrative machinery of the first British Empire provided two channels between Whitehall and the colonies. The formal link was the governor, usually subject to royal control, who transmitted orders to the provincial assemblies from the Privy Council and the executive boards. In addition legislative committees in America corresponded with colonial agents[12] resident in London and empowered by the colonial governments to represent the province before Parliament, the courts, individual ministers, and executive boards. In the seventeenth century the provinces had used the agencies only temporarily, when a crisis necessitated special pleading with the home government. By the middle of the following century the provinces usually chose residents in London, prominent lawyers, merchants, and politicians, to represent them on a continuing basis, although on occasion they might send an additional agent to England to re-enforce the regular appointee or to argue some particular cause.[13]

Despite more than a hundred years of practice, neither the specific powers of the agents nor the method of their appointment had been definitely established. They varied from colony to colony subject to political pressures and needs as they arose. Some provinces employed several men, assigning them different tasks. The agent had to be appointed by the province in its full legal or corporate sense to aid and represent the colony most effectively. Ideally his authority stemmed from an ordinance or law passed by both houses of the legislature and signed by the governor. But the vicissitudes of provincial politics often precluded cooperation in the choice of a nominee, so that in many cases the agent's usefulness in London was curtailed. When an agent served as the representative of one element of the colonial government—usually the elected lower house—the other branches considered him to be merely the spokesman of a faction or

12. By colonial agent I do not include Crown or royal agents such as those appointed for Georgia or the Floridas by the government in London for the dispersement of funds for infant colonies subsidized by the imperial government. William Knox and Charles Garth, colonial agents for Georgia and South Carolina, also served as Crown agents.

13. Edwin P. Tanner, "Colonial Agencies in England during the Eighteenth Century," *Political Science Quarterly*, XVI (1901), 24.

junto. Often the lower house would attempt to exclude the council from the committee of correspondence. In some cases a struggle among several factions in the lower house for control of patronage precluded any agreement; in others—and they were the more frequent—the assembly contested the right of the governor to share in nominating or ratifying the choice of agents.

Local political antagonisms over the agents became critical when the overriding dispute between the colonies and the mother country impinged on the selection process. The assemblies, often charging that the governors were merely spokesmen for the administration in London, attempted to exclude the executive from any role in the choice of agents and claimed this power for the lower house exclusively. Consequently the lower houses were prone to nominate men not because of their ability to work effectively in London or to influence British administrators, but because they happened to be on the right or "popular" side in the dispute between governor and assembly, or colony and mother country. The governors, for their part, tended to accuse the assemblies of impinging on executive prerogative when unilaterally investing an agent with authority to speak for the colony.

In colonies such as the corporate provinces of Rhode Island and Connecticut, where the assemblies clearly dominated the government, the choice of an agent created little difficulty. For some years both Rhode Island and Connecticut had employed Richard Partridge, an English Quaker, who was also agent for New Jersey. Early in 1759 Partridge, in ill health, recommended to his Rhode Island constituents that they name his friend Joseph Sherwood, a Quaker attorney of Austin-Freyers, to succeed him. When Partridge died in March, 1759, Sherwood, who had for some time assisted him, successfully solicited the post as Rhode Island agent.[14] Connecticut did not follow suit, however, but employed a provincial merchant and lawyer, Jared Ingersoll, on a temporary basis, and then in March, 1760 appointed two English solicitors, Thomas Life and Richard Jackson. Both had power to act as agents and attorneys for the

14. Richard Partridge to Governor Stephen Hopkins of Rhode Island, March 1, 1759; Sherwood to the Governor and Company of Rhode Island, March 17, 1759; Gertrude S. Kimball (ed.), *The Correspondence of the Colonial Governors of Rhode Island, 1723–1775* (2 vols., Boston and New York, 1902), II, 286–287.

colony.[15] In practice "Omniscient" Jackson, as he was known, was the effective agent while Life limited his activities to prosecuting before the Privy Council the colony's case in the Mohegan land dispute. The choice of Jackson was fortunate. A member of Parliament with good political connections, he soon became secretary to George Grenville at the Exchequer and later boasted of being on intimate terms with members of the Chatham administration.[16]

New Hampshire and Georgia were equally well represented in London. John Thomlinson, an English merchant born in Antigua with wide trading interests in the colonies, held the New Hampshire agency. Due to advanced age and poor health Thomlinson suggested that his son be named joint agent. The assembly complied in 1763, but also granted John Thomlinson, Jr. the power to act separately as agent.[17] The elder Thomlinson, a governmental contractor, was well connected with the British administration during the French war. The son was a member of Parliament and owned a plantation in

15. Connecticut Archives, War, 1675–1775, Colonial, X, Pt. 2, 1751–1775, Docs. 373, 374, 380. Jackson was appointed "Agent, or Attorney" in "all . . . Matters and Causes that are or may be Depending before any of his Majesty's Courts of Laws or Equity in Great Britain. . . ." *Ibid.*, Docs., 386, 397. In October, 1760 Thomas Life was named agent for the colony before the King, courts, minister, and executive boards. J. H. Trumbull and C. J. Hoadley (eds.), *Public Records of the Colony of Connecticut (1636–1776)* (15 vols., Hartford, 1850–1890), XI, 438–439. When Ingersoll left England in August, 1761, he turned the affairs of the colony over to both Jackson and Life. Ingersoll to Governor Thomas Fitch, Aug. 10, 1761, "The Fitch Papers. Correspondence and Documents During Thomas Fitch's Governorship of the Colony of Connecticut 1754–1766," 2 vols. of Connecticut Historical Society *Collections* (Hartford, 1918–1920), XVIII, 81–82.

16. On Jackson's connections and reputation see George Grenville to the Earl of Halifax, April 21, 1768, George Grenville Letter Book, Stowe Collection, Huntington Library, San Marino, Calif., St. 7 Vol. II; Jackson to Jared Ingersoll, Feb. 20, 1767, Franklin B. Dexter (ed.), "A Selection from the Correspondence and miscellaneous papers of Jared Ingersoll," New Haven Colony Historical Society *Papers*, IX (New Haven, 1918), 403; Eliphalet Dyer to Ingersoll, April 14, 1764, *ibid.*, p. 289; and Thomas Whately (Grenville's joint secretary at the Treasury) to Ingersoll, n.d. (but April 1764), *ibid.*, pp. 293–294.

17. James Nevin to Theodore Atkinson, Nov. 14, 1761, Belknap Papers, Force Transcripts, Library of Congress, II, 13A, 219–220; Theodore Atkinson to John Thomlinson, Sr., July 24, 1762, *ibid.*, p. 223. See also the action of the legislature in Nathaniel Bouton *et al.* (eds.), *Documents and Records Relating to the Province of New Hampshire* (40 vols., Concord, 1867–1943), VI, 854, 858, 868.

Grenada. They had two partners in their American business, Charles Apthorp and Barlow Trecothick. After 1765 the latter was to figure prominently in the consideration of American affairs in London. The agent with the most extensive contacts in administrative circles was William Knox. An Irish Protestant, he had served a political apprenticeship from 1756 to 1761 as Provost Marshal of Georgia and as a member of the provincial council under his patron, Governor Henry Ellis. Appointed agent in 1762, he solicited the assistance of Ellis, now unofficial colonial adviser in London to the Earl of Egremont, Secretary of State for the Southern Department. The former governor of Georgia was now "a veteran in soliciting and dancing attendance upon people in office." Knox also extended his contacts on his own initiative. Through John Huske, an American merchant in London, he became intimate with Charles Townshend, then president of the Board of Trade. When Townshend left office, the Georgia agent established relations with his successor, the Earl of Shelburne.[18] As provincial agent for Georgia, Knox enjoyed good relations with Charles Garth, who as Crown agent dispensed the subsidies granted by the royal government to the infant colony. A London solicitor related to the Colletons and Boones of South Carolina and the West Indies, Garth soon entered Parliament. On being appointed Crown agent, he offered his services to Georgia with the hope that he and Knox would cooperate. The two agents did, but Garth, possibly considering his post of Crown agent for Georgia and colonial agent for South Carolina

18. Knox to Lyttelton, March 5, 1760, "The Manuscripts of Captain Vicente Knox," H.M.C., *Report on Manuscripts in Various Collections*, VI (London, 1919), 81–83. See also Lyttelton to Knox, Jan. 2, 1761, *ibid.*, p. 85; Knox to Robert Knox, June 28, 1761, *ibid.*, p. 86; Knox to Lyttelton, Feb. 10, 1762, *ibid.*, p. 86; Ellis to Knox, April 30, 1762, *ibid.*, p. 87; Knox's "Recollections and Anecdotes," *ibid.*, pp. 279, 282; Allen P. Candler (ed.), *The Colonial Records of the State of Georgia* (26 vols., Atlanta, 1904–1916), XIII, 627, 650, 652; and William Knox, *Extra Official State Papers* (London edn., 1789), p. 19. Knox was to become an anathema to the colonists, but for several years he so ably performed his duties as agent that in May, 1765 the committee of correspondence of the Georgia legislature wrote him that they found "every part of your Conduct as Agent" sufficient proof of the interested part he took in the colony's welfare. They were no longer pleased later that year during the Stamp Act crisis. Committee of correspondence to Knox, May 14, 1765, Lila M. Hawes (ed.), "Letters to the Georgia Colonial Agent, July 1762, to January, 1771," *Georgia Historical Quarterly*, XXXVI (1952), 272.

incompatible, resigned the royal appointment.[19] An able man, he continued to serve the colonies as provincial agent for South Carolina, a post he received in 1762 probably on the recommendation of Governor Thomas Boone. Assuming his duties with zeal, Garth thoroughly identified himself with the interests of the province.[20]

Agency matters were not as easily resolved in other colonies, where partisan politics caused dissension. The contest between governor and lower house in New Jersey led the imperial administration to challenge the legal authority of an agent appointed unilaterally by the assembly. To ensure the selection of its own candidate the legislature of New Jersey in 1761 appointed Joseph Sherwood by tacking a clause onto a bill for the support of government. The Quaker lawyer viewed this tactic with some concern, fearing that such an appointment would not enable him to register his name as agent at the Plantation office in London.[21] The Board of Trade raised a more serious objection. By designating Sherwood as "Agent for the Province at the Court of Great Britain," the assembly was guilty of a "ridiculous Affectation" in clothing an officer—merely an attorney to transact their affairs, independent

19. Georgia committee of correspondence to Garth, July 27, 1764, Hawes (ed.), "Letters to the Georgia Colonial Agent," p. 265. Knox and Garth worked together. See the notation on their request to the Treasury for a continuation of the Act of 1755 setting a bounty on colonial indigo. T. 11/28:18. Perhaps Garth's position as colonial agent for South Carolina—then involved with Georgia in a boundary dispute—caused him to resign as Crown agent for Georgia. A Treasury minute for Jan. 11, 1765 (T. 29/36:231), indicates that he asked George Grenville to have the warrant of his appointment canceled. For Garth's position on the boundary dispute see his memorial to Egremont, dated July 5, 1763, P.R.O. 30/47/14:72.

20. Lewis B. Namier, "Charles Garth, Agent for South Carolina," *English Historical Review*, LIV (1939), 632–633. On the background of the dispute between the council and Commons House of South Carolina over the appointment of agents and the composition of the committee of correspondence see Beverley W. Bond, Jr., "The Colonial Agent as a Popular Representative," *Political Science Quarterly*, XXXV (1920), 384; and Ella Lonn, *The Colonial Agents of the Southern Colonies* (Chapel Hill, 1945), p. 77.

21. Sherwood requested a more authentic document, such as a copy of the vote of the assembly under the seal of the colony, to signify his appointment. Sherwood to Samuel Smith, Sept. 16, 1761, "Letters of Joseph Sherwood, Agent for the Province of New Jersey in Great Britain, 1761–1766," New Jersey Historical Society *Proceedings*, 1st Ser., V (1850–1851), 135.

of the general interest of the colony—with a character "that belongs only to the Minister of a Foreign Prince."[22] The assembly of New Jersey was acting as the government of a sovereign nation. The Commissioners of Trade repeatedly challenged comparable tactics employed by other assemblies in attempting to exclude the provincial councils and governors from selecting and investing the agents who were to represent the colonial governments. In time, disputes on these points between the administration in London and the lower houses limited the operations of the agents.

Friction between the governors and assemblies, in part, reflected a more pervasive political antagonism. The governor of New York complained that the house had encroached on the powers of the Crown (actually the governor) in the appointment of Robert Charles as agent,[23] by including his salary in a general bill for the support of government. The governor was obliged either to accept this appointment or do without the salaries of his own nominees in office. Furthermore, Charles was to act for the assembly, independently of the governor and council. The governor's objections were technically correct, as the Commissioners of Trade pointed out. The assembly should have passed a specific act appointing the agent subject to the concurrence of the other branches of government,

22. Commissioners of Trade to Governor William Franklin, July 13, 1764, Frederick W. Ricord and William Nelson (eds.), *Archives of the State of New Jersey* (36 vols., Newark, 1881–1941), 1st Ser., IX, 445–446.

23. Little is known of Charles, whom Professor Andrews called "a conspicuous busybody who was very sharply reprimanded by the Board of Trade for persistently demanding access to its files." Charles M. Andrews, *The Colonial Period of American History* (4 vols., New Haven, 1934–1938), IV, 295. Charles' appointment as agent for New York surprised Chief Justice Robert Hunter Morris of New Jersey, who described him as a "man of no Character equal to such an Employ . . ." extract of Morris to James Alexander, in Alexander Colden to Cadwallader Colden, Nov. 16, 1760, "The Letters and Papers of Cadwallader Colden," New York Historical Society *Collections* (11 vols., New York, 1877–1878, 1918–1924, 1935, 1937), LXVIII, 82. Charles had been secretary to Sir Peter Warren, the naval commander, and evidently secured the New York agency through his influence. In a memorial to the Board of Trade of 1765, Charles described himself as a "Secretary and naval Officer, for many years, in the Department of America. . . ." No man was more sincere than he, Charles claimed, in "Duty and Allegiance to his sovereign [and] more truly attached to the Religion & Laws of England, & to the Constitution of Britain, or more ardently wishes to see every true English Principle nourished & cultivated in America." C.O. 323/21:105.

but since the governor had already assented to the offensive measure, there was nothing to be done at this point.[24]

The situation in New York was not extreme, for in some colonies—Maryland and the three counties of Delaware—antagonism among the branches of government prevented the appointment of any agent.[25] An informal arrangement had existed for the counties since 1762, when Benjamin Franklin, agent for Pennsylvania, volunteered his services while in London. Two years later, before leaving for England on his second agency for the Quaker assembly, Franklin solicited a comparable position for the lower house of Maryland.[26] The Pennsylvania agency itself had a confused history. Factionalism in the legislature coupled with antagonism between proprietary governors and the assembly clouded the issue. Initially Franklin had shared the agency with Robert Charles, but when the latter declined serving after 1761, the lower house continued to employ Franklin alone. When Franklin left England in 1763 he entrusted the affairs of the province to his friend Richard Jackson, agent for Connecticut. The assembly then appointed Jackson a regular agent for the next two years. Franklin soon rejoined him in London, for although he failed to obtain a seat in the Pennsylvania assembly, his popularity among the dominant faction in the house was so great that he was sent back to England as joint agent to

24. Governor Clinton to the Commissioners of Trade, April 22, 1748, Edmund B. O'Callaghan and Berthold Fernow (eds.), *Documents Relative to the Colonial History of the State of New York* (15 vols., Albany and New York, 1856–1887), VI, 420; and Commissioners of Trade to Clinton, June 29, 1749, *ibid.*, VI, 427. Lieutenant Governor Colden in 1760 attempted to interest John Pownall, secretary to the Commissioners of Trade, in the New York agency. Because of the Board's rule prohibiting its personnel from acting as agents, Pownall declined the offer and, without prejudicing Charles, suggested Thomas Burke for the post. Colden did not have sufficient influence to effect the removal of Charles, who continued in office. See Pownall to Colden, Jan. 10, 1761, "the Letters and Papers of Cadwallader Colden," LIV (1921), 308; Pownall to Colden, Oct. 9, 1761, *ibid.*, LV (1922), 83; and Colden to Pownall, Nov. 11, 1760, April 5, Aug. 12, 1761, *ibid.*, IX (1876), 38, 80–81, 107.

25. Bond, "The Colonial Agent as a Popular Representative," pp. 376 and 376n3.

26. Governor Horatio Sharpe to Cecilius Calvert, May 11, 1762, June 11, 1764, William H. Browne *et al.* (eds.), *Archives of Maryland* (66 vols., Baltimore, 1883—), XIV, 53, 164.

13

solicit the Crown to assume Pennsylvania as a royal colony. With the opposition in Pennsylvania contesting the mission, Franklin's enemy, William Allen, wrote to the Quaker merchant David Barclay attempting to undermine Franklin with the ministry.[27]

Historians have stressed—perhaps exaggerated—Franklin's influence in English political circles. Apparently he had some connection with the Earl of Bute—enough to have his son, William, appointed Governor of New Jersey—but this contact was important only while Bute held office, and the Scottish favorite of George III resigned in April, 1763. There is some evidence to indicate that the Franklins deliberately circulated the impression in the colonies that they had great weight in British administrative circles. Several years later the Philadelphian Samuel Wharton, himself no mean lobbyist in London, bitterly complained that the Franklins had "not the smallest Share of Interest, with Administration; and all We were taught to believe, before I left America, was Bluff and Declamation."[28]

27. Votes of the assembly for Oct. 15, 1760, and the governor's message of Oct. 18, 1760, in Samuel Hazard *et al.* (eds.), *Pennsylvania Archives* (9 series, Philadelphia and Harrisburg, 1852–1935), 8th Ser., VI, 5159–5165; *Minutes of the Provincial Council of Pennsylvania, 1693–1776* (10 vols., Harrisburg, 1851–1852), VIII, 512–513; entry for Oct. 16, 1761, in Samuel Foulke, "An Account of the Proceedings of the General Assembly of Pennsylvania Commenc'd Oct. 14, 1761 . . . ," *Pennsylvania Magazine of History and Biography*, VIII (1884), 408; Isaac Norris to Franklin, Sept. 30, 1761, Benjamin Franklin Papers, American Philosophical Society Library, Philadelphia, I, 65; votes of the assembly for Sept. 21, 1762, April 2, 1763, and Oct. 15, 1764, Hazard *et al.* (eds.), *Pennsylvania Archives*, 8th Ser., VI, 5359, 5424, 5475–5476, VII, 5671; William Allen to David Barclay and Son, Oct. 24, 1764, *The Burd Papers: Extracts from Chief Justice William Allen's Letter Book Selected and Arranged by Lewis Burd Walker* . . . (Pottsville, Penn., 1897), p. 62; Franklin to Richard Jackson, Nov. 7, 1764, Carl Van Doren (ed.), *Letters and Papers of Benjamin Franklin and Richard Jackson, 1753–1785* (Philadelphia, 1947), p. 189; Charles Pettit to Joseph Reed, Nov. 3, 1764, William B. Reed, *Life and Correspondence of Joseph Reed* (2 vols., Philadelphia, 1847), I, 37. An extract of the assembly's resolution of October 26, 1764, appointing Franklin as joint agent is in the Franklin Papers, American Philosophical Society Library, LII, 46.

28. See Benjamin Franklin to William Franklin, March 22, 1775, Carl Van Doren (ed.), *Benjamin Franklin's Autobiographical Writings* (New York, 1945), p. 349; Thomas Cuming to Franklin, Oct. 7, 1763, Franklin Papers, American Philosophical Society Library, I, Doc. 81 1/2; and Samuel Wharton to George Croghan, Feb. 3, 1773, George Croghan Papers, John Cadwallader Collection, Historical Society of Pennsylvania, Philadelphia, Box 37.

Benjamin Franklin

Merchants, Agents, and Practical Issues

Residing on the same London street as Franklin was the agent for Virginia and North Carolina, James Abercromby,[29] a cousin to the general of the same name who had served in America during the late war, and holder of several executive offices in the southern colonies. Abercromby had been sole agent for the entire government of Virginia since 1753, but when he appeared to support Lieutenant Governor Robert Dinwiddie in the latter's dispute with the assembly over the pistole fee, the burgesses demanded the right to have their own agent. Dinwiddie denied the request but his successor, Francis Fauquier, acquiesced and persuaded the burgesses to allow members of the council to serve on the committee of correspondence. As the lieutenant governor explained the situation to the Commissioners of Trade, he could not see "the ill-Consequences" of allowing the lower house to have its own agent, particularly if it paid his salary.[30] Political factionalism underlay the constitutional issue, however, for one Virginian contemptuously referred to the new agent, Edward Montague, a master in Chancery and member of Parliament, as agent for "a Junto of the Council and Burgesses. . . ." Abercromby, accepting the decision with poor

29. On Abercromby see Andrews, *Colonial Period of American History*, IV, 216n2, 409–412; Namier, *England in the Age of the American Revolution*, p. 290n2; Governor William Bull of South Carolina to Lord Townshend, June 15, 1752, H.M.C., *Eleventh Report* (London, 1887), App., Pt. IV, p. 270; and Charles F. Mullett, "James Abercromby and French Encroachments in America," *Canadian Historical Review*, XXVI (1945), 48. An episode in 1765 when he offered to reveal new sources of revenue for the Crown from American quitrents showed that Abercromby's first loyalties were not to his Virginia constituents. Fearing that his offer to the royal government might cost him the Virginia agency, Abercromby proposed that the Crown grant him a sum from the Virginia quitrents "so as to make up to me my present income by way of an annuity for life. . . ." Abercromby to [Charles Jenkinson], Jan. 6, 1765, Add. MSS., British Museum, 38204, ff. 9–10.

30. Abercromby complained that he had not received the full support of Fauquier and that if the lieutenant governor had so desired, he might have diverted the prejudice held by the burgesses against the agent in their dispute with English merchants over Virginia paper currency. Abercromby to John Blair (private), July 6, 1759, James Abercromby Letter Book, 1746–1773, Virginia State Library, Richmond. See also the opinion of the English Attorney General, Charles Pratt, on the Virginia agency law, dated Dec. 24, 1759, T. 1/389:30–31; Fauquier to the Commissioners of Trade, Sept. 1, 1760, C.O. 5/1330:62–63; and Abercromby to Richard Corbin, June 29, 1759, Abercromby Letter Book.

grace, made light of the new appointee and thereafter did little for the colony.[31]

The patronage struggle in North Carolina over the agency was more acrimonious than that in Virginia, with both sides exchanging charges and recriminations over the right of the governor to share in the selection of an agent and councilors to sit on the committee of correspondence. Abercromby, the incumbent, complained that Governor Arthur Dobbs had "finess'd" him out of the post in hopes of appointing his own nominee, Samuel Smith, a London merchant.[32] Supporting first Abercromby and then Anthony Bacon, an English merchant engaged in the southern trade, the house attempted to name the agents through appropriations bills. The council, excluded from the committee of correspondence, twice rejected these measures. A compromise candidate agreeable to Dobbs, the council, and the assembly was finally found, Cuchet Jouvencal, a clerk in the office of the Secretary of State for the Southern Department. Nonetheless, in practice the assembly effectively controlled the committee of correspondence.[33]

The Commissioners of Trade in London, for their part, sought to limit the role of the governor in North Carolina and elsewhere merely to rejecting or approving the initial choice of the assembly. They did, however, support Dobbs to some extent by condemning the practice of the lower house of nominating an agent by appropriations bills. Consequently they instructed the governor to press for the passage of a separate agency bill when Jouvencal's term of

31. John Mercer to Charlton Palmer, July 27, 1762, Lois Mulkearn (ed.), *George Mercer Papers relating to the Ohio Company of Virginia* (Pittsburgh, 1954), p. 47; and Abercromby to Fauquier, Dec. 22, 1759, Abercromby Letter Book.

32. Abercromby to Fauquier, Dec. 22, 1759, Abercromby Letter Book. Bond, "The Colonial Agent as a Popular Representative," p. 378, and Samuel James Ervin, Jr., "The Provincial Agents of North Carolina," in *The James Sprunt Studies in History and Political Science*, XVI, ii, 68, both refer to Samuel Smith as Dobbs' private attorney in London, but an endorsement on a memorial by Dobbs to the Treasury lists Smith as a merchant in the Old Jewry (T. 1/433:333).

33. Throughout the affair Dobbs charged that the various nominations by the lower house concealed a conspiracy of a junto led by the attorney general of the colony, Thomas Child, to remove him from office and line their own pockets from the quitrents and funds voted to the province by Parliament. Dobbs to the Commissioners of Trade, May 28, 1760, C.O. 5/299:160–161; and Dobbs' answer to the charges of the assembly in C.O. 5/298:319–321.

office expired.[34] In March, 1764 an impasse was reached on the reappointment of the agent when the council refused to be excluded from membership in the committee of correspondence.

The situation became more confused when the new governor, William Tryon, even before leaving London became involved with both Jouvencal and Abercromby in the agency dispute. Tryon then appealed privately to the Board of Trade. Exasperated over the irregularity in the method of appointing agents in North Carolina and elsewhere, the board warned that if the assembly of North Carolina did not admit a proper number of councilors to the committee of correspondence, the home government itself would take action.[35] The assembly did not comply. Consequently when the affairs of the colonies most urgently required that a proper representative be present in London, factional disputes in North Carolina deprived the colony of an agent to present its case.

The controversy over the appointment of agents was most intense in Massachusetts, where the dispute between the governor and a faction in the House of Representatives later merged with the doctrinal disputes between England and America and virtually destroyed the agency itself as an institution.

William Bollan, for some years agent for the Bay Colony, at an early date fell victim to Massachusetts politics, the rivalry between the Otis and Hutchinson factions, and the animosities arising from colonial fears of the British government. Bollan, one-time advocate of the vice-admiralty court in Boston, was the son-in-law of the former governor, William Shirley, with whom he was closely connected in provincial politics. To make matters worse, he was an

34. Commissioners of Trade to Dobbs, April 4, 1761, Feb. 17, 1762, William L. Saunders (ed.), *Colonial Records of North Carolina* (10 vols., Raleigh, 1888–1890), VI, 539, 702 and entry for Feb. 10, 1762, Great Britain, Board of Trade, *Journal of the Lords Commissioners of Trade and Plantations* (14 vols., London, 1920–1938), 1759–1763, p. 249.

35. See Lord Hyde to the Earl of Dartmouth (president of the Board of Trade), Aug. 13, 1765, enclosing a letter from Tryon to the Board, June 24, 1765, and a further letter from William Hunter to Tryon, March 2, 1765, Dartmouth Papers, William Salt Library, Stafford, England, II, 78 (transcripts in English Records, North Carolina State Department of Archives and History, Raleigh). See also the Commissioners of Trade to Tryon, Nov. 29, 1765, Saunders (ed.), *Colonial Records of North Carolina*, VII, 132.

Anglican in Congregationalist Massachusetts. Although a new governor, Francis Bernard, had arrived in Boston in 1760, the struggle for patronage and power between James Otis and Thomas Hutchinson carried over from the previous regime. The younger Otis particularly resented Lieutenant Governor Hutchinson, apparently for having obtained an appointment as chief justice of the province after the new governor had promised the position to his father. The agent inadvertently became involved in the factional dispute. In the famous case against writs of assistance argued by Otis, Bollan had supplied the chief justice with the form of writs issued in the English Court of Exchequer. This led to his dismissal as agent by the House of Representatives in April, 1762, or so Bollan thought. His Anglicanism was also a factor, for the Congregationalist clergy feared that the British government was about to establish an Anglican bishop in the colonies.[36]

Although there was little to fear from an established Anglican bishopric, the memories of the seventeenth century—William Laud, the Clarendon Code, and the policy of religious conformity—lingered in the minds of many of the Puritan offspring in Massachusetts, who proposed Jasper Mauduit, a leading English dissenter, for the agency. Mauduit, an aged draper by trade, had little more than his associations in Dissenting circles to recommend him for the post. His more active and politically influential younger brother Israel would have been a better choice.[37] The elder Mauduit was, in fact, the candidate of only a faction within the House of Representatives. In the field of three candidates, the Otis faction backed the English dissenter, the governor's party favored Bernard's friend and agent for Connecticut and Pennsylvania, Richard

36. See Bollan's memorandum to the Duke of Newcastle, dated April 12, 1766, Add. MSS. 32974, ff. 364–369. On the question of the colonial bishops see Jack M. Sosin, "The Proposal in the Pre-Revolutionary Decade for Establishing Anglican Bishops in the Colonies," *Journal of Ecclesiastical History*, XIII (1962), 76–84.

37. A well-known pamphleteer, Israel Mauduit had enough influence with the Grenville administration to have Authur Savage of Massachusetts appointed comptroller of customs at Falmouth. Israel Mauduit to [Charles Jenkinson], March 1765, Add. MSS. 38304, f. 102; and Jenkinson to George Grenville, April 13, 1765, Add. MSS. 38304, f. 135. Among the Treasury papers (T . . . 11/27: 262) is a notation of Jan. 26, 1763, for a commission for Israel Mauduit to be Collector of Southampton. It is marked as canceled.

Jackson, while a third group supported Lieutenant Governor Thomas Hutchinson. When the opposition to Bernard's candidate agreed on the elder Mauduit, Hutchinson dropped out of contention. Inasmuch as Mauduit was in poor health, the House specified that Jackson was to act as agent if the regular appointee were incapacitated and instructed Mauduit to consult with the Connecticut agent in all legal matters relating to the province. In an effort to undermine the arrangement, Otis wrote privately to Mauduit that he was to consider himself responsible only to the House of Representatives, for "With a Governor we think our agent beyond meer [*sic*] civility has little to do."

Otis continued to agitate against Governor Bernard by attacking his friend Jackson, the alternate agent. Another opportunity was presented to Otis when Jasper Mauduit asked the House of Representatives to name his brother as joint agent and his eventual successor. Waiting until only forty-eight members out of one hundred and twenty-five were in attendance, Otis carried the nomination of Israel Mauduit through the house. However, the council after a bitter struggle rejected him due to the opposition of Hutchinson, who, Otis contended, wanted the position for himself. In any case, Israel Mauduit for a time often acted unofficially for his brother as agent. Otis temporarily abandoned the struggle, exclaiming in disgust: "but I hate that the L[ieutenant] G[overnor] should prevail in anything." [38] Before long he was to have another opportunity to agitate on the agency question.

In time the bitter factional struggle in Massachusetts compromised the agents in London. The agents for other provinces were also limited by the political nature of their appointments. But given greater latitude, many could have operated more effectively than they did. Even so they accomplished much. Influential lawyers, merchants, and members of Parliament such as Jackson, Thomlinson, Garth, Knox, and Jasper Mauduit (through his brother)

38. See Alice Vering, "James Otis" (Ph.D. dissertation, University of Nebraska, 1954), pp. 70–73, 93–95; Otis to Jasper Mauduit, April 23, Oct. 28, 1762, Feb. 14, 1763, *Jasper Mauduit, Agent in London for the Province of the Massachusetts Bay 1762–1765* (Massachusetts Historical Society *Collections*, LXXIV [Boston, 1918]), pp. 31, 32, 80, 95; Andrew Oliver to Jasper Mauduit (private), April 24, 1762, *ibid.*, p. 36; and Jasper Mauduit to Jonathan Mayhew, July 1762, Alden Bradford, *Memoirs of the Life and Writings of Jonathan Mayhew . . .* (Boston, 1838), p. 234.

worked well together on practical matters with the "men of business" who administered the Empire.

III

The most significant role played by the colonial agents and British merchants in the pre-Revolutionary decade related to the acts of the imperial government affecting the liberties of the North American colonies: those ill-fated measures which triggered a widespread colonial reaction and ruptured the empire. Before considering this aspect of their activities, it is worthwhile to examine the operations of this rudimentary lobby on particular commercial and economic issues to determine its methods of operation, strengths, and weaknesses, and the factors serving to divide it.

The agents and merchants often joined to apply for commercial legislation relating to a specific commodity produced in several colonies, or to the product of a single province. In either case the desired legislation was beneficial both to North America and the English merchants. Charles Garth joined with merchants trading to South Carolina and Georgia in a memorial to the Treasury requesting continuance of a bounty on indigo. The same merchants successfully petitioned for these colonies to export rice to South America, Africa, and southern Europe. Knox, agent for Georgia, and the merchants William Greenwood, James Crokatt, William Middleton, James Gordon, and John Nutt in 1764 testified before Parliament in favor of the measure.[39] Merchants trading to New England, including the firms of Anthony Merry, Lane and Booth, Champion and Haley, Trecothick and Thomlinson, and Tappenden and Hanbury, joined Jasper Mauduit, agent for Massachusetts, in requesting a reduction of the duty on whale fins imported by New England whalers from the Gulf of St. Lawrence. This proposal was

39. The memorial on the bounty for indigo is in T. 1/424:298. The petition on the export of rice is in T. 1/425:215; another to the Board of Trade in C.O. 323/17:111–122. See also Great Britain, Parliament, *Journals of the House of Commons* (London, 1547—), XXIX, 928 and "Reasons for permitting the exportation of rice from Carolina and Georgia to any part of America and to the African Islands," C.O. 323/17:261–280. Submitted by the merchants of London trading to those colonies. 4 Geo. III c. 27, passed in April, allowed the export of rice from Georgia.

included among the resolutions reported from the committee of the whole House of Commons on March 13, 1764, by Thomas Whately, joint Secretary to the Treasury.[40] The following year, the Committee of Ways and Means resolved in favor of bounties for lumber imported from America. Richard Jackson and the merchant firms of Trecothick and Thomlinson, Lane and Booth, David Barclay and Son, Mildred and Roberts, Capel and Osgood Hanbury, and Edward Athawes had lobbied for this measure.[41] The same merchants sought a bounty for American iron and although the Board of Trade approved, it was probably with the revenue question in mind that Charles Jenkinson, joint Secretary to the Treasury, wrote to the First Lord, George Grenville, suggesting an alternative duty on competing Swedish iron.[42]

One measure beneficial to many colonies—a bounty on colonial hemp and flax—had the support of almost all the merchants trading to America as well as many of the agents, among them Israel Mauduit, Robert Charles, Edward Montague, Charles Garth, Joseph Sherwood, and Cuchet Jouvencal. The memorial drawn by Garth and presented on November 20, 1763, bore the names of one hundred and two firms, including almost all of the merchants trading to America except those sitting in Parliament, who, as Garth put it, "being judges, could not with propriety or decency

40. *Commons Journal*, XXIX, 946. The petition is in C.O. 385/51 unfoliated, but endorsed as received on Feb. 9, 1764. See also Thomas Whately to John Pownall (secretary to the Board of Trade), Jan. 25, 1764, *ibid.*; Pownall to Jasper Mauduit, Feb. 2, 1764, C.O. 389/31:180; Charles Jenkinson (joint secretary to the Treasury) to the customs commissioners, Feb. 10, 1764, T. 11/27:385; and [Henry Saxby (secretary to the customs commissioners)], to Jenkinson, Feb. 25, 1764, Add. MSS. 38202, f. 161.

41. Officials at the Customs Board, Henry Saxby and John Tyton, and the Treasury would approve only a plan "which without occasioning two [*sic*] great a Charge upon the Revenue may prove beneficial to the Trade of his Majesty's Subjects in America." Saxby to [Jenkinson], March 27, 1765, C.O. 389/31:339; and Jenkinson to Pownall, March 19, 1765, C.O. 388/52 unfoliated, enclosing two memorials in favor of the bounties. Also Jackson to Governor Thomas Fitch, April 19, 1765, "The Fitch Papers," XVIII, 344.

42. Jenkinson to Grenville, April 13, 1765, Add. MSS. 38384, f. 135; the memorial of the London merchants on the iron bounty, dated April 2, 1765, C.O. 388/52 unfoliated, and three additional memorials read at the Board of Trade on April 22, 1765, in C.O. 323/18:243–254.

make themselves parties by signing it." Hemp was vital to the royal navy, and although the Admiralty Board on the basis of previous experience considered hemp produced in America inferior to the Petersburg product, it approved of the bounty so as to stimulate colonial production and free England of her dependence on Russian hemp—an uncertain source in case a northern war should close the Baltic Sea. National security and commercial benefits being thus combined, Parliament granted the bounty.[43]

There is no evidence that these specific commercial measures relating to iron, hemp, lumber, or rice marred relations between the agents and merchants, but paper money was a divisive issue between the lobbyists for a relatively short time, and the disagreement on this issue extended to classes and individuals within the colonies as well. The merchants did not support the agents when the matter came before the Board of Trade, in part because the economic ramifications of paper currency were so complex that the merchants themselves could not agree on its effects in the payment of transatlantic trade.[44] Since the issue of paper money continued to exacerbate colonial-imperial relations for almost a decade, it is well worth analyzing the question in detail.

Colonial legislatures, during and after periods of war, issued paper bills of credit to defray emergency expenses. Ordinarily an assembly would pass legislation issuing such bills—sometimes as legal tender—for a specified number of years, at the same time pledging future taxes for the redemption of the paper. Several factors led to almost inevitable depreciation of this currency: failure to vote or collect sufficient taxes to retire the bills, an extension of the period for redemption, and, most often, too great an issue for normal commercial

43. Charles Garth to the South Carolina committee of correspondence, Nov. 20, 1763, quoted in Namier, *England in the Age of the American Revolution*, p. 292; Admiralty Board to John Pownall, Jan. 2, 1764, C.O. 5/65:447–448. See also the petition in C.O. 323/17:106–110 and the memorial of the agents and London merchants, C.O. 5/65:439–445. Although William Knox is not listed in the later document, undoubtedly he was influential. See his undated paper, "Reasons for granting a Bounty on the importation of Hemp & Flax from the British Colonies in America," William Knox Manuscripts, Clements Library, Ann Arbor. Knox's name is listed in another memorial sent by Jenkinson to the Board of Trade and read by the Commissioners on January 26, 1764 (C.O. 323/17:233–238). The act granting the bounty on hemp is 4 Geo. III, c. 26.

44. Abercromby to James Blair, May 3, 1759, Abercromby Letter Book.

needs.[45] Tempted by political considerations, colonial legislatures sometimes issued paper bills without future taxes as security; devaluation followed with devastating effects on prices, credit—the whole money market.[46] Provincial merchants used this paper in clearing transatlantic debts between the colonies and Great Britain. Since the entire economic complex determined the exchange rate, the prices of bills of exchange depended on the volume and value of colonial produce as against imported British goods, supply and demand for bills of credit, and the value of provincial currency. The price of bills of exchange was linked to the value of bills of credit and reflected the total condition of transatlantic trade as it related to local conditions in the colonies and in Great Britain. Consequently rates of exchange between provincial and English currency, despite attempts by colonial legislatures to fix them arbitrarily, fluctuated considerably and often depended on market conditions, the quantity of money in circulation, and the number of bills brought to the market.[47]

The British government attempted to regulate colonial issues of paper money since both colonial and British creditors protested the practice of debtors paying their obligations in depreciated currency. In 1751 Parliament had passed an act regulating the New England

45. Curtis P. Nettels, *The Money Supply of the American Colonies Before 1720* (*University of Wisconsin Studies in the Social Sciences and History*, No. 20 [Madison, 1934]), pp. 253, 255, 268, 269, 277.

46. John A. Schutz, "Succession Politics in Massachusetts, 1730–1741," *William and Mary Quarterly*, 3rd. Ser., XV (1958), 511.

47. Robert A. East, "The Business Entrepreneur in a Changing Economy, 1763–1795," *The Journal of Economic History, Supplement*, VI (1946), 22; and James H. Soltow, "The Role of Williamsburg in the Virginia Economy, 1750–1775," *William and Mary Quarterly*, 3rd Ser., XV (1958), 474–475. While some in Virginia attributed the great rise in the rate of exchange exclusively to the new emissions of paper money, Lieutenant Governor Francis Fauquier thought there was a more fundamental cause: the Virginians were importing more goods than their exports of tobacco would cover. According to Fauquier, "the most thinking Gentlemen of the Colony" acknowledged this, but the situation was "so disagreeable a truth to the generality that they obstinately shut their eyes against it." He could suggest no remedy, for he feared that the Virginians "are not prudent enough to quit one Article of Luxury, till Smart obliges them." Fauquier to the Earl of Egremont, May 1, 1762, Petworth House Archives, Sussex, England, Vol. 163, f. 98; and Fauquier to the Board of Trade, Nov. 3, 1762, C.O. 5/1330: 339–340.

colonies in their emissions of paper money. No steps were taken against the southern colonies. But the practices of Virginia and North Carolina brought further complaints, especially from English creditors.[48] For six years, between 1759 and 1764, they sought redress of their grievances from the provincial legislatures. Nor were the British merchants the only creditors to suffer, for the depreciation of the Virginia currency in 1762 meant losses to not a few merchants in the northern colonies.[49] Discontent in Great Britain, mainly in administrative circles, over the recalcitrance of the legislatures of Virginia and North Carolina to amend their laws fixing the procedures for determining exchange rates led in 1764 to the passage of an act by Parliament limiting the conditions for emitting paper money.

The British merchants as a group did not want this act, for they could not agree on the consequences of paper money in the payment of transatlantic debts. They merely asked the Board of Trade to instruct the governors of North Carolina and Virginia to recommend to their legislatures that they pass an act providing that sterling debts be discharged in sterling, or in paper bills of credit only if the creditor would accept them, and not according to the nominal value of such bills but at the actual difference of exchange at the time of payment. In their petition they pointed out that £133 North Carolina currency would not buy the legal rate of £100 sterling but only £70 in the market. The assembly of North Carolina

48. The opinion of some Virginians toward British merchants as parasites who fleeced the planters and kept them in perpetual debt is well known. But J. H. Soltow, "Scottish Traders in Virginia, 1750–1775," *Economic History Review*, 2nd Ser., XII (1959), 83–98, noting the anti-merchant feeling in Virginia, points out that they performed necessary economic functions in marketing and mobilizing credit. Furthermore, the Virginians enjoyed a high standard of living, and many of the perpetually debt-ridden planters led a luxurious life. The debts owed the British planters may have reflected tardiness in repaying debts. As Dora Mae Clark, *British Opinion and the American Revolution* (New Haven, 1930), pp. 28–29, points out, while Dutch and German customers enjoyed only six months' credit, and the French even less, the colonists demanded and received from one to three years, and many British merchants had to wait even longer for the payment of colonial debts.

49. William S. Sachs, "Interurban Correspondence and the Development of a National Economy Before the Revolution: New York as a Case Study," *New York History*, XXXVI (1955), 331.

refused to act, admitting that the "Depretitation [*sic*] of our currency is too well known and felt, but all remedies hitherto proposed have proved Abortive. . . ."[50] The legislature of Virginia was more amenable. It had previously set the discount rate at 25 per cent advance on sterling for the difference of exchange. In practice, however, depreciated Virginia currency was discounted as much as 50 to 60 per cent to purchase bills of exchange.[51] The assembly now provided that the colonial courts set the discount rate between bills of exchange (fixed, in part, by the amount of paper bills of credit in circulation) and sterling. At the same time the House of Burgesses sent to its agent, Edward Montague, a lengthy justification of the colony's paper currency issues to be used by Montague before the Board of Trade.[52] The British merchants were still dissatisfied, for a significant margin could exist between the rate set by the provincial courts and the market rate at the time a debtor finally settled his account. An exchange rate between Virginia currency and British sterling set by statutory or judicial procedures did not reflect the real market value of paper money.

In the winter of 1762–1763 merchants from London, Glasgow, and Liverpool presented memorials to the Board of Trade. Among the more prominent traders were James Buchanan, Anthony Bacon, Edward Athawes, and Capel and Osgood Hanbury. On

50. See the royal instructions to the executives of Virginia and North Carolina in Leonard W. Labaree (ed.), *Royal Instructions to British Colonial Governors, 1670–1776* (2 vols., New York, 1935), I, 229–230, 236–238; also Board of Trade, *Journals*, 1759–1763, pp. 24–25, 26, 37–38; James Munroe (ed.), *Acts of the Privy Council, Colonial Series* (6 vols., Edinburgh, 1908–1912), IV, 415–416. The petitions of the British merchants and the report of the Board of Trade are printed in Saunders (ed.), *Colonial Records of North Carolina*, VI, 17–18, 22–24. See also Henry R. McIlwaine and John P. Kennedy (eds.), *Journals of the House of Burgesses of Virginia* (13 vols., Richmond, 1905–1913), 1758–1761, pp. 40–41, and James Abercromby to John Blair, May 3, 1759, Abercromby Letter Book. The reply of the North Carolina House, dated Nov. 28, 1759, is in C.O. 5/299:18. See also the speech of Governor Dobbs, C.O. 5/299:10 and Dobbs to the Commissioners of Trade, Jan. 19, 1760, C.O. 5/299:3.

51. E. James Ferguson, "Currency Finance: An Interpretation of Colonial Monetary Practice," *William and Mary Quarterly*, 3rd Ser., X (1953), 160.

52. See the Virginia committee of correspondence to Montague, Dec. 12, 1759, "Proceedings of the Virginia Committee of Correspondence," *Virginia Magazine of History and Biography*, X (1903), 345–347; and their instructions to the agent, *ibid.*, XI (1903–1904), 2–5.

receiving the petition of the London merchants on December 22, 1762, the Commissioners promptly set a hearing on Virginia paper currency issued the previous spring. Since Edward Montague, the agent for the House of Burgesses, was then ill, with the "kindly" consent of Edward Athawes, chairman of the merchants' committee, the board granted a postponement until February 1, 1763. Both sides offered testimony and the commissioners read an additional memorial from the London merchants as well as one from Glasgow presented by Athawes and another from Liverpool delivered by Sir Ellis Cunliffe.[53] The following day the board decided in favor of the merchants, charging that issuing paper bills of credit as legal tender was destructive of the public credit of the colonies and contrary to the sense of Parliament as contained in the Act of 1751 regulating the bills of credit of the New England provinces. Moreover, the emission of large quantities of paper money on insufficient and uncertain funds had been the principal cause of the fluctuating rate of exchange—an unstable rate operating to the prejudice of the public credit of Virginia and the British merchants. If the House of Burgesses neglected to vote sufficient taxes and fix a definite expiration date for its paper money issues, the commissioners would apply to Parliament for legislation extending the provisions of the Act of 1751 to Virginia.[54]

Despite this strong warning the Virginia burgesses flatly refused to pass any additional legislation. No laws, they declared, could guard against the fluctuating exchange rate. Moreover, the British merchants had no cause to complain about the excessive rise of the rate, for that would be "sufficiently balanced by the Advantage they must inevitably receive from its present declining State." Although the taxes voted to retire the bills at the date of expiration were sufficient, the burgesses maintained, the laxness of the sheriffs in failing to remit the money they collected had prevented the retirement of bills of credit on schedule. These bills must be declared

53. The memorial of the London merchants received on Dec. 22, 1762, in C.O. 5/1330:261–264; the petitions of the Glasgow and Liverpool merchants received on Feb. 1, 1763, in C.O. 5/1330:277–278, 279.

54. Edward Montague to John Pownall, Jan. 17, 1763, C.O. 5/1330:269; Montague to Pownall, Jan. 24, 1763, C.O. 5/1368:214–216; and Board of Trade, *Journals*, 1759–1763, pp. 328, 330–332, 333, 334.

legal tender to ensure their circulation. In some instances determining the rate of exchange for the payment of sterling debts had proved faulty inasmuch as the rate had risen between the time of the court judgment and the actual remittance of the money, but the consequences had been "small and inconsiderable, of a casual nature, against which no human Laws can provide, and for which therefore we cannot suggest a Remedy. . . ."[55]

The uncompromising attitude of the Virginia House of Burgesses did not impress the merchants in London; but neither did it lead them to close the door on any compromise. On December 8, 1763, with a committee of the London merchants trading to Virginia and the agent for the House of Burgesses also present, the Board of Trade conducted a hearing on Virginia currency. The merchants declared that they would be "well satisfied" if the provincial bills were so regulated that judgments for sterling debts would be discharged in sterling money either in Great Britain or Virginia. The board evidently decided to allow the colonials another opportunity, but warned that any further neglect by the House of Burgesses in redressing the grievances of the merchants would be neither just nor equitable. If it did not comply, the only alternative would be legislation by Parliament. The "Candour of the Merchants" in agreeing once more to appeal to the "Equity of the Legislature of Virginia" for a solution which the board would otherwise have taken to Parliament would, the commissioners hoped, "induce the Gentlemen of the House of Burgesses to comply with what is required of them."[56]

55. See the speech by Lieutenant Governor Fauquier, May 19, 1763, McIlwaine and Kennedy (eds.), *Journals of the House of Burgesses of Virginia*, 1761–1763, pp. 171–172; reply by the burgesses, May 20, 1763, *ibid.*, pp. 173–174 and also their report of May 28, 1763, *ibid.*, pp. 188–192 (manuscript copy, "The Representation to the Governor of Virginia by the House of Burgesses May 1763, concerning the Paper Currency," Shelburne Papers, Clements Library, Ann Arbor, 49:455–464. See also Fauquier to the Board of Trade, May 24, 1763, C.O. 5/1330:431–433; the printed address of the burgesses, C.O. 5/1330:443; and committee of correspondence to Montague, June 16, 1763, "Proceedings of the Virginia Committee of Correspondence," XI (1903–1904), 345–349.

56. John Pownall (secretary to the Board of Trade) to Edward Athawes, Nov. 7, 1763, C.O. 5/1330:243; Athawes to Pownall, n.d. (but endorsed as received on Nov. 24, 1763), C.O. 5/1330:519; Board of Trade, *Journals*, 1759–1763, p. 418; and Commissioners of Trade to Fauquier, Dec. 9, 1763, C.O. 5/1368:246.

27

For some unexplained reason, however, the Board of Trade abandoned the procedure suggested by the merchants—a referral to the colonial assembly. The following month, after notifying Montague and the London merchants to submit evidence, and without waiting to hear from the Virginia legislature, the commissioners began considering the question of paper money in *all* of the colonies. At the request of the Virginia agent, who was again ill, the board granted a delay until early February, 1764. Among the merchants invited to attend were James Crokatt, Edward Athawes, John Lidderode, Capel and Osgood Hanbury, Aufrere and Sargent, Trecothick and Thomlinson, Sir William Baker and John Nutt. Representing the colonies were William Knox of Georgia, Charles Garth of South Carolina, Edward Montague of Virginia, Robert Charles of New York, and Joseph Sherwood of New Jersey. The Board also called to attend a hearing on February 2, various officials familiar with the colonies: General Robert Monckton and Sir Charles Hardy of New York, Thomas Pownall and Joseph Hardy of New Jersey, Henry Ellis of Georgia, Thomas Penn and Richard Jackson (agent) of Pennsylvania, Dinwiddie and Ludwell of Virginia, and James Glen of South Carolina.[57]

Unfortunately we do not know fully what transpired at the hearing on February 2, 1764. All present agreed, however, that it would be "highly expedient and proper" to prohibit by act of Parliament all further emissions of paper bills of credit as legal tender, to remove the quality of legal tender from all bills then circulating after the period fixed for their redemption, and to set a terminal period for legal-tender bills not having a specified date for their redemption. Thomas Penn and Richard Jackson requested that Parliament not pass such an act until the following session to allow the colonies an opportunity to express their views.[58]

57. Pownall to Edward Athawes and Montague, Dec. 23, 1763, C.O. 5/1368: 208; form letter from Pownall to James Crokatt, Jan. 18, 1764, C.O. 324/17:338–339; Pownall to the several executives, n.d., C.O. 324/17:341; and Board of Trade, *Journals*, 1764–1767, pp. 3–4, 6, 11.

58. In his account of this episode, Richard Jackson also mentioned that Monckton and another individual had "agreed that they had seen the good Effects & even Necessity of Paper Money. . . ." Jackson to Franklin, n.d. (but post April, 1764), Van Doren (ed.), *Letters and Papers of Franklin and Jackson*, pp. 116–117.

Merchants, Agents, and Practical Issues

On February 7, the agents had their chance. Garth, Sherwood, Montague, Jouvencal, Charles, and William Knox attended the board. They asked that the colonies might be informed of the commissioners' intention to press for an act of Parliament so that they might receive further instructions from their constituents. After pointing out the supposed inconvenience of this procedure, the commissioners asked if the agents intended to oppose such a bill in Parliament. The agents did not reply immediately, but instead asked for time to consider. Four days later Charles, acting as spokesman for the group, announced that they would not support the board's proposal. They agreed unanimously that a certain quantity of paper currency ought to circulate in the colonies as legal tender in all contracts and dealings *within* each province and that each colony be allowed to report on the amount it required.[59] The arguments of the agents seem to have had little effect on the commissioners. Two days later, on February 9, 1764, the board issued a formal representation condemning the practices of the colonies in emitting paper money and calling for the extension of the Act of 1751 to all of the provinces.[60] The agents did not give up. On February 13, Knox and Garth submitted a counterproposal: first, no bills of credit issued by a colonial legislature were to be legal tender for debts contracted with residents of Great Britain; second, these bills were not to be legal tender for the discharge of any debt whatsoever until the Privy Council of Great Britain approved the law creating such money.

What followed next is not entirely clear. Apparently the Commissioners of Trade dropped the idea of bringing a bill into Parliament that year, as the agents had earlier requested. But late in March, Anthony Bacon, acting not as a member of the merchants'

59. Knox evidently compiled the arguments used by the agents. See his sixteen-page memorandum, "The Proposition of the Board of Trade to take away the lawful tender from all Paper Currency in the Colonies," Knox Manuscripts. In connection with Knox's arguments see also Price, "Rise of Glasgow in the Chesapeake Tobacco Trade," pp. 194–198; and Richard M. Jellison, "Antecedents of the South Carolina Currency Acts of 1736 and 1746," *William and Mary Quarterly*, 3rd Ser., XVI (1959), 556–567.

60. Board of Trade representation, February 9, 1764, C.O. 324/17:343–366; Order in Council, March 9, 1764, C.O. 5/65:397–398; and Munroe (ed.), *Acts of the Privy Council, Colonial Series*, IV, 623–645.

committee but in the private capacity of a member of Parliament, "unexpectedly revived" the question of paper money in the House of Commons.[61] On April 4, he moved for permission to bring in a bill to prevent future emissions of paper money as legal tender and to regulate the legal tender clauses of bills of credit then in circulation. In substance this was the proposal made by the Board of Trade in its representation of February 9. Consequently Edward Rice, a Commissioner of Trade, seconded Bacon's motion.

At this point the agents and merchants in the House of Commons were able to work out a compromise with the administration forces. Sir William Meredith and Peregrine Cust—a London merchant and brother to the Speaker of the House—opposed Bacon's motion, with Garth, the agent for South Carolina, supplying them with arguments against Bacon's proposal. Charles Townshend supported them, arguing that the colonies ought to be allowed paper currency as legal tender, but under proper regulation. The issue then went to a committee consisting of Townshend, Sir William Baker, Rice, Bacon, Meredith, and Soam Jenyns, another Commissioner of Trade. After some discussion Rice and Jenyns proposed to Meredith and other friends of the agents that they should confine the proposed bill "to the single point of preventing the Colonies for the future from passing Acts issueing paper bills with the clause of legal tender," but not to set an expiration date for any then circulating. Since the "sense" of the House of Commons favored "restraining the provinces of this power," the agents thought it best to accept this compromise.[62]

In its final form, the Currency Act of 1764[63] was much less severe

61. Hillsborough to Grenville, March ?, 1764, George Grenville Papers, in the possession of Sir John Murray, 50 Albemarle St., London; Board of Trade, *Journals*, 1763–1767, p. 21; Jackson to Franklin [April ?, 1764], Van Doren (ed.), *Letters and Papers of Franklin and Jackson*, p. 116; and Joseph Sherwood to Jacob Spicer of the New Jersey committee of correspondence, March 24, 1764; Sherwood to Samuel Smith, April 19, 1764, Joseph Sherwood Letters, New Jersey Historical Society, Newark, 1752–1768.

62. *Commons Journal*, XXIX, 1027; and Garth to the South Carolina committee of correspondence, March ?, 1764, as quoted in Namier, *England in the Age of the American Revolution*, p. 293 and Namier, "Charles Garth, Agent for South Carolina," p. 640.

63. The Currency Act of 1764 is 4 Geo. III, c. 34.

than the proposal originally suggested by the Board of Trade in its report of February 9, 1764. The commissioners had then advocated extending the curbs imposed in 1751 on the New England colonies to the other provinces. The statute of 1751 had not abolished paper money, as is sometimes thought, but merely established rules for retiring bills according to the specifications included in the provincial legislation creating the currency. The Currency Act of 1764— a compromise reached by the Commissioners of Trade, the agents, and the merchants in the House of Commons—did not ban paper money in the colonies or legal-tender currency then circulating; it merely prohibited further legal-tender laws and required that the provinces retire existing legal-tender currency on the dates specified for their expiration.

Only at this time on the question of paper money as legal tender for sterling debts were the agents and *some* merchants to disagree. Within a short time, particularly after legal tender issues then outstanding were retired in the colonies, the merchants were fully to support the agents in their efforts to lessen the restrictions imposed by the imperial legislature in the act of 1764. They later cooperated in order to obtain remedial legislation satisfactory both to the colonists and the merchants in Great Britain.

The bills of credit issued by the colonial assemblies to help finance the French and Indian War served as currency while this paper was outstanding. As the provinces retired these bills between 1766 and 1768, and the amount of money available as a medium of exchange consequently decreased, the assemblies of the middle and southern colonies invariably sought to issue fresh bills as legal tender. As some British politicians aligned with George Grenville were then quick to point out, "Their want of paper in circulation is, therefore, an evidence of their having no public debts outstanding; and that their ordinary expences are too inconsiderable to supply them with a medium equal to their trade."·Further attempts by the colonies to issue paper money indicated that they had retired their war debts and could indeed afford to pay the taxes proposed during the Grenville administration in 1764–1765.[64]

64. [Thomas Whately and/or William Knox], *The Present State of the Nation Particularly with Respect to its Trade, Finances, &c. &c.* (London, 1768), p. 74.

CHAPTER II

Prologue to Revolution:
Constitutional Issues during the
Grenville Ministry

I

AT the close of the French and Indian War, a costly conflict waged primarily for the protection of the American colonies,[1] several colonial agents informed their constituents of the decision of the British government to station 10,000 troops in North America and the West Indies [2] for the defense of the newly expanded empire and to raise revenue from the colonists to pay part of the cost. From this decision, made during the administration of the Earl of Bute in the winter of 1762–1763, stemmed the constitutional disputes of the administration of George Grenville destined to disrupt the

1. For the British motives in waging the French and Indian War, or the Great War for Empire, see J. M. Sosin, *Whitehall and the Wilderness: The Middle West in British Colonial Policy, 1760–1775* (Lincoln, Nebr., 1961), pp. 5–25.

2. See Joseph Sherwood to the governor of Rhode Island, Aug. 4, 1763, Rhode Island Agents, Official Letters, Brown University Library, Providence; Sherwood to Samuel Smith of the New Jersey committee of correspondence, Aug. 4, 1763, Joseph Sherwood Letters, New Jersey Historical Society Library, Newark; and Jasper Mauduit to the speaker of the Massachusetts House of Representatives, Feb. 11, 1764, Massachusetts Historical Society *Collections*, 1st Ser., VI (Boston, 1794, 1800), 194. Mauduit referred to his previous letter of March 12, 1763.

first British Empire. The Grenville ministry, faced with a staggering war debt incurred for the security of America and the need to find revenue for the protection of newly acquired buffer territories—Canada, the North American interior, and the Floridas—initially sought only to devise ways to increase the American contribution for the expanded defense establishment. Seeking practical solutions to this immediate problem, the administrators on the executive boards invariably consulted the colonial agents and, to a lesser extent, British merchants. To understand the success or failure of the lobbyists it is essential to appreciate how and why the imperial administration formulated its solutions. When the agents and merchants were able to offer feasible alternatives or compromises, the Board of Trade and the Commissioners of the Treasury were often receptive to their suggestions. But the colonial assemblies limited the agents' freedom of action and their effectiveness by challenging the political authority of the mother country. The issue as seen by Grenville was no longer only raising revenue from the colonies, but at the same time meeting the constitutional challenge by affirming the principle of British sovereignty.

The presence of British troops in North America almost immediately gave rise to major constitutional and political questions involving the rights and liberties of the colonists. As part of the Revolutionary Settlement of 1688–1689 Parliament, in order to ensure civil control of the army and prevent the arbitrary use of military force, periodically passed Mutiny Acts, comparable to the modern Articles of War or the Uniform Code of Military Justice. When the imperial legislature in 1765 attempted to extend the Mutiny Act to America it gave rise to serious constitutional questions involving the personal liberties of individuals and the respective powers of Parliament and the colonial assemblies.

The extension of Parliamentary jurisdiction resulted from the peculiar position of the British Army in America. Except for small headquarters detachments, no soldiers were permanently stationed in the settled areas of the provinces, and consequently there were no regular facilities to accommodate troops. In order to reach their interior stations from the coast, however, troops had to march through populated areas, where they might be billeted for brief intervals. In many colonies the civil authorities refused to provide

33

housing and such incidental supplies as vinegar, salt, rum, firewood and bedding. Some provincials, having been told that the British Mutiny Acts did not extend to America, or so the British Commander-in-Chief Thomas Gage and his deputy Barracksmaster James Robertson complained, threatened to prosecute magistrates who attempted to quarter soldiers. To rectify the situation Gage suggested to officials in London that clauses be incorporated into the Mutiny Act scheduled to be passed by Parliament in 1765. By the additions Gage proposed, civil magistrates in the colonies might quarter the troops in private homes if there were no barracks. The Secretary at War, Welbore Ellis, concurred in the suggestions [3] and on orders from the Secretary of State, the Earl of Halifax, early in April, 1765 brought into the House of Commons a bill extending the Mutiny Act to America. But on the motion from printing the bill, the administration suffered a setback. As reported by the agent for Rhode Island, "many of the Members of the House opposed this measure as Arbitrary and Contrary to the natural Liberty of the Subject. . . ." Richard Jackson, agent for Connecticut, a member of Parliament and Grenville's Secretary at the Exchequer, predicted that from what he knew of the disposition of the administration it would be willing to drop the objectionable clause. [4]

3. Gage to the Earl of Halifax, Jan. 23, 1765, Clarence E. Carter (ed.), *Correspondence of General Thomas Gage* (2 vols., New Haven, 1931–1933), I, 49; Gage to Welbore Ellis, Jan. 22, 1765, *ibid.*, II, 262; two enclosures from Gage, *ibid.*, II, 263–264, 266; Halifax to Ellis, March 2, 1765, and Ellis to Halifax, March 7, 1765, S.P. 41/25:4, 5. See also the account of the later Secretary at War (Viscount Barrington), sent to the Earl of Chatham, endorsed "Account of the Recent Mutiny Act in America." P.R.O. 30/8/97:23–24. The account is endorsed as received on Feb. 10, 1765, but the correct date probably is February, 1767. While Halifax and Ellis evidently had no qualms about quartering troops in private domiciles, the King did. George III complained to George Grenville, the administration spokesman in the House of Commons, that the Secretary of State appeared to have disregarded the "noise that may be made here in Parliament" over the clause. Grenville agreed that it might cause difficulty, especially as the quartering of soldiers "upon the people against their wills is declared by the petition of right to be contrary to law," but, he pointed out, a precedent in Scotland might justify the procedure now contemplated for the colonies. George III to Grenville, March 9, 1765, Grenville to George III, March 9, 1765, William J. Smith (ed.), *The Grenville Papers* (4 vols., London, 1852–1853), III, 11–12, 13.

4. Halifax to Ellis, March 11, 1765, S.P. 4/25:6; Sherwood to Governor Stephen Hopkins, April 11, 1765, Gertrude S. Kimball (ed.), *Correspondence of the*

With Parliament adjourned until April 19, the agents and merchants took up the cause. Garth of South Carolina, now a member of Parliament, and Montague of Virginia contacted the London merchants trading to North America. At a joint meeting where the South Carolina agent supplied objections to the Mutiny bill, the merchants appointed a committee consisting of Garth and Richard Glover, member for Weymouth, to wait on Grenville, the administration spokesman in the House of Commons. In a two-hour conference with the First Lord of the Treasury they discussed their objections to the proposed measure. Grenville assured them that he would speak to the Secretary at War about amending the bill. At a subsequent meeting attended by Garth, Glover, Franklin, Barlow Trecothick, and Jared Ingersoll, special agent from Connecticut, Ellis altered the objectionable clauses. The entire committee of the London merchants trading to America subsequently approved the amended bill, and the agents were able to assure their constituents that by the modifications they had secured with the assistance of the merchants, the civil magistrates in the colonies would quarter troops in barracks, and if those were insufficient, then in empty houses, barns, and other facilities, but there was "to be no Billeting in Private Houses."[5] Here was an excellent example of cooperation between the lobby and the administration in eliminating an infraction against personal liberties.

Colonial Governors of Rhode Island, 1723–1775 (2 vols., Boston and New York, 1902), II, 362; and Jackson to Governor Thomas Fitch, April 19, 1765, "The Fitch Papers," Connecticut Historical Society *Collections* (2 vols., Hartford, 1918–1920), XVIII, 343–344.

5. See Garth to the South Carolina committee of correspondence, April 5, May 25, 1765, printed in Lewis B. Namier, "Charles Garth, Agent for South Carolina," *English Historical Review*, LIV (1939), 641–642 and Lewis B. Namier, *England in the Age of the American Revolution* (London, 1930), pp. 294–295; and Sherwood to Hopkins, May 2, 1765, Kimball (ed.), *Correspondence of the Colonial Governors of Rhode Island*, II, 363. See also the undated draft of a letter to Welbore Ellis requesting an appointment on the Mutiny bill for Glover and Trecothick, Benjamin Franklin Papers, American Philosophical Society Library, Philadelphia, L-2, pp. 55. It is clear that "Governor" Thomas Pownall also had a hand in amending the Mutiny Act. See Charles Jenkinson to Grenville, April 11, 1765, Ninetta S. Jucker (ed.), *The Jenkinson Papers, 1760–1766* (London, 1949), pp. 358–359; and Grenville to Jenkinson, April 13, 1765, George Grenville Letter Book, Huntington Library, Stowe Collection, San Marino, Calif., St. 7, Vol. II.

Ironically the agents seem to have given little thought to one clause of the Mutiny Act which later provoked a major constitutional dispute: the power of Parliament to *require* the colonial assemblies by specified procedures to furnish barracks or hired houses with bedding, candles, small beer or rum. Before the act had been passed, Grenville had discussed the clause containing this provision with Glover and Trecothick, who "seem'd to acquiese in it"; consequently Grenville hoped there would be no substantial objections.[6] Subsequent developments did not fulfill his hopes. The requirement by Parliament that the provincial legislatures provide services for the army later raised the constitutional question of the authority of the imperial legislature to issue orders to the colonial assemblies. But Grenville had at least been open-minded and flexible in his attitude on the act governing the royal army in America. He demonstrated the same mentality when dealing with the problem of revenue to support the military forces.

II

In the spring of 1763 it fell to George Grenville, as First Lord of the Treasury, to implement the decisions of the preceding Bute administration. Colonial revenue was the key problem. Initiating an exhaustive investigation of the sources of colonial revenue, the Treasury officials then drew up a comprehensive program based on a realistic examination of the patterns of colonial trade, the inadequacies of existing revenue sources, and the financial condition of the colonies. So well informed were Grenville and his assistants and so comprehensive was their program that the colonial agents and British merchants were to find it difficult to induce the administration to abandon the project.

A difficult problem in financing the American defense establishment faced Grenville and his Secretaries at the Treasury, Charles Jenkinson and Thomas Whately. The basic establishment for 7,500 troops in North America (2,500 were stationed in the lesser islands of the West Indies) came to roughly £200,000 a year, but uncertain additional expenses increased the amount. The Indian departments and the cost of the civil establishments of the "infant" colonies such

6. Grenville to Ellis, April 27, 1765, Grenville Letter Book, St. 7, Vol. II. For the controversial clauses of the Mutiny Act of 1765 (5 Geo. III c. 33), see the first, seventh, and eighth paragraphs of the statute.

Courtesy of New York Public Library

George Grenville

as Nova Scotia, Georgia, and the Floridas also fell within the military budget. The disposition of many of the garrisons in the interior, remote from the settlements and consequently difficult to provision, increased the military budget. The cost of the North American military establishment placed an added burden on the already overloaded English finances. As a result of the late war with France and Spain, the national debt had risen from £73 million to £137 million, with the funds borrowed at 3 to 4 per cent drawing nearly £5 million a year interest at a time when the annual national budget stood at £8 million. The financial situation in Great Britain contrasted greatly with that in the colonies. Investigation by the Commissioners of the Treasury and Trade indicated that the provinces had relatively few and slight financial obligations. The cost of the civil establishment was only £75,000 a year. Although the colonies had expended £2,500,000 during the war, Parliament had reimbursed them with grants of £1,500,000 and the provinces were now retiring the remaining war debt rapidly. Indeed the Treasury estimated they would be cleared by 1769. These figures indicated that the colonies could contribute some financial aid to relieve the mother country of a portion of the burden in supporting the new North American military establishment.[7]

The Treasury Board under Grenville attacked the problem on a broad front. It was apparent almost at once that the existing trade and revenue laws were not yielding their full potential in duties. The royal navy, armed with instructions from the Privy Council, was ordered to patrol American waters to check smuggling, while the Commissioners of Customs were requested to report on further possible remedies.[8]

7. T. 1/433:404 has the military charge for the American garrisons in 1765. Originally the Treasury limited the outlay for surveys and the Indian departments to £15,000 a year (Jenkinson to the Earl of Hillsborough, Jan. 4, 1764, Add. MSS., 38304, f. 7), but this proved inadequate. See also Thomas Whately, *Considerations of the Trade and Finances of this Kingdom, and on the Measures of Administration with respect to those great National Objects since the conclusion of the Peace* (3rd edn., London, 1769), p. 79. For the estimates of the colonial civil list and the provincial war debt see C.O. 324/17:497, 498.

8. Jenkinson to the Commissioners of Customs, May 21, 1763, T. 11/27:282; 3 Geo. III c. 22; minute of the Privy Council, June 2, 1763, S.P. 30/47:21 and circular letter from Egremont (Secretary of State for the Southern Department) to the colonial governors, July 9, 1763, "The Fitch Papers," XVIII, 247–248.

Much of the later Grenville program for the colonies was based on two reports issued by the Commissioners of Customs. The first, issued on May 19, 1759, in an effort to halt illegal trading with the enemy during the French war, had not been acted upon by the imperial government, and the Customs Board now incorporated it into a supplemental report of July 21, 1763. In these reports the Commissioners of Customs suggested additional legislation by Parliament to better ascertain, identify, and estimate the quantity of goods shipped, the duties paid, and the arrival and clearance of ships in colonial ports. The irregularity of the American coastline made it difficult to check smuggling, if the colonists sought to violate any trade statute, but the Customs Commissioners emphasized violations of two Acts of Trade and Revenue: 25 Charles II, c. 87 and particularly 6 Geo. II, c. 2, which imposed a duty of sixpence on a gallon of foreign molasses. Violations of this last act were all the more prevalent since customs collectors in the colonies engaged in collusive practices with local smugglers. For their part, revenue officials in America had for some time suggested the "Expediency" of allowing the produce of the foreign West Indies to be imported at lower duties in exchange for fish and lumber since molasses, in particular, was necessary to the distilleries of New England. Although the Customs Board realized that procedures in the colonies for enforcing trade and revenue laws were lax, they suggested only that absentee officials be ordered to their posts in the provinces and declined recommending the enforcement of these acts in vice-admiralty courts rather than in the common-law courts, which employed provincial juries.[9]

Despite the hesitancy of the Customs Board to abandon the existing system, Grenville's Treasury was to expand the jurisdiction in trade and revenue cases of the vice-admiralty courts in the colonies. Ironically, a former colonial agent, William Bollan, had unwittingly contributed to the Treasury's decision. Bollan, when advocate of the vice-admiralty court in Massachusetts, had proposed legislation to extend the powers of the prerogative court over all violations of the Acts of Trade. There were "Scarce any hopes of Success" in the common-law courts, he had argued, for the prosecution could not

9. Report of the Commissioners of Customs, July 21, 1763, T. 1/426:269–272 (copy in the Jenkinson Papers, Add. MSS. 38335, ff. 144–147).

compel witnesses to testify. Trial by jury, he had observed sarcastically, was "only trying one Illicit Trader by his Fellows, or at least
his well wishers. . . ." The Customs Commissioners had treated his
recommendations lightly, dismissing what they termed "small
Inaccuracies" in the current laws and foreseeing new difficulties
with legislation aimed at expanding the powers of the vice-admiralty
courts.[10] However, the Treasury took Bollan's recommendations
more seriously and later incorporated some of his proposals into its
American program. In July, 1763 Charles Jenkinson wrote to the
secretary of the Customs Board for copies of the correspondence
which had occasioned the Customs report of 1759, and specifically
the opinion of the solicitors to the Customs Board on Bollan's
recommendations.[11] At the same time the Treasury ordered the
Customs Commissioners to set up administrative procedures for
determining the volume and channels of colonial trade, maintaining
records of incoming and outgoing vessels, cargoes, destinations,
and bonds issued for enumerated goods as required by the Acts of
Navigation. Officials were to tally these and note any discrepancies
so that possible collusion between shippers and customs officials
in the colonies could be detected.[12]

On September 16, 1763, the Customs Commissioners presented a
detailed plan incorporating the procedures required to restrain
illegal trade detrimental to the revenue service. One aspect of this

10. See the report of the Commissioners of Customs of May 10, 1759, T.
1/392:38–39; and the report of their solicitors on Bollan's observations of Feb. 26,
1742–1743, Oct. 24, 1749, and June 9, 1755. Bollan's letter of 1743 is printed in
Worthington C. Ford (ed.), "Letters of Governor Shirley and William Bollan
to the Lords of Trade, respecting the disregard in New England of the Navigation
Laws, 1743," Publications of the Colonial Society of Massachusetts *Transactions*,
VI (1899–1900), 300–301. Bollan, who had been dismissed as agent for Massachusetts, at this time appeared before the Board of Trade and offered his assistance
on the problem of illicit trade. See Bollan to John Pownall, May 2, 1763, C.O.
323/15:97; Pownall to Bollan, May 6, 1763, C.O. 324/14:201; and Great Britain,
Board of Trade, *Journals of the Lords Commissioners of Trade and Plantations* (14 vols.
London, 1920–1938), 1759–1763, p. 364.
11. Jenkinson to William Wood, July 23, 1763, T. 11/27:283.
12. Treasury Board minutes for July 22, 29, 1763, T. 29/35:125–126, 135;
Jenkinson to the Customs Commissioners, July 25, 1763, T. 11/27:304; and three
letters from Thomas Whately to the Customs Commissioners, July 25, 1763, T.
11/27:424, 425.

second report of 1763, relating to the duties on the produce of the foreign West Indies imposed by the Sugar Act of 1733, was particularly important. Although smugglers were evading or compounding for the duties originally intended to halt trade with the French Islands, the Customs Commissioners suggested that the trade of the British colonies with the foreign Indies should not now be interrupted. The North American provinces "being now augmented" required "very great additional" quantities of sugar and molasses, which would be supplied principally from the French Indies. Moreover, the French planters, no longer having recourse to their own colonies in North America, would require still greater quantities of provisions, lumber, and livestock from the British provinces on the mainland. The remedy lay in reducing the six-penny tax. A lower duty on molasses and sugar would still raise revenue and not destroy the vital trade between the mainland and the foreign islands.[13]

13. Customs report of Sept. 16, 1763, T. 1/426:289. Evidently Edward Hooper did most of the work on this report, but Richard Jackson, Grenville's Secretary at the Exchequer, was also consulted. See Jackson to Jenkinson, Sept. 18, 1763, Jucker (ed.), *Jenkinson Papers*, p. 191. The British colonies in North America were indeed vital to the economy of the French sugar islands, as the Customs Board thought. The French had no other major market for their produce, and no other source for provisions, livestock, and lumber. As early as 1681 the planters of Guadeloupe and Martinique had sought the permission of Colbert to trade with New England (Agnes M. Whitson, "The Outlook of the Continental American Colonies on the British West Indies, 1760–1775," *Political Science Quarterly*, XL [1930], 60, and Stewart L. Mims, *Colbert's West Indian Policy* [New Haven, 1912], pp. 222–224). In 1763, with the conclusion of hostilities, the French court granted permission to the island governors to allow British ships to enter and take off rum and molasses. Governor George Thomas of Antigua pointed out that the French allowed this trade under regulations, for "without Lumber, Provisions, and Horses, the French Sugar Colonies must sink; and yet those valuable Articles are to be paid for only with Molasses and Rum, which would otherwise be useless to them. . . ." A few months later Thomas noted that Dominica since the conclusion of the peace treaty had become the market for the produce of the French islands. Local British customs officials admitted and cleared French sugar, rum, and molasses as the produce of the British islands without payment of duties. Naval officers attempting to enforce the law had "met with great discouragements in the execution of their Duty, from the Persons concerned in this fraudulent Trade. . . ." Thomas to Egremont, Sept. 9, 1763, C.O. 152/47:35 (enclosing copies of two sets of regulations, dated Aug. 18, 1763, issued by Governor General de Bourlamaque and Intendant de Peiner at Guadeloupe based on the order of the French King of April 18, 1763, C.O. 152/47:37–40); and Thomas to Halifax, March 28, 1764, C.O. 152/47:59.

Almost immediately the Commissioners of the Treasury took action to draft a law incorporating the provisions for lowering the duties on foreign molasses and sugar and tightening the procedures for enforcing the Revenue Acts.[14] They presented a memorial to the Privy Council stating their findings and recommending a new procedure for prosecuting violations of the trade and revenue laws by a new vice-admiralty court having concomitant jurisdiction over all America with the courts already established there. But it would have no jurisdiction in cases where particular acts of Parliament had confined the recovery of penalties and forfeitures to the local courts.[15]

Closer supervision and enforcement of the existing Acts of Trade and Revenue under the authority of the imperial legislature, an expansion of the jurisdiction of the vice-admiralty courts, and a reduction by statute of the duties imposed by the act of 1733: these were the elements of the new program to be presented to Parliament early in 1764. The increase in revenue expected from this program was still insufficient to defray the colonial share of the burden of North American defense. An additional source of revenue was needed. On September 23, 1763, Charles Jenkinson informed the Commissioners of the Stamp Office that they were to prepare for the consideration of the Commissioners of the Treasury the draft of an act "for imposing proper Stamp Duties upon his Majesty's Subjects in America and the West Indies."[16] The decision to impose stamp duties was to have tremendous consequences in the future, but needing time to formulate a stamp bill, the Treasury did not immediately proceed with stamp duties in 1764.

14. Treasury Board minute, Sept. 21, 1763, T. 29/35:164; and three letters from Whately to the Customs Board, Sept. 23, 1763, T. 11/27:320, 321, 331. To centralize the administration of the new regulatory program, the following month Henry Hulton was appointed Plantations Clerk to receive all reports from American ports, prepare and dispatch documents, and "keep a constant and strict attention to the conduct & correspondence of the officers of the customs in the plantations. . . ." Treasury order, October 19, 1763, T. 11/27:359.

15. The memorial of the Treasury, Oct. 4, 1763, T. 29/35:68–73; order in council, Oct. 5, 1763, and the reference to the Law Officers on the Admiralty court and their report, C.O. 5/67:249–255, 256–259; representation of the Admiralty, March 14, 1764, C.O. 5/67:259–264; order in council of March 26, 1764, T. 1/429:156–159, and the commission for the new admiralty court, June 15, 1764, Add. MSS. 35190, ff. 225–228.

16. Jenkinson to the Commissioners of Stamps, Sept. 23, 1763, T. 27/28:432.

Agents and Merchants

While the Grenville ministry was thus formulating its American program throughout 1763, the colonial agents had not been idle. Many realized that at best they could only persuade the ministers to modify, not abandon, the program. Richard Jackson, agent for Connecticut and Pennsylvania, as Grenville's Secretary at the Exchequer seems to have worked on some aspects of the Grenville legislation for America. He was ópposed to certain facets of the program, considering the "inland duty" or stamp tax levied by Parliament as having a "very dangerous Tendency," and had recommended a tax of three half pence on foreign molasses. He would not object to a rate of twopence, however. Although Jackson had lobbied privately with the ministry he had not succeeded in making any appreciable impression, and he was convinced that it was useless to argue against raising revenue in the colonies for the support of the British garrisons. It would "answer no purpose to do so." Jasper Mauduit emphasized the same point with his Massachusetts constituents. Everyone in the administration agreed that the government should impose and enforce a practical duty. The agent hoped that the British ministers would be generally disposed "to serve the colonies, and not to distress them." The Treasury had originally decided on a tax of fourpence on foreign molasses, but Grenville now seemed satisfied with half that rate. In conjunction with the other agents, Mauduit had been left to pursue an independent course since the Massachusetts General Court had "not been pleased to instruct" him after he had twice warned the provincial assembly of the intended British measures.[17]

17. Jackson to Franklin, Nov. 12, 1763, Franklin Papers, American Philosophical Society Library, I, 83; Jackson to Franklin, Dec. 23, 1763, Jan. 26, 1764, Carl Van Doren (ed.), *Letters and Papers of Benjamin Franklin and Richard Jackson, 1753–1785* (Philadelphia, 1947), pp. 123, 138; and Jasper Mauduit to the Speaker of the Massachusetts assembly, Dec. 30, 1763, Massachusetts Historical Society *Collections*, 1st Ser., VI, 194. Although the Massachusetts legislature did not act officially, late in 1763 Thomas Cushing, later Speaker of the House, privately informed Mauduit of the Bay Colony's objections to the enforcement of the Sugar Act of 1733. He cleverly pointed out to the new agent that the supporters of Bollan who had been dismissed from the post were contending that had he still been agent, Bollan would have strenuously protested the contemplated tax on molasses. The best way to settle the issue, he advised, would be to lower the duty to one half penny per gallon. By this time the merchants of Massachusetts had begun to react. In 1763 they organized "The Society for encouraging Trade and Commerce

Generally the colonial assemblies were slow in reacting to the warnings of the agents. Although Governor Francis Bernard corresponded with the home government on the vital role of foreign molasses in the New England economy, and the House of Representatives of the Bay Colony in the spring of 1763 appointed a committee to consider the revision in the imperial regulations on trade, it was not until December that the committee adopted a petition of the Massachusetts merchants and sent Mauduit their views on the tax rate imposed on foreign molasses. Other colonial legislatures were also tardy in transmitting their protests against the intended modifications of the Acts of Trade and Revenue. Governor Stephen Hopkins waited until January 13, 1764, before issuing a call to the Rhode Island assembly, and not until the following month did it send to London its analysis of the role of the molasses trade in the New England economic complex. The General Court of Connecticut did not act until March, 1764.[18] The "lazy" committee of correspondence of New York, according to one councilor,

----

within the Province of Massachusetts Bay" for the express purpose of preventing the renewal of the Act of 1733, due to expire in 1763. The society adopted a "State of the Trade" written by Thomas Gray and Edward Payne aimed at showing the condition of New England commerce. It sent copies to the merchants of the other New England colonies, and to Mauduit and Bollan. The burden of their argument was that the molasses and rum trade was the vital element of the New England economic complex, involving the traffic in fish, provisions, lumber, and livestock with the West Indies and Africa. A duty of sixpence on foreign molasses, they contended, was prohibitive; indeed the vital molasses trade would "not bear any Duty at all." This last contention was not true, as events later proved, but for the present the merchants persuaded the various New England legislatures to adopt their arguments and support their cause. Cushing to Mauduit, Oct. 28, 1763, *Jasper Mauduit Agent in London for the Province of the Massachusetts Bay 1762–1765* (Massachusetts Historical Society *Collections*, Vol. LXXIV [Boston, 1918]), p. 131. Copies of the "State" are printed in Connecticut Historical Society *Collections*, XVIII, 263, and Publications of the Colonial Society of Massachusetts *Transactions*, XIX (1916–1917), 382–390. See also committee of the Boston merchants to the merchants of New London, Connecticut, Jan. 19, 1764, "The Fitch Papers," XVIII, 261–262.

18. Alice Vering, "James Otis" (Ph.D. dissertation, University of Nebraska, 1954), pp. 107–109, 111; J. H. Trumbull and C. J. Hoadley (eds.), *Public Records of the Colony of Connecticut (1636–1776)* (15 vols., Hartford, 1850–1890), XII, 240; Board of Trade, *Journals*, 1764–1767, pp. 77, 79. The Rhode Island remonstrance is in C.O. 5/1276:701–714.

wrote neither to the agent Robert Charles, nor to Governor Robert Monckton, then in Britain. Finally in March, 1764 Lieutenant Governor Cadwallader Colden, at the insistence of the council and provincial merchants, transmitted to the Board of Trade a petition from the New York mercantile community.[19] The New York remonstrance, as the other colonial protests, arrived in London too late to be used in determining the new tax rate on foreign molasses set by Parliamentary statute in March, 1764.

The agents consequently were left to their own resources. But it made little difference since the Treasury, well aware of the need for foreign molasses in New England, was operating on the assumption that the new duty would not harm the trade with the foreign West Indies. The specific rate imposed on foreign molasses was the result of a compromise effected by the Treasury between the claims of the West Indian planter interest and the New England agents. Joseph Sherwood initially reported that the administration would introduce a bill lowering the duty to twopence, but in the House of Commons, Rose Fuller, "a West Indian," reported the resolutions of the committee on expiring laws that the Act of 1733 with the duty of sixpence be continued. Both Israel and Jasper Mauduit, as well as Joseph Sherwood, claimed that the West India interest exerted influence to have the rate increased.[20] The Massachusetts agent on February

19. John Watts to Monckton, Dec. 29, 1763, "Letter Book of John Watts, Merchant and Councillor of New York . . . ," New York Historical Society *Collections*, LXI (1928), 211–212; Colden to the Commissioners of Trade, March 9, 1764, "The Letters and Papers of Cadwallader Colden," New York Historical Society *Collections* (New York, 1877–1878, 1918–1924, 1935, 1937), IX (1876), 312.

20. Jasper Mauduit to the Massachusetts House of Representatives, Feb. 11, 1764, Massachusetts Historical Society *Collections*, 1st Ser., VI, 194–195; Joseph Sherwood to Samuel Smith, Feb. 4, 1764, Sherwood Letters, New Jersey Historical Society; and Great Britain, Parliament, *Journal of the House of Commons* (London, 1558—), XIX, 825. Israel Mauduit claimed that there was little to be done on the molasses duty since "this is a very bad Session for any such attempt, when the state of parties is such that 50 or 60 West Indian votes can turn the balance on which side they please." Mauduit to ?, March 3, 1764, *Jasper Mauduit Agent in London*, p. 149n. Sherwood also saw the West Indian lobby at work. He wrote: "I have Intelligence that the West Indian Traders are forming a Scheme to prevent or Abridge the Trade of the American Colonies to the French Islands. . . ." Sherwood to Gov. Stephen Hopkins, Sept. 12, 1763, Kimball (ed.), *Correspondence of the Colonial Governors of Rhode Island*, II, 352. Two points may be noted: first,

27, 1764, presented to the Treasury a memorial drawn up by his brother as well as the statement of a private merchant (perhaps Thomas Cushing of Massachusetts) that the trade would bear no more than one penny per gallon. The Mauduits themselves were content to represent against any duty higher than twopence, arguing that a higher duty would destroy the New England fisheries. This was not the case, as the Treasury officials knew and as was later proved. The Treasury set the final rate at threepence. According to Thomas Whately, who drew up the Trade and Revenue Act of 1764, this figure represented a compromise between the four-pence asked by the West Indians and the two pennies suggested by the agents for North America.[21]

The agents had another opportunity when the ministry introduced the revenue bill into the House of Commons on March 14. Sherwood and several others tried unsuccessfully to have the molasses duty reduced to twopence. For a week John Thomlinson, Jr., agent for

---

Mauduit exaggerated the numerical strength of the West Indian group; and second, the Act of 1764 was intended to raise revenue from, not prohibit, the trade with the foreign islands. A duty cannot be extractive and prohibitive at the same time.

21. Mauduit's memorial is in T. 1/430:204–205, but cf. the Treasury Board minute for February 27, 1764, T. 29/35:320. See also Whately, *Considerations on the Trade and Finances of this Kingdom*, p. 197. Edmund S. and Helen M. Morgan, *The Stamp Act Crisis. Prologue to Revolution* (Chapel Hill, 1953), p. 26, and Allen S. Johnson, "The Passage of the Sugar Act," *William and Mary Quarterly*, 3rd Ser. XVI (1959), 511, both contend that the Treasury chose the three-penny tax because it would yield the most revenue. They cite an undated and unsigned document in the Treasury Papers (T. 1/434:52—Johnson says it is in Whately's hand) in which it was estimated that the annual importation of foreign molasses was roughly 800,000 gallons. A duty of twopence per gallon would yield £66,667, while a duty of threepence would reduce the volume by the ratio of nine to seven, but would produce a greater revenue, £77,775. Thus the higher duty was adopted although it would adversely affect the colonial economy by reducing the amount of molasses imported. This analysis does not agree with the account published by Whately in describing the method by which the figure of threepence was selected. Secondly, even incomplete figures compiled by the Treasury and Customs showed that more than 900,000 gallons of foreign molasses were imported on which the three-penny duty was paid (T. 1/447:164). Finally, as will be shown below, the two men who worked out the details of the new tax, Whately and Jenkinson, both operated on the assumption—and it proved correct—that the French would have to absorb the tax by accepting a lower price for their molasses, since they depended on the mainland colonies as a market for their produce and as a source of provisions, lumber, and livestock.

New Hampshire, attended the House of Commons and met with other American agents. On March 25 they decided to have a "private Audience" with the First Lord of the Treasury. Unfortunately the minister had gone to his "Levee" when they called that day. They scheduled another meeting two days later to draw up a memorial to the Treasury,[22] but again they were too late, since the bill was ordered engrossed on March 26. Four days later it passed the House of Commons. The agents and merchants need not have bothered about the three-penny duty on foreign molasses. As officials at the Treasury expected, it did not harm colonial trade despite dire predictions in America.

The act for "granting certain Duties in the British Colonies" (4 Geo. III, c. 15) contained several significant provisions. The duties imposed by this statute, including the threepence tax on foreign molasses,[23] were to provide revenue toward defraying the

22. Jasper Mauduit to the speaker of the Massachusetts House, March 13, 1764, Massachusetts Archives, State House, Boston, XXII, 359; Israel Mauduit to ?, Massachusetts Archives, XXII, 357; *Commons Journal*, XIX, 934–935; William Cobbett (ed.), *The Parliamentary History of England from the Earliest Period to the Year 1803* (36 vols., London, 1813), XV, 1431; Sherwood to Joseph Clark, March 20, 1764, papers of Joseph Sherwood, agent for Rhode Island in London, Brown University Library, Providence; Sherwood to Jacob Spicer, March 24, 1764, Sherwood Letters, New Jersey Historical Society; and John Thomlinson, Jr. to John Thomlinson, Sr., March 26, 1764, Robert Mowbray Howard (ed.), *Records and Letters of the Family of the Longs of Longville, Jamaica, and Hampton Lodge, Surrey* (2 vols., London, 1925), I, 226. An unfinished memorial mentioned by Thomlinson may have some connection with the undated, five-and-one-half page paper on the molasses question among the William Knox Manuscripts, Clements Library, Ann Arbor.

23. It is impossible to hold, as some scholars have, that the Molasses Act of 1764 was identical in purpose with the Sugar Act of 1733, which set a duty of sixpence to restrict trade, or that the Grenville ministry with the support of the British West India planters "attempted to limit rigidly the overseas commerce of the Americans." The contention that the "chief purpose" of both the acts of 1733 and of 1764 "was to aid the British West Indian molasses producers and rum distillers by cutting off from their New England competitors their chief source of molasses," is untenable. (See, for example, John Richard Alden, *The South in the American Revolution, 1763–1789* [Baton Rouge, La., 1957], p. 59 and Gilman M. Ostrander, "The Colonial Molasses Trade," *Agricultural History*, XXX [1956], 77.) The preamble of the statute of 1764 states that act was intended to raise revenue—not to prohibit trade. Furthermore, the West Indian islands and the northern colonies were not competitive. As John Temple, Surveyor General for

cost of defending, protecting, and securing the colonies. The law also contained provisions to insure the full collection of revenue suggested by Commissioners of the Customs in their report of September 16, 1763. To check smuggling carried on under the guise of intercolonial or coastal trade, the statute specified that no goods could be shipped without a cocket purchased at the port of discharge listing every item carried. Goods having no cockets were liable to seizure. Finally, penalties and forfeitures could be recovered in courts of record or vice-admiralty either in the colony where the offense was committed or in a vice-admiralty court having jurisdiction over all America.[24] The court was established at Halifax, Nova Scotia that summer.

The "Black Act," as the Boston merchants called it, went into effect on September 29, 1764. From the protests previously registered by colonial merchants one might conclude, as did John Temple, Surveyor General of the Customs at Boston, that the colonial trade would either decline with catastrophic results to the colonial

---

the Customs of the Northern District in America, pointed out, the quantity of molasses exported by the British West Indies to the mainland colonies was "inconsiderable"—less than 10,000 hogsheads annually. Their molasses was "all turned into rum & principally" sent to Great Britain. Moreover, West India rum was a better article, commanding a much higher price than the American produce —"country" rum. The American merchant Thomas Clifford noted that "when there is so much difference in the price . . . the country buys the cheapest sort and makes a little West India serve." Finally, it should be noted that the British West Indian distillers were as anxious as the New Englanders to obtain French molasses for their distilleries. John Temple to Thomas Whately, Sept. 10, 1764, "The Bowdoin and Temple Papers," Massachusetts Historical Society *Collections*, 6th Ser., IX (Boston, 1897), 24; and Richard Pares, *Yankees and Creoles: The Trade between North America and the West Indies before the American Revolution* (Cambridge, Mass., 1956), p. 133. Richard B. Sheridan, "The Molasses Act and the Market Strategy of the British Sugar Planters," *The Journal of Economic History*, XVII (1957), 70, notes that although sizable quantities of British rum "continued to be consumed in the northern colonies . . . by far the greatest part of the market was supplied with cheap rum which was distilled in the New England colonies from foreign molasses, but in all of the colonies there were some discriminating customers who insisted upon the quality of rum that was imported from the British sugar colonies."

24. For a fuller explanation of the provisions dealing with bonds and cockets see Thomas Whately, *The Regulations lately Made concerning the Colonies and the Taxes Imposed upon Them, Considered* (London, 1765), pp. 95–97.

economy, or that the merchants would find some means through corrupt officials in the West Indies and America to naturalize foreign produce and bring it into the mainland as of British origin. But neither happened. Due to the vigilance of the customs officials in the West Indies [25] and America there was little, if any, smuggling. The new act was executed with "great exactness." As a result Temple, then revising his pessimistic view, reported that the New Englanders seemed reconciled to the new law. Within a week several vessels had entered Boston harbor with foreign molasses and the three-penny tax had been duly paid. The comptroller of the port sent still more encouraging news to London: despite the new duty, the price of molasses had not increased. This confirmed for Charles Jenkinson, joint Secretary to the Treasury, what he had expected. "The French who have no other Method of disposing" of their produce would be "forced to pay the Duty & not the People of the Colonies who purchase them." [26] Modern research confirms this analysis. An examination of the wholesale price of molasses in the colonies does not disclose any noticeable change attributable to the

25. Governor Charles Pinfold of Barbados reported that due to the vigilance of the customs and naval officials there was very little illicit trade in the West Indies. The "small Remains of Clandestine Commerce" would be easily surpressed, he predicted. According to Governor George Thomas there was very little illicit trade in the Leeward Islands. Officials had detected the practice of forging clearances at Angilla and had warned the customs officers on the mainland. All appeared most attentive in their duty. See Pinfold to the Commissioners of Trade, June 22, 1764, C.O. 28/32: unfoliated, and Thomas to Halifax, March 26, 1765, C.O. 152/47:98–99.

26. Temple to Whately, Sept. 10, Oct. 3, 1764, "The Bowdoin and Temple Papers," IX, pp. 24, 30; Jenkinson to Benjamin Hallowell, Jr., Jan. 12, 1765, Add. MSS. 38304, f. 112; and Benjamin Harrison to Jenkinson, May 3, 1765, Add. MSS. 38339, f. 119. A more detailed explanation of the analysis of the Treasury in concluding that the new tax would not harm the colonial economy is found in a pamphlet by Whately. The French West Indian planters had no other source for provisions and lumber except the British mainland colonies. They could pay for these provisions only with the produce of their own islands. Could they then refuse to exchange their produce except "upon our own Terms?" Whately asked, "since they have no other way to dispose of it." The trade of the West Indies, he maintained, "is always under the Controul of the Nation that is in Possession of North America. . . ." The island planters depended on the continent for the "Subsistance of their Inhabitants, and for the Means of disposing of their Produce. . . ." Whately, *The Regulations lately Made concerning the Colonies*, pp. 84–85.

legislation of 1764.[27] Indeed, the stability of the wholesale price index indicates that the Treasury officials under Grenville were correct in their estimates. French planters had to absorb the cost of the threepence tax by accepting a lower price for their molasses; consequently the wholesale price after the duty was paid in the mainland colonies did not rise.

Yet provincial politicians and merchants continued to protest through their colonial agents against the economic consequences of the three-penny duty. This "prohibitive" tax was purportedly ruining their trade. Perhaps they did not know their business, although this seems unlikely. Or a political motive may have lain behind the colonial argument, for they coupled their objections to the molasses duty with their complaints against another revenue measure, the proposed stamp duty.

III

Stamp duties as a source of revenue had been used with good results in England for some time. Consequently it was natural, in searching for a further source of money to finance the colonial defense establishment, for various officials such as Governor William Keith of Pennsylvania, Lieutenant Governor Robert Dinwiddie of Virginia, and the ubiquitous lobbyist Henry McCulloch of North Carolina to advocate extending this revenue law to include America. These suggestions had little consequence until September, 1763, when the Treasury under Grenville ordered the Commissioners of Stamps to draft a bill to extend stamp duties to the provinces.[28]

27. Lawrence A. Harper, "Mercantilism and the American Revolution," in "The American Revolution: A Symposium," *Canadian Historical Review*, XXIII (1942), 11. See also the tables of monthly prices for molasses in Arthur C. Cole, *Wholesale Commodity Prices in the United States 1700–1861 Statistical Supplement* (Cambridge, Mass., 1938), pp. 50–54; and Ruth Crandall, "Wholesale Commodity Prices in Boston during the Eighteenth Century," *Review of Economic Statistics*, XVI (1934), 127. For an analysis of the cycle in molasses and rum prices see Anne Bezansom, R. D. Gray, and Miriam Hussey, *Prices in Colonial Pennsylvania* (Philadelphia, 1935), pp. 201–204, 403–406; and Pares, *Yankees and Creoles*, pp. 126, 129.

28. Treasury minute, Sept. 22, 1763, T. 11/35:165; Jenkinson to the Commissioners of Stamps, Sept. 23, 1765, T. 27/28:432. Initially McCulloch worked on the project assisting Thomas Cruwys, solicitor to the Stamp Office. McCulloch seems

Agents and Merchants

When Grenville presented his plan for an American revenue to the House of Commons on March 10, 1764, he asked for and received approval for stamp taxes in the colonies.

The First Lord of the Treasury, needing more time to collect information, at this time deferred the matter. Consequently he had no objections when John Huske, an American merchant sitting for Maldon, argued in the House of Commons that since a stamp bill was a "peculiar step," the colonies ought to be notified and given an opportunity by their agents to voice their objections before Parliament adopted such a novel revenue measure.[29] Joseph Sherwood then notified his New Jersey constituents that the ministry had

to have had in mind a fund in the colonies to establish security for issues of Exchequer Bills of Union as a medium of exchange. The money would serve as a defense fund. But he later claimed that the Treasury took the matter out of his hands and based its plan on the stamp duties in England, "very different from what ought to have been observed in America." "Minutes taken in conference with Mr. H. McCullo . . ." (possibly by Charles Yorke), Add. MSS. 36226, f. 358; and "Mr. McCulloh's general thoughts on the Right the Legislature has to *Tax* the British Colonies, in all Cases of Public & General Concern," Wentworth-Woodhouse Muniments, Sheffield City Library, England, R65–66.

29. Jenkinson to Grenville, July 2, 1764, Smith (ed.), *Grenville Papers*, II, 373; Cecilius Calvert to Governor Horatio Sharpe, April 3, 1764, William H. Browne, *et al.* (eds.), *Archives of Maryland* (66 vols., Baltimore, 1883—), XIV, 144. Calvert wrote "Hurst" but there was no M.P. by that name. See the list in Gerrit P. Judd, IV, *Members of Parliament 1734–1832* (New Haven, 1955). Some claimed Richard Jackson obtained the postponement. See Dyer to Jared Ingersoll, April 14, 1764, Franklin B. Dexter (ed.), "A Selection from the Correspondence and miscellaneous papers of Jared Ingersoll," New Haven Colony Historical Society *Papers*, IX (New Haven, 1918), 289. Claims for Jackson as well as William Allen of Pennsylvania were made in an anonymous article circulated in several colonial newspapers early in May, 1764. Fred J. Ericson, "Contemporary British Opposition to the Stamp Act, 1764–1765," Michigan Academy of Science, Art, and Letters, *Papers*, XXIX (1943), 490, describes it as a "rather complete story." It is not. On little or no evidence Ericson claims that considerable opposition existed in Parliament to the proposed stamp bill and that Grenville was forced against his will to postpone the measure. This is not the case. He postponed the bill simply because he needed more information from the colonies on items to be taxed. Furthermore, as the agent for South Carolina noted, "the sense of Parliament appear'd so strongly in approbation of the principle of some tax in America for its own support and protection." Charles Garth to the South Carolina committee of correspondence, June 5, 1764, Namier, "Charles Garth, Agent for South Carolina," p. 648.

postponed the bill until the next Parliamentary session so that the colonists might "make their objections and shew Cause against it if they can." Jasper Mauduit was more specific when he informed the Massachusetts House of Representatives that in postponing the stamp duty Grenville was willing to give the colonies "their option to raise that [i.e., a stamp duty] or some equivalent tax [*sic*], Desirous as he express'd himself to consult the Ease, the Quiet, and the Good will of the Colonies."[30] Mauduit's account is particularly significant since it indicates that Grenville gave the colonies an option between the stamp duty and some other tax, and not an alternative between paying stamp duties levied by Parliament or themselves raising money by the traditional requisition system to help defray the cost of the army in America.[31] The distinction is critical, since Grenville has been accused of hoodwinking the agents and offering the colonists a spurious option of raising revenue themselves. Not knowing the specific sum each was to raise or the proportion of the total sum each was to contribute, the colonial assemblies, it has been suggested, could not take advantage of this impractical alternative and thus avoid the burden of Parliamentary taxation.[32]

Since the option to the stamp bill had been made to the colonies through their agents, following the Parliamentary session they conferred with the merchants of London trading to America. By ascertaining the debts owed to the merchants by the North Americans, they hoped to argue that the colonies were unable to pay additional taxes. Evidently this approach proved unfruitful. The agents then called on Grenville in order to obtain for their constituents the best possible

30. Joseph Sherwood to Jacob Spicer, March 24, 1764, Sherwood Letters, New Jersey Historical Society Library; Jasper Mauduit to Thomas Cushing, March 13, 1764, Massachusetts Archives, XXII, 359.

31. Of all the known accounts of the debate in the House of Commons that day, only that of the Virginia agent indicated that Grenville might have presented the option in terms of a requisition. According to Edward Montague, Grenville suggested that "it would be satisfactory to him if the several provinces would among themselves, and in modes best suited to their circumstances raise a sum adequate to the expence of their own defence." [Montague to the Virginia committee of correspondence], April 11, 1764 (extract), *Virginia Gazette* (Purdie and Dixon), Oct. 3, 1766.

32. Edmund S. Morgan, "The Postponement of the Stamp Act," *William and Mary Quarterly*, 3rd Ser., VII (1950), 353–392; and Edmund S. and Helen Morgan, *The Stamp Act Crisis*, pp. 60–61.

51

information on the intended revenue bill and to demonstrate "a mark of respect" to the First Lord of the Treasury for the "candour" he had shown in not hurrying through the measure.[33]

There are five accounts written by three participants as to what Grenville said during this controversial conference on May 17, 1764.[34] According to Jasper Mauduit, the First Lord of the Treasury argued that stamp duties required the fewest officials, were the most equal in application, and were the least expensive to collect. In postponing the stamp bill he had left it to each colony either to assent to the measure or to request modifications. Israel Mauduit then pointed out that without having specific information on the proposed bill, it would "be asking the province to Assent to they did not know what. . . ." Grenville, who did not have a bill ready, replied that such details were not necessary since the Treasury would model the American bill after the English stamp law, familiar to everyone.[35] The most extensive account of this May, 1764

33. William Knox, *The Claim of the Colonies to an Exemption from Internal Taxes Imposed by Authority of Parliament, Examined* (London, 1765), 23; and Garth to the South Carolina committee of correspondence, June 5, 1764, Namier, "Charles Garth, Agent for South Carolina," p. 646.

34. There are other accounts, but not by individuals who were present at the time. Charles Lloyd, Grenville's private secretary, may have been in a position to know what happened, but unfortunately the pamphlet ascribed to him (*The Conduct of the Late Administration, Examined* [London, 1767], p. 13), sheds little light on the incident. Burke in his famous speech of April 19, 1775, on taxation (Cobbett (ed.), *Parliamentary History*, XVII, 1242–1243) confused the option to the stamp tax with the molasses duty of 1764. He argued that Grenville might have offered an option in the form of another method of taxation. The agents, he claimed, had no authority to consent to the colonists taxing themselves by requisition which had been declared that day (April 19, 1775) in the House of Commons. Burke, who was not present at the conference with Grenville in May, 1764, confused the issue. A somewhat inaccurate rebuttal to his argument was written by Israel Mauduit (*A Short View of the History of the New England Colonies, with Respect to their Charters and Constitution* [4th edn., London, 1776], pp. 95–100).

35. Jasper Mauduit to Andrew Oliver, May 26, 1764, Massachusetts Archives, XXII, 375. The younger Mauduit, Israel, himself left two accounts of Grenville's "option" to the stamp bill, but he wrote them ten or more years after the event and in these two almost identical versions, he seems to have confused the two conferences the agents had with Grenville—one in May, 1764 and the other the following February. His manuscript account is in the Jenkinson Papers, Add. MSS. 38447, ff. 259–260 (printed in Jucker (ed.), *Jenkinson Papers*, pp. 306–307) and his published account is in his *Short View of the History of the New England Colonies*, pp. 97–100.

conference[36] left by an agent makes it clear that Grenville did not offer an option in the form of a requisition by which the colonial legislatures needed to have specific sums or quotas assigned to them. Indeed, from the narrative of Charles Garth, the fullest and most explicit account written at the time by a participant, it is evident that Grenville specifically objected to any form of requisition. It was doubtful if all of the colonies would agree to this system, and if any refused, it would then be necessary to resort to enforcement by Parliamentary authority. The First Lord of the Treasury, by delaying the stamp bill, intended to learn the views of the colonial assemblies on the matter. If they could "point out any system of plan as effectual and more easy to them," he would be "open to every proposition" from America.[37]

36. I do not refer here to the account of William Knox which was second-hand, based on some other agent's version. In his *The Claim of the Colonies to an Exemption from Internal Taxes*, p. 35, Knox stated that Grenville told the agents that "if the colonies thought any other mode [*sic*] of taxation more convenient to them, and make any proposition which should carry the appearance of equal efficacy with a stamp-duty he would give it all due consideration." But Knox confused the issue again in another pamphlet (*The Controversy Between Great Britain and her Colonies, Reviewed* [London, 1769], p. 198). Knox here stated that "Mr. Grenville, indeed, went so far as to desire the agents to acquaint the Colonies, that if they could not agree among themselves, upon raising a revenue by their own assemblies, yet if they all or any of them disliked stamp duties, and would propose any other sort of tax which would carry the appearance of equal efficacy, he would adopt it, but warmly recommended to them the making of grants by their own assemblies, as the most expedient method for themselves on several accounts."

37. Garth to the South Carolina committee of correspondence, June 5, 1764, Namier, "Charles Garth, Agent for South Carolina," p. 647. For further objections by Grenville to the requisition system see his letter to William Knox, July 15, 1768, H. M. C., *Report on Manuscripts in Various Collections*, VI (London, 1919), 101–102. A few further observations may be made on the analysis of Grenville's option to the stamp bill contained in Morgan, "The Postponement of the Stamp Act," pp. 353–392. In pointing out the impracticability of a requisition there was nothing deceitful in Grenville's asking the agents if they could suggest quotas, since they had previously agreed at the Treasury on the division of Parliamentary grants to the colonies for their previous military contributions. (See, for example, Sherwood to Stephen Hopkins, May 21, 1763, Rhode Island Agents, Official Letters.) Only a requisition need be made through the "regular" channel of the Secretary of State. As head of the Treasury, Grenville could act through the agents. John Huske had suggested this procedure

Agents and Merchants

While awaiting the response of the colonial assemblies, the ministry went ahead with the tentative stamp bill in case the provincial assemblies should not propose a practical alternative. From officials in the colonies the Treasury obtained data on the incidence and circulation of documents appropriate for stamp duties. By December 17, 1764, it had approved a tentative stamp bill drawn up by Thomas Whately with the assistance of Thomas Cruwys and John Bretell of the Stamp Office, and Henry McCulloch.[38]

IV

In no case did the provincial legislatures of North America propose a practical alternative to the stamp bill or allow their agents grounds for compromise. Instead most saw no need for the military garrison, posed constitutional objections to the revenue measure, and instructed their agents to cooperate in having the Molasses Act of 1764 repealed.[39] Although the Pennsylvania assembly tentatively indicated it would submit a suitable alternative, it ordered Richard Jackson to remonstrate against a stamp duty or any other tax by Parliament as "repugnant to our Rights and Priveleges as Freemen and *British* subjects." The South Carolina legislature also objected to any tax imposed by Parliament as contrary to the inherent right of every British subject to be taxed only by his own consent or that of his representatives. The committee of correspondence instructed Charles Garth to join with the other agents "to make all opposition you possibly can" to such a measure. The Virginia House of Burgesses objected on more narrow grounds.

in the House of Commons in March, and it was common practice during the Grenville ministry for the executive boards to consult with the agents on American affairs.

38. The information on stamps solicited in a circular letter from Halifax, Secretary of State for the Southern Department, to the colonial governors of Aug. 11, 1764, are in T. 1/430:175–291. See also "Mr. Whately's Plan of a Stamp Act for the Colonies & Plantations in America and the West Indies approved by the Lords Comm. of the Treasury," Dec. 17, 1764, Add. MSS. 35910, ff. 310–323.

39. The Georgia committee of correspondence did not mention the proposed stamp bill, however, when on July 27, 1764, it instructed its agent, William Knox, to work for repeal of the Act of 1764. Lila M. Hawes (ed.), "Letters to the Georgia Colonial Agent, July, 1762, to January, 1771," *Georgia Historical Quarterly*, XXXVI (1952), 266. See also the resolution of March 25, 1765, Allen P. Candler (ed.), *The Colonial Records of the State of Georgia* (26 vols., Atlanta, 1904–1916), XIV, 252.

Stamp taxes were "internal" or "inland" duties. If money must be raised, why not by the old requisition system, to which the Virginians had "always with the greatest Cheerfullness submitted . . . & comply'd . . .?"[40] This had hardly been the case, but the New England colonies, certainly Connecticut, could claim to have met adequately the requisitions sent them during the French war. Now Governor Thomas Fitch and a committee of the assembly drew up a pamphlet against stamp duties or "any other internal Tax," and the General Court appointed Jared Ingersoll, then about to depart for London on private business, as special agent to assist Richard Jackson. Neighboring Rhode Island joined Connecticut in opposition to the stamp bill. A committee of the General Court, headed by Governor Stephen Hopkins, urged collective action in London. Joseph Sherwood was to work either singly or with the other colonial agents in preventing passage of the new revenue measure.[41]

The administration in London did not consider the protests of these colonies especially significant, but it did react strongly to the tactics of the New York and Massachusetts assemblies. Couched in excessive language, their remonstrances and instructions to their agents confirmed the decision to pass the Stamp Act. Robert Charles thought the New York remonstrance so offensive that he

40. Votes of the assembly, Sept. 18, 22, 1764, Samuel Hazard *et al.* (eds.), *Pennsylvania Archives* (9 series, Philadelphia and Harrisburg, 1852–1935), 8th Ser., VII, 5635, 5643–5645; instructions to Jackson, Sept. 22, 1764, Van Doren (ed.), *Letters and Papers of Franklin and Jackson*, pp. 183–186; South Carolina committee of correspondence to Charles Garth, Sept. 4, 1764, Robert Wilson Gibbs (ed.), *Documentary History of the American Revolution: consisting of letters and papers relating to the contest for liberty, chiefly in South Carolina* (3 vols., New York, 1853–1857), II, 2; proceedings of the Virginia committee of correspondence, Dec. 19, 1764, "Proceedings of the Virginia Committee of Correspondence," *Virginia Magazine of History and Biography*, IX (1902), 353–354, 368; and the Virginia committee of correspondence to Montague, July 28, 1764, *ibid.*, XII (1904–1905), 9–11.

41. Trumbull and Hoadley (eds.), *Public Records of the Colony of Connecticut*, XII, 256, 299–300; a copy of the Connecticut pamphlet (*Reasons why the British Colonies, in America, Should not be charged with Internal Taxes, by authority of Parliament* . . . [New Haven, 1764]) is in T. 1/436:29–47. See also Thomas Fitch to Jackson, Dec. 7, 1764, "The Fitch Papers," XVIII, 304–305; committee of the Rhode Island assembly to George Wyllys, Oct. 8, 1764, *ibid.*, XVIII, 290–292; and John Russell Bartlett (ed.), *Records of the Colony of Rhode Island and Providence Plantations* (10 vols., Providence, 1856–1865), VI, 403–404, 412. The Rhode Island petition which Sherwood presented on March 1, 1765 is in C.O. 5/1280:13–20.

refused to present it.[42] Equally offensive was the letter that the committee of the House of Representatives of the Bay Colony sent to Jasper Mauduit on June 13, 1764. It insisted that the Molasses Act of 1764 imposed a heavy burden on the trade of the colony. The agent should have interpreted the previous silence of the lower house on this act and the proposed stamp bill as indicating their opposition to unwarranted taxation without representation. The committee saw no need for revenue simply because it considered the military establishment as unnecessary. Flatly rejecting any option to the stamp bill, the committee belittled Grenville's offer and ordered Mauduit to obtain a repeal of the Act of 1764 and to prevent the imposition of further taxes. Ordinarily instructions to the agent were also approved by the governor and council. In this instance the committee, headed by James Otis, acted only on the authority of the lower house. Twelve days later it sent a strongly worded circular to the other assemblies, urging them to unite against the ministerial program. Later that summer the Boston members of the house requested Governor Bernard to call a meeting of the General Court ostensibly to take steps to prevent Parliament from imposing an internal tax, although they had previously refused to see the need for any taxation to support the troops. When the assembly met that fall it drafted and sent to Jasper Mauduit a petition to be presented to the House of Commons. The legislature of the Bay Colony predicted that the new duty on molasses would have a prohibitive effect on trade and requested that the colonies continue to enjoy the privilege of laying internal taxes.[43]

42. On the New York assembly see the entry for Aug., 1764, William H. W. Sabine (ed.), *Historical Memoirs From 16 March 1763 to 9 July 1776 Of William Smith* ... (New York, 1956), pp. 23–24; Smith to Governor Robert Monckton, Nov. 5, 1764, "The Aspinwall Papers," Massachusetts Historical Society *Collections* (2 vols., Boston, 1871), 4th Ser., X, 541; John Watts to Sir William Baker, March 30, 1765, Watts to James Napier, April 15, 1765, and Watts to Monckton, April 16, 1765, "Letter Book of John Watts . . . ," pp. 341, 344, 346. The Assembly's address to Colden, Sept. 11, 1764, in T. 1/434:185–187 (copy in the Jenkinson papers, Add. MSS. 38338, ff. 39–40); the address of Sept. 12, 1764, in Charles Lincoln (ed.), *Messages from the Governors [of New York]* (11 vols., Albany, 1909), I, 683; the address of Oct. 18, 1764, in *ibid.*, I, 687; the address to the King, Lords, and Commons, in *ibid.*, I, 688–700.

43. A manuscript copy of the House's initial letter of June 13, 1764, to the agent Jasper Mauduit is in the Dartmouth Papers, William Salt Library, Stafford,

Developments in Massachusetts proved decisive in England when the governor in July transmitted the proceedings of the lower house to the Board of Trade. Bernard suspected that the Boston faction headed by Otis intended to split the General Court and organize a movement "to connect" the demagogues of the several governments in America to join together in opposition to all orders from Great Britain which "don't square with their notions of the rights of the people."[44] The imperial government reacted quickly to these events in Boston and New York. In December, the Commissioners of Trade under the Earl of Hillsborough condemned the resolutions of the Massachusetts assembly, the circular letter to the other provincial legislatures, and the initial instructions to the agent. In these documents, the board declared, the Massachusetts house had treated the acts and resolutions of the British legislature with "the most indecent disrespect," and had openly avowed principles of the "most dangerous nature and tendency," while inviting the assemblies of the other colonies in a "most extraordinary manner" to adopt the same opinions. The following month they charged that the New York assembly had passed an "extraordinary order" tending to "excite a combination in the several colonies to oppose particular Acts and resolutions" of Parliament.[45] Having been

---

England, II, 51 (extracts printed in William Tudor, *The Life of James Otis* [Boston, 1823], pp. 166–169). See also extracts in the Jenkinson Papers, Add. MSS. 38202, ff. 343–344 endorsed "Assembly's Refusal of Mr. Grenville's optional offer." T. 1/434:181–184 has the Treasury's copy of the proceedings of the House. See also Hutchinson to ?, July 11, 1764, *Jasper Mauduit Agent in London*, p. 163. A manuscript copy of the House's circular letter to the other assemblies, June 25, 1764, in Benjamin Franklin Papers, Library of Congress, Ser. II, 42 (printed in Connecticut Historical Society *Collections*, XVIII, 284–285). The petition of Nov. 3, 1764, to the House of Commons is in Alden Bradford (ed.), *Speeches of the Governors of Massachusetts from 1765 to 1775 and The Answers of The House of Representatives To the Same . . .* (Boston, 1818), pp. 21–23. Hereafter cited as *Massachusetts State Papers*. The House's letter to Mauduit, dated Nov. 28, 1764, is in the Arthur Lee Papers, Harvard College Library, Cambridge, Mass. (printed in Massachusetts Historical Society *Collections*, LXXIV, 174–175).

44. Bernard to the Board of Trade, June 29, 1764, Bernard Papers, Harvard College Library, Cambridge, Mass., III, 157.

45. Board of Trade, *Journals*, 1764–1767, p. 139. The representations on Massachusetts and New York, dated Dec. 11, 1764, and January 17, 1765, respectively, are in C.O. 5/1130:270, 275.

challenged in its authority, the imperial government reacted. Since the colonial assemblies had denied the right of Parliament to tax them, the Privy Council decided to establish that right by "a new execution of it, and in the strongest instance, an internal Tax, that of the Stamp Duty."[46]

The agents had warned their constituents that neither Grenville nor Parliament would accept a denial of the right of the British legislature to impose a stamp duty. All of their efforts in the future were to falter on this point. They could and did win many practical concessions from British ministries, but they could do nothing when the colonists protested against measures of the imperial government by denying its authority.

Since the colonial assemblies had left the agents no alternative, there was little for them to do in 1765 but offer negative opposition. The agent for Georgia bitterly summed up the situation. Some of the legislatures, "supposing that obstinacy and strong expression" would have the same effect on the imperial government as it had on colonial governors, directly questioned the authority of Parliament instead of allowing the agents to use their own discretion. Other, "less violent," assemblies had instructed their agents to petition against internal taxes. But not a single colony had authorized its agent to consent to the stamp duty[47] or to offer any precise equivalent. Two colonies had asked their agents to signify their willingness to contribute a portion of the money needed by methods of their own choosing, but when their colleagues asked these agents if they could undertake for any particular sum, they confessed that they had no authority from America to do so. To Knox it seemed best for the agents simply to establish a precedent of being heard on behalf of their constituents against the tax. Yet after he had drawn

46. Edward Sedgwick (Undersecretary of State) to Edward Weston, Feb. 14, 1765, H.M.C., *Tenth Report*, Appendix, Pt. I (London, 1885), p. 382. Charles Lloyd, Grenville's private secretary, corroborates this in his pamphlet, *The Conduct of the Late Administration, Examined* (London, 1767), p. 15.

47. If the debates on March 5, 1770, relating to the Stamp Act recorded by Sir Henry Cavendish are correct, then Grenville was misrepresenting the case to the House of Commons when he reportedly stated: "some of the assemblies applied to me, by their agents, to collect this very tax." John Wright (ed.), *Sir Henry Cavendish's debates of the House of Commons, during the thirteenth parliament . . . 1768–1774* (2 vols., London, 1841–1843), I, 494.

William Knox

up a petition which did not question the jurisdiction of Parliament, several other agents professed that they were not free to sign the document or present any other remonstrances but those sent by their assemblies.[48] Jasper Mauduit also realized that no one in the House of Commons would support any colonial claim founded on charter right or custom to an exemption from Parliamentary taxation. Although he did not relinquish the American legal argument, he attempted to mitigate any move by the imperial legislature against the colonists. Evidently he considered the government resentful of colonial claims. Initially he drew up a pamphlet against the intended stamp bill which he circulated among many members of Parliament, but his hopes were dashed when Richard Jackson advised him that the legislature would not allow any claim against its authority.[49]

The agents then sought to take their case directly to the administration. At the request of his colleagues, Charles Garth arranged a meeting with Grenville in order "to ward off," if possible, the "intended blow. . . ." This conference with the First Lord of the Treasury, although scheduled for thirty minutes, lasted for almost two hours. Franklin, Jackson, Garth, and Jared Ingersoll attended as a committee for the agents.[50] Grenville, speaking with "great

48. William Knox, *Claim of the Colonies to an Exemption from Internal Taxes*, pp. 33–35. Initially Knox's constituents approved his action, for they feared "it may prove of fatal consequences to some of the Colonys should they go too great lengths in denying the authority of Parliament for we believe more may be gained by humbly and dutifully remonstrating than by any other method . . . you should join with the other colony agents in any and every petition or remonstrance that may be thought right to prefer provided the subject matter of them is properly expressed." Georgia committee of correspondence to Knox, July 18, 1765, Georgia Miscellaneous Manuscripts, 1732–1796, Force Transcripts, Library of Congress.

49. Jasper Mauduit to the Massachusetts committee of correspondence, Feb. 19, 1765, Bradford (ed.), *Massachusetts State Papers*, p. 31; Mauduit to the Massachusetts committee of correspondence, Jan. 11, 1765, *Jasper Mauduit Agent in London*, p. 168n; Mauduit to Andrew Oliver, Jan. 16, 1765, Massachusetts Archives, XXII, 426.

50. Garth to the South Carolina committee of correspondence, Dec. 26, 1764, Namier, "Charles Garth, Agent for South Carolina," pp. 648–649; Garth to Franklin, n.d., Franklin Papers, American Philosophical Society Library, XL, 35; and Jackson to Jared Ingersoll, March 22, 1766, Dexter (ed.), "A Selection of the Correspondence . . . of Jared Ingersoll," p. 383. Franklin, who by the other accounts seems to have remained silent during this conference, wrote to Joseph Galloway almost two years later that when Grenville challenged the agents to

tenderness and regard for the colonies," told the agents that he was honor bound to move the stamp bill in the House of Commons, but if Parliament should think of any other method of deriving financial aid from America he would not object. As a counter-argument Jackson raised a political point: by means of the Stamp Act the Crown would be able to pay the civil list in the provinces and subvert the assemblies. Having no need to call on the legislatures, the governors would never convene them. The Pennsylvania agent must have known, of course, that the governors did not assemble the legislatures merely to vote salaries. In any case Grenville, "warmly" rejecting the idea, declared that the ministry had no such intention. When the agents then suggested that the administration raise money in America by the old requisition system, Grenville in turn asked them if they could agree on quotas for each colony. When they could not, the minister pointed out that neither could anyone in England. Even if quotas could be agreed on, there was no guarantee that the provinces would meet them, or that they would remain equitable, since the uneven rate of development of the various provinces would alter their capacity to contribute financially. Convinced of the merits of a stamp bill, Grenville left it to the agents to present further objections in Parliament.[51]

The issue went to the House of Commons in the second week of February, 1765. Although Garth, Isaac Barré, Alderman William Beckford, Sir William Meredith, Jackson, and General Henry Conway, an opposition politician with a personal grudge against

submit an alternative to the stamp bill, he, Franklin, presented "a Plan for a General Loan Office in America . . . to be established by Act of Parliament, appropriating the Interest to the American Service. . . ." But Grenville, according to Franklin, was "besotted with his Stamp Scheme" and paid little attention to the proposal. Franklin to Galloway, Oct. 11, 1766, Carl Van Doren (ed.), *Benjamin Franklin's Autobiographical Writings* (New York, 1945), p. 156. By the time Franklin wrote this letter, the Stamp Act had stirred the passions of both sides. His language reveals that the agent himself was not immune from strong feelings. His story is questionable, for the very full account left by Jared Ingersoll, written at the time of the interview, mentions no proposal of this nature.

51. Garth to the South Carolina committee of correspondence, Feb. 8, 1765, Namier, "Charles Garth, Agent for South Carolina," p. 649; Ingersoll to Thomas Fitch, Feb. 11, 1765, "The Fitch Papers," XVIII, 324–326; and Sherwood to Stephen Hopkins, March 11, 1765, Rhode Island Agents, Official Letters.

Grenville, spoke against internal duties, they treated the issue lightly. Montague and Charles offered petitions from Virginia and New York, but no member would accept them. The spokesmen for the colonists lost on a motion for adjournment by a margin of 245 to 49, an indication of the great strength of the ministry. During the second reading of the stamp bill, on February 13, the agents and merchants made a concerted effort to petition against the measure. The West Indian Rose Fuller, Meredith, Jackson, and Garth had petitions from the colonies and the London merchants, but they failed to make any impression, since these remonstrances denied the authority of Parliament. The language of the New York petition was so "inflammatory" that Robert Charles could not prevail on anyone to present it.[52] So strong was the sense of the House of Commons that the bill easily passed the second reading. The House of Lords concurred without a division, and the King signed the bill on March 22.[53]

The agents and merchants had failed to block the Stamp

52. Ingersoll to Fitch, Feb. 11, March 6, 9, 1765, "The Fitch Papers," XVIII, 316, 317, 321; Jackson to Fitch, Feb. 9, 1765, *ibid.*, pp. 317, 334; Garth to the South Carolina committee of correspondence, Feb. 8, 17, 22, 1765, Namier, "Charles Garth, Agent for South Carolina," pp. 649–650, 651, 652; Whately to John Temple, Feb. 9, 1765, John Temple Correspondence, Stowe Americana, Stowe Collection, Huntington Library, San Marino, Calif.; Mauduit to Andrew Oliver, Feb. 9, 1765, Bradford (ed.), *Massachusetts State Papers*, p. 30; Joseph Sherwood to Stephen Hopkins, Feb. 23, 1765, Rhode Island Agents, Official Letters; and Mauduit to the Massachusetts committee of correspondence, Feb. 19, 1765, Bradford (ed.), *Massachusetts State Papers*, p. 31; and *Commons Journal*, XXX, 148.

53. A unique provision was incorporated into the Stamp Act. Doubtful if the ordinary courts of record in the colonies could be reliable in cases dealing with inland or internal taxes, the Treasury solicited the opinion of the recent attorney general, Charles Yorke. Evidently Yorke, in conjunction with Whately and Jenkinson of the Treasury, and Jeremiah Dyson, a Commissioner of Trade, worked out the enforcement procedures of the new revenue measure. By the terms of the Stamp Act (5 Geo. III c. 12) the government at the discretion of the informer or prosecutor could sue for penalties and forfeitures in violation of *all* acts of trade and revenue in the vice-admiralty court of the colony where the offense was committed, a court of record, or a vice-admiralty court having concurrent jurisdiction over all America. See Whately to Yorke, Feb. 16, 1765, Add. MSS. 35911, f. 1; Yorke to Grenville, Feb. 17, 25, 1765, George Grenville Papers—in the possession of Sir John Murray, 50 Albemarle St., London, W.1; and the 56th and 57th clauses of 5 Geo. III c. 12.

Act[54] because the colonial assemblies had not presented a practical alternative, and because they had challenged the authority of the imperial legislature. At best, Garth and Ingersoll, personally familiar with Treasury officials, were able to obtain a reduction in rates on some items before final enactment of the bill.

Unable to persuade the Grenville ministry to forego the Stamp Act, the agents and merchants were yet able in many cases to nominate the stamp distributors appointed by the Treasury so that the new duty could be collected with as little inconvenience as possible by reputable colonists. William MacKensie, Adam Drumond, and Anthony Bacon had the nominations for Quebec and Barbados; Ingersoll himself was distributor for Connecticut, while Barlow Trecothick named George Meserve for New Hampshire. Trecothick and Bacon also nominated James MacEvers as distributor for New York. Edward Montague selected George Mercer, a lobbyist for the Ohio Company of Virginia, as distributor for the Old Dominion, while Benjamin Franklin secured the appointments of John Coxe and Jonathan Hughes as distributors for New Jersey and Pennsylvania.[55]

Inasmuch as the Grenville ministry in the spring of 1765 was reviewing the operation in the colonies of the legislation passed the previous years, the agents and London merchants trading to North America still hoped to persuade the Treasury and Parliament to reduce the three-penny duty on foreign molasses, to mitigate the restraints on colonial trade, and to lessen the hardships imposed

54. To ensure that the money raised by the new Revenue Acts would be used to defray the cost of the military establishment and would not leave the colonies and thus impair their economy, the Treasury issued orders that collectors and stamp distributors pay over the funds directly to the military in America. See J. M. Sosin, "A Postscript to the Stamp Act. George Grenville's Revenue Measures: A Drain on Colonial Specie?" *American Historical Review*, LXIII (1958), 918–923.

55. See Whately to Grenville, April 11, 1765, Grenville-Murray Papers; Whately to John Temple, May 10, 1765, "The Bowdoin and Temple Papers," p. 52; Franklin to Josiah Tucker, Feb. 26, 1774, Albert H. Smyth (ed.), *The Writings of Benjamin Franklin with a Life and Introduction* (10 vols., New York, 1907), VI, 200, and Lloyd, *The Conduct of the Late Aministration, Examined*, pp. 25, 28. Evidently Henry McCulloch was also consulted by the English stamp commissioners in apportioning stamps for each colony and in fixing proper security to be paid by each distributor. See John Brettel (secretary to the stamp commissioners) to Charles Jenkinson, March 25, 1765, Add. MSS. 38204, f. 166.

by the enforcement of the new legislation in the new vice-admiralty court at Halifax.[56] The colonists had two principal objections to the vice-admiralty court system: first, such prerogative courts rendered judgment without trial by jury, and second, the location of the court with general jurisdiction over all America might impose hardships on colonists who had to travel great distances to plead before it. In evaluating these complaints Whately pointed out that the same procedures were followed in England, where, for example, violations of the Revenue Acts (including the stamp laws) were also "triable in a summary Way, without Jury, before the Justices of the Peace." The appointed judges of the vice-admiralty courts were far better magistrates than the annually elected provincial judges.[57] Appointed officials, not as responsive to popular pressure and prejudices, consequently would be more likely to enforce the law. The Grenville ministry did prove responsive, however, to colonial complaints over the single vice-admiralty court at Halifax. It instituted proceedings to substitute three more conveniently located courts at Boston, Philadelphia, and Charleston, with jurisdiction over the northern, middle, and southern colonies respectively.[58] But before Grenville could put this plan into effect he left office, and it fell to a·later administration to relocate the vice-admiralty court jurisdiction.

Grenville's Treasury Board also responded to some complaints against the enforcement provisions of the new Acts of Trade and Revenue by adopting modifications suggested by the London merchants trading to America. Strict enforcement of the Navigation Acts by the royal navy and custom officials in America to prevent

56. Joseph Sherwood to Stephen Hopkins, March 11, 1765, Rhode Island Agents, Official Letters.

57. Whately, *Considerations on the Trade and Finances of this Kingdom*, p. 227. For a discussion of this court system and the colonial reaction see Carl Ubbelohde, *The Vice-Admiralty Courts and the American Revolution* (Chapel Hill, 1960). The colonial assemblies protested against the court at Halifax even though it transacted little or no business. After the American Revolution the independent states found that trial by jury was impractical in cases involving maritime law and reverted to the former law of nations.

58. See the memorial of the Treasury Board and the plan for the revised admiralty courts, C.O. 5/67:277–280, 281–283. Also Whately to John Temple, May 13, 1765, "The Bowdoin and Temple Papers," p. 56, and Whately, *Considerations on the Trade and Finances of this Kingdom*, pp. 227–229.

smuggling had resulted in petty restrictions and harassment of coastal and intercolonial shipping. To alleviate these difficulties the merchants proposed two clauses amending the Revenue Act of 1764, one allowing goods being shipped from one colony to another to be carried without a cocket, and another allowing ships arriving in America from Great Britain to be exempt from search until they reached port in the colonies. The Commissioners of Customs agreed to allow goods produced in America and not subject to import or export duties to be conveyed in the coastal trade without cockets, if they were carried in small, undecked vessels easily surveyed. But they would not allow any ship bound from Great Britain to the colonies to be exempt from search until reaching port. Fearing to dampen the vigilance of the naval officers, the commissioners felt that it would be sufficient to instruct the customs and naval officials to search with discretion and not to interrupt vessels proceeding to port in a regular fashion.[59] With regard to coastal trade and the vice-admiralty courts, the merchants were able to obtain partial satisfaction.

Nothing was done to reduce the threepence duty on foreign molasses—a tax the Americans claimed was prohibitive and would thus impair the economy of the northern colonies. The ministry did not accept the colonial analysis and preferred to see what effect the duty would have in practice. Whately correctly predicted that the three-penny tax would not be found "on experience so grievous" as had been represented. Having put through a program to raise revenue in the colonies and to assert the sovereignty of the mother country, the Treasury officials appeared to be generally satisfied with the situation both in England and in the colonies. On the basis of information sent by John Temple, Surveyor General of the Customs in Massachusetts, Whately wrote to the First Lord that "ye People are much reconciled to ye Mollasses & Stamp Duty." Still, Temple had warned, there had been some difficulty—a riot concerning a seizure and the imprisonment of the official executing the Parliamentary law.[60] But Benjamin Hallowell, Jr., the comp-

59. Customs report of March 22, 1765, T. 1/441:324; and Treasury minute of April 22, 1765, T. 29/36:315–316.

60. Whately to Temple, Nov. 5, 1764, "The Bowdoin and Temple Papers," p. 37; Whately, *The Regulations lately Made*, p. 83; and Whately to Grenville, June 15, 1765, Grenville-Murray Papers.

troller at Boston, was sending gratifying news to Charles Jenkinson. The joint secretary at the Treasury was confirmed in his view that "Temper & Firmness will make this Business end well, & that the People of the Colonies will after due Consid[eratio]n discover that the Taxes imposed on them by the Legislature of this Country are by no means oppressive but such as they very well can & ought to bear." George Grenville, less certain than Jenkinson, was more apprehensive. But he was no longer in office when news came later that year of the colonial demonstrations against the Stamp Act. Whately then wrote to his chief that the violent, open challenge to Parliamentary authority was "the strongest proof" of the propriety of the Stamp Act, for it demonstrated that "y' Step ought to have been taken some fifty years ago."[61]

The views of Thomas Whately aptly reflected the attitude of the hard-headed administrators of the Grenville ministry entrusted with the responsibility of governing a nation and an empire. Whately, Jenkinson, and their colleagues, initially facing the practical problem of financing the British garrisons in North America, had provoked a full-scale challenge to the authority of the mother country. They sought to meet the constitutional crises not merely by an affirmation but also by the exercise of authority. British merchants and colonial agents seeking to mitigate the imperial program were limited in their efforts by the insistence of the American legislatures that the constitutional question be the key issue. Future ministries, less experienced and cohesive, were to be content merely with the declaration, not the exercise, of authority. In attempting to influence such administrations the merchants and agents were able to obtain practical concessions by apparently avoiding the explosive question of sovereignty. But in the last analysis, the issue could not be avoided.

61. Jenkinson to Grenville, July 13, 1765, Add. MSS. 38305, ff. 13–14; Jenkinson to Grenville, June 19, 1765, Add. MSS. 38305, f. 11; Philip Lloyd to Jenkinson, June 20, 1765, Add. MSS. 38204, f. 285 (Grenville was suffering from an inflammation of the eyes and Lloyd served as his amenuensis); and Whately to Grenville, Oct. 10, 1765, Grenville-Murray Papers.

CHAPTER III

Accommodation under Rockingham

I

COLONIAL agents and British merchants in the few short months during the winter of 1765–1766 achieved their greatest cohesion and success in influencing British colonial policy. Their efforts directly resulted in repeal of the Stamp Act, a reduction in the duties on produce imported into North America, and a modification of the laws hampering colonial trade. This modification in British policy for the colonies was of greater significance than the mere accommodation of specific colonial grievances. It instituted a pattern of colonial response to British legislation which contributed to the final break with the mother country. The Whigs in America attributed their success in the winter of 1765–1766 during the Stamp Act crisis in great measure to their boycott on British goods and the resultant economic distress in the mother country. British merchants reflecting this distress in turn applied pressure on the government. To the American patriots, then, the lesson of the Stamp Act crisis was clear. Economic boycott would force the British to back down. They failed to appreciate that to successive British administrations economic distress was the excuse for, not the cause of, reversals of colonial policy. When the final crisis approached, they would not react as they had apparently done in the past. Fully expecting that a program of coercion in 1774–1775 would be as effective as it had been a decade before, the patriot leaders grossly miscalculated the situation. This was, perhaps, the most important consequence of the accommodations won by the agents and merchants during the Stamp Act crisis.

Other factors explain the success of the agents and merchants better than the economic boycott recommended by the Stamp Act Congress at New York in the fall of 1765. The composition and nature of the British administration under the Marquis of Rockingham were critical. Most important, the young, inexperienced Rockingham Whigs were intimidated by the mass violence which erupted in the urban centers of North America. Rockingham himself felt that he simply could not enforce the Stamp Act and contented himself with the mere affirmation of authority. Moreover, conditioned by partisan politics to view with disfavor the program of their factional opponents, the Whigs were susceptible to the arguments of the agents and merchants that the program of the Grenville ministry was detrimental to Anglo-American trade. The British merchants reacting to the widespread economic distress caused by the colonial boycott exerted themselves more strongly. And finally the agencies themselves were better organized and staffed as a direct result of the recommendations of the Stamp Act Congress.

To meet the challenge of the Stamp Act the congress of colonial delegates meeting in New York in September, 1765 had recommended that the provincial legislatures take concerted action through special as well as regular colonial agents.[1] Moreover, the crisis demanded that a colony be represented by men of demonstrated ability and weight in British administration circles. Consequently the colonial legislatures now rejected those agents who had been lax or incompetent and replaced them, in some instances, with more influential men. But in each case local political alignments in the colonies continued to influence the selection of an agent. The assembly of New Hampshire nominated Barlow Trecothick and John Wentworth as special agents to present the petitions and memorials of the Stamp Act Congress to the British government.[2]

1. Journal of the Stamp Act Congress, Oct. 24, 1765, Hezekiah Niles (ed.), *Principles and Acts of the Revolution in America* (Baltimore, 1822, reprinted New York, 1876), p. 168.

2. Journal of the New Hampshire Assembly, Nov. 22, 1764, Nathaniel Bouton *et al.* (eds.), *Documents and Records Relating to the Province of New Hampshire* (40 vols., Concord, 1867–1943), VII, 92. The exact status of the agency is not clear. The

Agents and Merchants

Trecothick, the key figure among the London merchants trading to America, had close connections with Rockingham, the head of the new British ministry, while Wentworth was distantly related to the Marquis. In a short time Trecothick replaced John Thomlinson, Jr. as standing agent. New Jersey also obtained a new agent as Joseph Sherwood fell victim to provincial poltics.[3] His successor was Henry Wilmot, an English lawyer on intimate professional and personal terms with Charles Pratt and Robert Henley. Pratt was Lord Chief Justice of the Court of Common Pleas, and Henley, Lord Northington, was Lord Chancellor during the Rockingham ministry. While Sherwood was dismissed in part for not having acted more vigorously

following summer both Wentworth and Trecothick were appointed "joynt & separate Agents . . . with or without" the two Thomlinsons. See the Journal of the Assembly, June 20, 1766, *ibid.*, VII, 105; and Theodore Atkinson to Wentworth and Trecothick, July 12, 1766, Belknap Papers, Force Transcripts, Library of Congress, Vol. II, 13, A, p. 231.

3. As early as 1761 Sherwood had suspected that a local magnate, William Alexander (the self-styled Lord Sterling) had sought the agency for his own nominee. With the crisis over the Stamp Act, the New Jersey legislature suddenly dismissed Sherwood not because of any offense he had committed, according to Governor William Franklin, but because the proprietors of East New Jersey on the council wanted their own nominee, Henry Wilmot, appointed as agent. They simply took advantage of Sherwood's apparent dereliction of duty; while Parliament was enacting the stamp bill his letters had been "short & trivial" compared to the "full & sensible" accounts sent by Wilmot. The speaker of the Assembly, Cordlandt Skinner, who was in the proprietary interest, then proposed Wilmot as agent. Unaware of the Speaker's connection with the proprietors, the Assembly elected the new agent. The choice was fortuitous, for as the Governor observed, Sherwood was in "no ways equal" to Wilmot in ability. Still Governor Franklin feared that Wilmot had accepted the post only to serve the proprietors and to add to his own influence with the ministry in London. Franklin may have been right, for in accepting the position Wilmot warned Skinner that he would not have refused the New Jersey agency if for no other reason than to comply with Alexander's wishes. While he promised to serve the colony to the best of his ability, he pointed out that he was also agent for the four Leeward Islands. In case of conflict of interest—"which probably will never happen," he interjected—his New Jersey constituents must allow him to "preserve my allegiance" to the West Indian islands. Sherwood to Samuel Smith, June 6, 1761, Joseph Sherwood Letters, New Jersey Historical Society Library, Newark; William Franklin to [Benjamin Franklin], Nov. 13, [1766], Benjamin Franklin Papers, American Philosophical Society Library, Philadelphia, XLII, 3; Wilmot to Skinner, Sept. 25, 1766, Frederick W. Ricord and William Nelson (eds.), *Archives of the State of New Jersey* (36 vols., Newark, 1881–1941), 1st Ser., IX, 571.

to prevent passage of the Stamp Act, William Knox lost his post as agent for Georgia for having acted too forcefully. Realizing that there was nothing to be gained by protesting the right of Parliament to tax the colonies, Knox had sought to prevent passage of the Stamp Act by advancing practical arguments. Although his constituents had agreed with his tactics at the time and had given him full discretion, Knox did more than merely abstain from denying the right of Parliament to tax the colonies. He published a pamphlet[4] positively asserting that right and lavishly praising George Grenville. The Commons House then dismissed him and appointed Charles Garth to present the petitions of the Stamp Act Congress. Garth, who had also been asked by the Maryland assembly to present its grievances against the Stamp Act, thus represented three southern legislatures. Knox temporarily remained agent for the Georgia council, but embittered at the treatment accorded him by the lower house[5] he soon became one of George Grenville's leading pamphleteers and a vociferous defender of the authority of Parliament over the colonies. In a few years Knox was to play an important role in colonial administration as an Undersecretary of State for the American Department.

The Stamp Act crisis reopened the agency dispute in Massachusetts, where the political factions in the General Court had advanced two rivals for the position, Israel Mauduit and Thomas Hutchinson.

4. William Knox, *The Claim of the Colonies to an Exemption from Internal Taxes Imposed by Authority of Parliament, Examined* (London, 1765), pp. 2, 38; Knox to Grenville, Nov. 28, 1765, William J. Smith (ed.), *The Grenville Papers* (4 vols., London, 1852–1853), III, 109.

5. Georgia committee of correspondence to Knox, July 18, 1765, Georgia Miscellaneous Manuscripts, 1732–1796, Force Transcripts, Library of Congress (printed in Lila M. Hawes (ed.), "Letters to the Georgia Colonial Agent, July 1762, to January, 1771," *Georgia Historical Quarterly*, XXXVI [1952], 272); James Habersham to Knox, Oct. 28, 1765, Georgia Miscellaneous Manuscripts, Habersham Correspondence, II, 36; Journal of the Commons House, Nov. 15, 1765, Jan. 22, 1766, Allen P. Candler (ed.), *The Colonial Records of the State of Georgia* (26 vols., Atlanta, 1904–1916), XIV, 293–294, 316–318, 337; Wright to the council, the council to Wright, Dec. 19, 1765, *ibid.*, XVII, 241, 268; and Habersham to Knox, Dec. 4, 1765, "The Letters of Hon. James Habersham, 1756–1775," *Georgia Historical Society Collections*, VI (1904), 50; extract of Knox to James Habersham (president of the Georgia Council), May 20, 1766, Candler (ed.), *Colonial Records of the State of Georgia*, XVII, 375.

Agents and Merchants

A compromise candidate, Richard Jackson, was appointed for one year.[6] Due to his connection with Governor Francis Bernard and George Grenville, Jackson, who was perfectly acceptable to the assemblies of Connecticut and Pennsylvania, nonetheless was suspect to the extreme members of the Massachusetts House of Representatives. When the Stamp Act Congress recommended the appointment of special agents to present petitions against the Grenville program, the lower house had an opportunity to circumvent Jackson and, in time, entirely eliminate the governor's friend. Dennys DeBerdt, an aged Flemish Hugenot who had settled in England and who had extensive personal and business contacts in the colonies, was named by the lower house as special agent ostensibly to assist Jackson. Later the representatives dealt only with DeBerdt and refused to join with the council in selecting an agent for the entire government. Such political factionalism in the Bay Colony was to jeopardize the agency. This development was foreshadowed in December, 1765, when a committee of the house including Samuel Adams, James Otis, Thomas Cushing, and Thomas Gray wrote privately to DeBerdt with instructions and thus bypassed the council. The choice of DeBerdt as special agent was an effort not only to circumvent the governor and council, but also to gain influence with the new British administration, for while the aged Flemish merchant enjoyed a good reputation in the Bay Colony, he was also thought to have the favor of the Earl of Dartmouth, a "nobleman of the highest Repute" and president of the Board of Trade in the administration newly formed by the Marquis of Rockingham in the summer of 1765.[7]

6. Jackson for some reason found the appointment embarrassing. He feared that if he refused the post, however, it would then go to a nominee of Sir William Baker, the London merchant. Jackson deferred to the minister's judgment, for Grenville might find that his acceptance of the Massachusetts agency "would be of service to Government. . . ." After a conference with Grenville, who considered the point a "Matter of some Delicacy," Jackson accepted the position. Jenkinson to Grenville, April 11, 1765, Add. MSS., 38304, f. 134; Grenville to Jenkinson, April 13, 1765, George Grenville Letter Book, Stowe Collection, Huntington Library, San Marino, Calif., St. 7, Vol. II; and Jackson to Andrew Oliver, June 13, 1765, *Jasper Mauduit Agent in London for the Province of the Massachusetts Bay, 1762–1765* (Massachusetts Historical Society *Collections*, Vol. LXXIV [Boston, 1918]), p. 180n.

7. Samuel White to DeBerdt, Nov. 7, 1765, *Papers Relating to Public Events in Massachusetts Preceding the American Revolution*, printed for the Seventy-Six Society

70

Accommodation under Rockingham

Had the Whigs of the Bay Colony been better informed on the Methodist-inclined First Lord of Trade, they would not have been so hopeful. On assuming his new post, Dartmouth devoted some time to reading John Locke's "plan for the government of the Colonies," and he noted with disapproval that the colonial governors, dependent on the provincial assemblies for their salaries, had no authority over the legislatures. Dartmouth thought that an imperial fund should be established for the executives to correct the situation. Otis and Adams would have been appalled at the idea. A neophyte in office, Dartmouth had to spend some time reviewing the state papers relating to the colonies dating from the reign of Charles II.[8] The First Lord of Trade was not an exception. Four of the most important ministers in the new government, Rockingham, First Lord of the Treasury, William Dowdeswell, Chancellor of the Exchequer, and Henry Seymour Conway and the Duke of Grafton, both Secretaries of State, were all relatively young men who had never held high civil office before.

Faced with widespread rioting in the urban centers of America—the first overt, mass challenge to British authority—the inexperienced Rockingham ministry relied heavily on the advice of the colonial "experts," the provincial agents, and British merchants. Furthermore, conditioned by partisan politics, the Whigs did not look with favor on any measure of the preceding Grenville ministry. Indeed, as soon as the Rockingham administration was formed, the agent for Rhode Island reported that the recent change in government "will produce great ease to the Inhabitants of America." That summer Dartmouth kept a schedule of appointments with certain agents and merchants, among them Richard Jackson, DeBerdt, Anthony Bacon, and Capel Hanbury. In August, DeBerdt's daughter and secretary wrote an American correspondent, "We are in great hopes something will be done,to relieve you, as Lord Dartmouth seems bent on taking some steps to undo what the late Ministry have done." As early as November, rumor had it that the

---

(Philadelphia, 1856), pp. 4–5 (hereafter cited as *Massachusetts Revolutionary Papers*); Otis, Adams, Cushing, and Gray to DeBerdt, Dec. ?, 1765, Henry A. Cushing (ed.), *Writings of Samuel Adams* (4 vols., New York, 1904–1908), I, 61–66; and Adams and Cushing to G[eorge] W[hitefield], Nov. 11, 1765, *ibid.*, I, 33.

8. Entry for Aug. 18, 1765, Dartmouth Papers, William Salt Library, Stafford, England, Dartmouth memorandum book, V, 221B.

Rockingham administration intended to repeal the Stamp Act. The final impetus came in December, when word of the riots in New York arrived. "... dreadful News from America," wrote one Whig politician, "Nothing less than a Rebellion in New York." Rockingham himself complained that the news of the outbursts would force the administration to broach the situation in America at the opening session of Parliament.[9]

II

Intimidated by the violence in the colonies, the inexperienced Whigs were susceptible to the arguments and pleadings of the agents and merchants. Indeed, the ministry may have deliberately sought their help. For their part the agents, under orders from the respective assemblies to press for repeal of the Grenville program, took full advantage of the situation. The agents for the Bay Colony were particularly active. Jackson relayed a statement of colonial rights drafted by Thomas Hutchinson, Lieutenant Governor of Massachusetts, to Henry Conway, Secretary of State for the Southern Department. He also delivered a Pennsylvania petition to Dartmouth.[10] Although William Bollan had no official standing at

9. Joseph Sherwood to Governor Ward of Rhode Island, July 16, 1765, Gertrude S. Kimball (ed.), *The Correspondence of the Colonial Governors of Rhode Island, 1723–1775* (2 vols., Boston and New York, 1902), II, 367; Grenville to the Duke of Bedford, Nov. 28, 1765, Grenville Letter Book, St. 7, Vol. II; George Onslow to the Duke of Newcastle, Dec. 11, 1765, Add. MSS. 32972, f. 202; Rockingham to Newcastle, Dec. 12, 1765, Add. MSS. 32972, f. 214; entries for July 18, 21, August 5, 30, 1765, Dartmouth Papers, Dartmouth memorandum book, V, 221B, ff. 3, 12, 16; Esther DeBerdt to Joseph Reed, William B. Reed, *Life of Esther Reed* (Philadelphia, 1853), p. 59.

10. See the instructions to Jasper Mauduit of Nov. 28, 1764, with a copy to Jackson sent the following spring, Arthur Lee Papers, Harvard College Library, Cambridge, Mass.; Otis, Samuel Adams, Thomas Gray, Thomas Cushing, and Edward Sheaf to DeBerdt, Dec. 21, 1765, *Massachusetts Revolutionary Papers*, p. 6; and entries for Nov. 8, 11, 1765, Dartmouth Papers, Dartmouth memorandum book, V, 221B. An extensive fragment of Hutchinson's paper was printed by Edmund S. Morgan in *The New England Quarterly*, XXI, 480–492. See also the entries in Hutchinson's diary for June 20, 1775, and March 20, 1776, Peter Orlando Hutchinson (ed.), *The Diary and Letters of Thomas Hutchinson* (2 vols., London, 1883–1886), I, 473, II, 26.

this time, the former agent for Massachusetts worked directly with the head of the administration. He sent the First Lord of the Treasury letters from Hutchinson and other Bay Colonists describing the resistance to the Stamp Act and advising of the impossibility of enforcing the revenue measure in America. Hutchinson had written: "It would be as much as a man's life is worth to touch a stamp if it was in his power to come at them."[11] In order further to convince the Treasury of the impossibility of enforcing the Stamp Act, Benjamin Franklin and Barlow Trecothick, agents for Pennsylvania and New Hampshire, transmitted to the Board letters from various stamp distributors in the colonies, pleading to be allowed to resign their posts in the face of the hostile reaction to the onerous revenue law.[12]

Seeking to create as wide an impression as possible, Franklin undertook a campaign in the English press in behalf of the colonial cause. In time he became "the engineer of the American propaganda machine in London," reprinting the more notable pamphlets from America, encouraging others to write, and himself contributing many pieces.[13] Dennys DeBerdt was active earlier than Franklin

11. See Bollan to Rockingham, Oct. 12, Nov. 4, Nov. 13, 1765, and Feb. 7, 1766; and Hutchinson to Bollan, Dec. 20, 1765, Wentworth-Woodhouse Muniments, Sheffield City Library, Sheffield, England, R24-10, 28, 1, 66, 67.

12. These letters may be found in T. 1/439:63, 65; T. 1/440:229; and T. 1/442:345-346. A few are printed in the *Maryland Historical Magazine*, IV (1909), 134.

13. William Strahan to David Hall, Jan. 11, 1766, "Correspondence between William Strahan and David Hall, 1763-1777," *Pennsylvania Magazine of History and Biography*, X (1886), 92; Verner W. Crane, "Benjamin Franklin and the Stamp Act," Publications of the Colonial Society of Massachusetts *Transactions*, XXXII (1937), 56-57. There were those who doubted Franklin's contribution. DeBerdt charged that in the struggle over the repeal of the Stamp Act, Franklin "stood entirely neuter till he saw which way the cause would be carried, and then broke out fiercely on the side of America." Thomas Hollis, the "Strenuous Whig" dissenter, accused Franklin of being "*A Trimmer*"; he had not come out strongly against the Stamp Act until after the administration had decided to repeal the measure. Even more damaging was the story circulated in Pennsylvania by the agent's political enemies: Franklin had helped instigate the offensive Act! Evidently many believed the allegation, for the Philadelphia mob threatened to hang in effigy both Franklin and his nominee as stamp distributor, John Hughes. The young and impressionable Benjamin Rush bemoaned: "O *Franklin, Franklin*, thou curse to Pennsylvania and America, may the most accumulated vengeance

and anticipated many of the arguments the Pennsylvania agent later used. As early as September, 1765, DeBerdt had tried to convince the First Lord of Trade that the revenue measure was unnecessary. Evidently unaware that the legislatures of Virginia and Massachusetts, as well as the colonial delegates to the Albany Congress, had requested British aid at the outbreak of the late French war, DeBerdt maintained that the army had never served a useful purpose in America. Britain had sent "an useless, nay . . . a dissolute sett of Men to live in Idleness" among the colonists. This intemperate and unfounded analysis, appearing in several Massachusetts newspapers, received wide circulation.[14]

The agents and merchants attacked not only the military garrisons and the revenue measures intended for their support but other aspects of the Grenville program: the restriction on paper money as legal tender, the vice-admiralty courts, and the limitations on colonial coastal trade. John Huske, the American merchant living in London, made the most sweeping challenge in a proposal for a free port system. If adopted it would have undermined the carrying provisions of the traditional navigation system.[15] Huske based the plan

burst speedily on thy guilty head!" Perhaps Franklin subsequently adopted a stronger position against the Stamp Act in order to counter such impressions and protect his political standing in the colony. Esther DeBerdt to Joseph Reed, Dec. 12, 1766, Reed, *Life of Esther Reed*, p. 107; Hollis to Jonathan Mayhew, June 19, 1766, Bernard Knollenberg (ed.), "Thomas Hollis and Jonathan Mayhew: Their Correspondence," *Massachusetts Historical Society Proceedings*, LXIX (1947–1950), 190; John Reed to Franklin, June 17, 1766, Franklin Papers, American Philosophical Society Library, II, 27; Joseph Galloway to Franklin, June 7, 16, Nov. 14, 1766, *ibid.*, I, 170, II, 23, 26; and Benjamin Rush to Ebenezer Hazard, Nov. 8, 1765, L. H. Butterfield (ed.), *The Letters of Benjamin Rush* (2 vols., Philadelphia, 1951), I, 18. See also John J. Zimmerman, "Benjamin Franklin and the Pennsylvania Chronicle," *Pennsylvania Magazine of History and Biography*, LXXXI (1957), 351–352.

14. DeBerdt to Dartmouth, Sept. 3, 1765, Dartmouth Papers, II, 83 (printed in Albert Mathews [ed.], "Letters of Dennys DeBerdt, 1757–1770," Publications of the Colonial Society of Massachusetts *Transactions*, XIII [1910–1911], 435–436). See also the entry for Jan. 1, 1766, in John Adams' diary, Charles Francis Adams (ed.), *The Works of John Adams* (10 vols., Boston, 1850–1856), II, 171.

15. As early as 1763 Campbell Dalrymple, military governor of Guadeloupe, and Francis Moore, a British resident of St. Eustatius, had suggested opening Dominica as a free port. Francis Armytage, *The Free Port System in the British West Indies. A Study in Commercial Policy 1766–1822* (London, 1953), pp. 36–37. Dalrymple

Dennys DeBerdt

he presented to the Secretary of State for the Southern Department on the thesis that the trade and revenue measures of the Grenville ministry threatened the interdependent trade of England, North America, and the West Indies. He advocated instead a system of free ports, warehouses for the deposit of tax-free goods transshipped from the colonies, and a reduction of the tax on molasses.[16] The Rockingham ministry did not act immediately on this plan inasmuch as the Stamp Act crisis took priority over all other American affairs. But a modified, limited version of Huske's scheme to rationalize and relieve Atlantic commerce was made the basis of new trade and revenue legislation shortly after the repeal of the Stamp Act.

The administration, the merchants, and the agents cooperated closely in meeting the crisis precipitated by the legislation of the previous Grenville regime. At the end of the year DeBerdt, a member

had recommended the importation of goods free of duty into Dominica from any part of the world provided they were carried in British bottoms. Dalrymple to Bute, Feb. 27, 1763, Add. MSS. 38200, f. 261. Huske's scheme, based on entirely different principles, came closer to the plan finally enacted in 1766.

16. Huske advocated a total drawback of the taxes on foreign sugar imported into the colonies and a tax of only one penny per gallon on foreign molasses. In addition, Parliament should declare Port Royal in Jamaica, Basse Terre in Grenada, Prince Rupert and Reseau bays in Dominica, Pensacola, St. Augustine, New York, Portsmouth, and Halifax "free ports" to all nations for the importation of African slaves and all produce and manufactures legally brought from Europe under current regulations. These ports would still be under regulations, but "free" in the sense that they would be open to British and foreign vessels carrying the produce of an American colony of that foreign country. Foreign ships could not bring in enumerated goods—except rice—from the British colonies. Huske would place sugar and rum in a special category. These items, imported either in British or foreign ships, were to be stored in government warehouses and not released until the duty on them was paid. They could then be reshipped only after bond had been given that they would not be relanded in any other British dominion. All other foreign colonial produce imported into the "free" ports was not to be subject to additional duties or further restrictions than were currently imposed by Parliament. No produce of a foreign colony, except molasses, could be imported—even in British vessels—into any colony, until previously reshipped from a "free" port. "Observations on the Trade of Great Britain to her American Colonies & their Trade to Foreign Plantations with a Plan for retrieving, extending & Securing thereof," C.O. 5/66:127–139 (copies in Chatham Papers, P.R.O. 30/8/97:27–31 and Newcastle Papers, Add. MSS. 33030, ff. 318–323. See also Huske to Conway, Oct. 27, 1765, C.O. 5/66:123.

of the committee of London merchants, having called on Rockingham, Grafton, Dartmouth, and Conway to deliver the official protests of Massachusetts against the Stamp and Molasses Acts, reported to his constituents that the ministers "are intirely convinced of the Bad Tendency of the late regulations & disposed to relieve you. . . ."[17] On December 4, the merchants of London trading to America met in response to a newspaper advertisement. Their committee, headed by Trecothick, included DeBerdt, David Barclay, Jr., Charles Crokatt, Capel Hanbury, and Edward Athawes. Two days later, in an effort to organize the entire British mercantile community for the repeal of the Stamp Act, they dispatched to the trading and manufacturing towns of the kingdom a letter composed by Trecothick and the First Lord of the Treasury. According to Rockingham's private secretary, Edmund Burke, this circular was "the principal instrument in the happy repeal of the Stamp Act. . . ."[18]

A concrete program for the ministry was concerted between the administration leaders and the lobbies outside formal governmental circles. Over the holidays while Parliament was recessed, Rockingham held two private dinner parties to discuss American affairs. Dowdeswell, Conway, and Dartmouth represented the administration, and Trecothick, Sir William Baker, and George Aufrere, the merchants. Trecothick was the liaison with the provincial agents. Apparently as a tactical maneuver to win enough votes in Parliament, they agreed at these sessions on a general declaration of the right of the imperial legislature to legislate for the colonies, and at the same time to grant the Americans "every possible Relief in

17. DeBerdt to Samuel White, Dec. 14, 1765, Mathews (ed.), "Letters of Dennys DeBerdt, p. 308.
18. George Thomas Keppell, sixth Earl of Albemarle, *Memoirs of the Marquis of Rockingham and his contemporaries. With original Letters and Documents now first published* (2 vols., London, 1852), I, 319. For the preliminary organization of the committee of the London merchants, see "At A General Meeting of the Merchants of London pursuant to public Advertisement on Wednesday the Fourth day of December 1765," Add. MSS., Jenkinson Papers, 38339, f. 166. A copy of the circular letter of Dec. 6, 1765, is among the Rockingham Papers, Wentworth-Woodhouse Muniments, R1–537. See also John Harrison to John Temple, April 15, 1766, "The Bowdoin and Temple Papers," Massachusetts Historical Society *Collections*, 6th Ser., IX (Boston, 1897), 72.

Trade & Commerce. . . ." But they were not unanimous on the Stamp Act; all supported various amendments to the measure, some a suspension of the act, but very few initially favored outright repeal. Yet Rockingham after these meetings was hopeful, noting "Treycothick & the Merchants Trading & Manufacturing Towns &c. go on well."[19] The campaign he and Trecothick had organized to focus mercantile pressure on Parliament was proceeding as expected.

In January the administration introduced this well-conceived plan to the House of Commons. Despite the hours and days devoted to constitutional rhetoric the question would not be resolved on any point of jurisprudence, but by the pressure the administration would bring to bear on the members of Parliament. Realizing the situation, Rockingham and Trecothick had organized the protest movement of the British mercantile community. By the middle of the month the petition of the London merchants calling for relief from the Stamp Act boycott had arrived. In the days following, similar petitions poured in from other trading and manufacturing towns and were referred to the House committee on American affairs chaired by the "West Indian" Rose Fuller.[20] The Rockingham ministry now used these protests by the merchants to achieve a political end. These petitions and the subsequent testimony by agents and merchants at the bar of the House of Commons were the result of careful organization by the ministers, who "encouraged, channelled, and directed this mercantile pressure," and who in reality had so committed themselves before they actually concluded to repeal the Stamp Act that in the end they had "no other choice."[21] On the evening of January 17, Rockingham met with Charles Townshend, Conway, Dowdeswell, and Grafton to concur on a

19. Rockingham to Newcastle, Dec. 31, 1765, Jan. 2, 1766, Add. MSS. 32972, f. 384; Add. MSS. 32973, ff. 11–13.

20. The petition of the London Merchants which set the pattern for those of the other towns is in Chatham Papers, P.R.O. 30/8/73:154–155. See also Great Britain, Parliament, *Journal of the House of Commons* (London, 1547—), XXX, 442, 443, 445, 485, 489, 501, 503, 611; William Cobbett (ed.), *The Parliamentary History of England from the Earliest Period to the Year 1803* (36 vols., London, 1813), XVI, 133–135, 480; and DeBerdt to Samuel White, Jan. 16, 1766, Mathews (ed.), "Letters of Dennys DeBerdt," p. 310.

21. Carl B. Cone, *Burke and the Nature of Politics. The Age of the American Revolution* (Lexington, Ky., 1957), p. 85.

final course of action discussed earlier that day with the Attorney General, Charles Yorke. The administration would press for one bill repealing the Stamp Act on the grounds of its adverse consequences in England; and to gain sufficient votes in Parliament it would introduce another bill declaring the legislative authority of Parliament in all cases over the provinces.[22]

The colonial agents now did not need to present the petitions from the various colonial assemblies to the imperial legislature in order to secure repeal of the Stamp Act. They had already laid the foundations for repeal with the merchants and ministers. While they went through the empty formality of submitting these remonstrances, the House of Commons went through the equally empty gesture of rejecting petitions submitted by George Cooke, member for Middlesex, Edward Montague, William Knox, and Stephen Fuller, brother of Rose Fuller and agent for Jamaica. However, these petitions entrusted by Dennys DeBerdt to the former Speaker of the House, Arthur Onslow, were used "privately" with the administration.[23] But petitions were unnecessary. Rockingham was determined to repeal the Stamp Act simply because he was not strong enough to enforce it. He would "wish no Man so great a Curse—as to desire him to be the person to take Administration & be obliged to enforce the Act."[24]

The climax came when the House of Commons went into a committee of the whole on American affairs until February 21.

22. Rockingham to Yorke, Jan. 17, 1766, Add. MSS. 35430, f. 32. In the House of Commons, William Pitt had drawn the distinction between internal and external taxation. He argued that Parliament had the right to legislate for the colonies in all cases except internal taxation. I cannot agree with Allen S. Johnson, "British Politics and the Repeal of the Stamp Act," *South Atlantic Quarterly,* LXII (1963), 188, that anything was to be accomplished by rejecting a general declaratory act and adopting Pitt's theory that Parliament had no right of internal taxation in America. As was shown within two years, the colonists themselves were to make a mockery of this distinction, and Pitt's theory satisfied no one, neither the Americans, the British, nor least of all, Pitt himself.

23. DeBerdt to Samuel White, Jan. 16, 1766, Mathews (ed.), "Letters of Dennys DeBerdt," p. 310; Garth to the South Carolina committee of correspondence, Jan. 19 (but with postscript of Jan. 30), 1766, "Correspondence of Charles Garth," *S.C.H. & G.M.,* XXVI (1925), 73–74; Cobbett (ed.), *Parliamentary History,* XVI, 136; and *Commons Journal,* XXX, 479, 499–500.

24. Rockingham to Charles Yorke, Jan. 25, 1766, Add. MSS. 35430, ff. 7–8.

The almost daily sessions lasted for eight or ten hours, with the administration subjecting the members to some forty witnesses testifying on the detrimental effects of the Stamp Act. The parade included merchants, Americans then in London, and agents. Among the agents and former agents were Sherwood, Thomas Life, Robert Charles, Franklin, Henry Wilmot, Stephen Fuller, William Knox, William Bollan, and Edward Montague. The merchants, both British and American, included Trecothick, James Crokatt, Beeston Long, chairman of the merchants trading to the West Indies, Edward Athawes, Capel Hanbury, William Kelly of New York, and Daniel Mildred. Other Americans testifying were George Mercer, a lobbyist for the Ohio Company of Virginia, Stephen Sayre, and John Wentworth. The administration managed the entire affair. As Newcastle's Parliamentary reporter informed the Duke after one session, Trecothick was examined for "four hours & gave a full clear & Satisfactory account of the distress at home & abroad and stated everything as he did to Your grace this morning. . . ." Capel Hanbury and Daniel Mildred "confirmed him in every thing. . . ."[25] In an equally staged performance Franklin gave a noteworthy exhibition. His testimony, like that of Trecothick, chairman of the committee of London merchants, was rehearsed. By design certain members asked him particular questions to allow him to convey just the information or attitude he wanted to put before the House of Commons. Anthony Bacon contributed three questions intended to demonstrate how harmful continuance of the Stamp Act would be to British trade.[26] Just as William Pitt, Richard

25. James West to Newcastle, Feb. 11, 1766, Add. MSS. 32973, f. 411. For the list of witnesses, see *Commons Journal*, XXX, 513, 532, 538, 546, 574, 786. The testimony of Trecothick, Hanbury, Kelly, Franklin, and Beeston Long, chairman of the West Indian committee, is in Add. MSS. 33030, ff. 88–106, 113, 130–140. Mercer's testimony is edited by J. E. Tyler in "Colonel George Mercer's Papers," *Virginia Magazine of History and Biography*, LX (1952), 414–420. Tyler claims for this document that "It would, for example, throw light on the suggestion that the agitation among the merchants for the repeal was a face-saving device on Rockingham's part. Rockingham was much better informed on American affairs than is sometimes suggested." *Ibid.*, p. 407n5. The present writer can find nothing in the document to substantiate these conclusions.

26. Verner W. Crane, "Certain Writings of Benjamin Franklin on the British Empire and the American Colonies," Bibliographical Society of America *Papers*, XXVIII (1934), 23–24; Lewis B. Namier, "Anthony Bacon, M.P., An

Jackson, and many colonists before him, Franklin distinguished between internal and external taxes in denying the right of Parliament to levy stamp duties. He now publicly took the same line DeBerdt had privately used with Dartmouth in denying the need for revenue to defray the cost of an unnecessary British military establishment in North America. The late war had been fought for British, not American interests, he claimed; consequently it had been a British war.[27] Within a short time Franklin's testimony was well publicized in England and in America, and the agent became a hero in Pennsylvania and the colonies generally.

Votes and organization, not rhetoric, decided the fate of the Stamp Act in Parliament. A preview of the outcome came on February 7, when the House of Commons by a decisive margin rejected a motion by George Grenville to enforce the revenue measure. After the vote, a Parliamentary observer noted Trecothick, Hanbury, and "a great number of Merchants with the Agents full of thanks" in the lobby of the House.[28] The decisive vote for repeal of the Stamp Act came on the night of February 21/22, after the Commons had sat until two o'clock in the morning. By a margin of 275 to 167, the members voted for repeal. The joy of the considerable body of merchants in the lobby "was extreme."[29] In order to win support the administration had coupled repeal with an act declaring the power of Parliament to legislate for the colonies in all cases whatsoever. The two bills passed the Commons on March 14; the action of the House of Lords was anticlimactic. Both measures received the royal assent on March 18.

Eighteenth-Century Merchant," *Journal of Economic and Business History*, II (1928), 38. The queries put to Franklin and his replies are printed in Albert H. Smyth (ed.), *The Writings of Benjamin Franklin with a Life and Introduction* (10 vols., New York, 1907), IV, 434–435. See also Franklin's memorandum, *ibid.*, X, 323.

27. Franklin's testimony in Smyth (ed.), *Writings of Franklin*, IV, 419–421, 446, Cobbett (ed.), *Parliamentary History*, XVI, 154. But cf. Franklin to Lord Kames, Jan. 3, 1760, Smyth (ed.), *Writings of Franklin*, IV, 4.

28. James West to Newcastle, Feb. 7, 1766, Add. MSS. 32973, f. 377.

29. William Rouet to Baron Mure, Feb. 22, 1766, William Mure (ed.), *Caldwell Family Papers* (Maitland Club, *Publications* [2 vols., in 3 pts., Glasgow, 1854]), II, Pt. ii, 73–74; Rockingham to the King, Feb. 22, 1766, Sir John Fortescue (ed.), *The Correspondence of King George The Third, from 1760 to … 1783 …* (6 vols., London, 1927), I, 275.

The agents and merchants had won a great victory primarily because they were dealing outside formal governmental channels with inexperienced, politically unstable ministers who were at a loss in enforcing British authority in North America. The lobbyists now extended their campaign with the administration to "relieve" American commerce of the "burdens" imposed by other regulations of the Grenville ministry. Evidently they operated with the tacit consent of the current administration, for even before the repeal of the Stamp Act, Edmund Burke, Rockingham's private secretary, revealed that the Whigs were preparing a "compleat revision of all the Commercial Laws"—from the "act of Navigation downwards" —dealing with the British and foreign colonies. Committees of the London merchants trading to North America and the West Indies were already meeting to decide on an extensive modification of existing legislation. The preliminary plan would then be concerted among the merchants' committees, the administrative boards, and the independent members of Parliament before being brought into the House of Commons as a "regular and Digested Scheme." Burke expected to be as fully occupied in managing the evidence and testimony in this affair as he had been in the repeal of the Stamp Act.[30]

The West Indian and North American merchants reached a final agreement on trade regulations at a meeting held at the King's Arms Tavern on March 10. Under this program, designed to relieve Anglo-colonial commerce, all molasses imported into North America from the British and foreign West Indies would be subject to a duty of only one penny per gallon. This placed foreign molasses on an equal footing with the British West Indian product and sharply reduced the tax to the rate previously suggested by the colonial agents and John Huske. To protect the colonial distiller the importation of foreign rum into North America would be prohibited. Certain articles from the foreign islands such as sugar, coffee, and cocoa would be landed in North America in ports having a regular customs house. After storage in government warehouses they could then be exported to Europe under such

---

30. Burke to Charles O'Hara, March 1, 3, 1766, Thomas W. Copeland (ed.), *The Correspondence of Edmund Burke Volume I April 1744–June 1768* (Cambridge and Chicago, 1958), pp. 239–240.

regulations as might be deemed proper. If landed in Great Britain, however, they were to be deposited duty free until re-exported under the existing regulations governing enumerated articles. The consumption of foreign sugar in North America would be permitted on payment of a duty of five shillings per hundredweight, but when re-exported to Great Britain the sugar was to be considered as foreign produce and the tax paid in England.[31] The provisions of this plan generally reduced import taxes in the North American colonies and relieved the provincial merchants and shippers of many restrictions in the regulations for the carrying trade. Coupled with the proposal for allowing foreign shipping into Dominica and Jamaica as "free" ports, the program followed basically the scheme submitted the previous October by the American merchant John Huske.

The next stages involved reaching an agreement with the administration and arranging the tactics for presenting the revised trade regulations to Parliament. Two days after concluding their sessions at the King's Arms Tavern, the merchants conferred with Rockingham. They were nearly in complete accord. The First Lord of the Treasury then reported to the King that "there is the Greatest Prospect of an Advantageous System of Commerce being established for the Mutual & General Interest" of Great Britain, the North American colonies, and the British West Indies. The regulations were then referred to the Treasury and Customs Commissioners, and with their approval on March 24, the committee on American papers in the House of Commons was instructed to admit the merchants to testify on American trade.[32]

Since the evidence of the merchants before the House of Commons was to be the foundation of the new American trade act, the administration considered their claims essential to its case. The statements of two traders were particularly significant. William Kelly, a retired New Yorker now living in London, claimed that the duty imposed by the Act of 1764 had raised the price of molasses one

31. This agreement is found in the Chatham Papers, P.R.O. 30/8/97:47–48; Add. MSS., Jenkinson Papers, 38229, f. 235; Treasury Board Papers, T. 1/452:211; Shelburne Papers, Clements Library, Ann Arbor, Vol. 49, ff. 521–522 (printed in Lillian M. Penson, *The Colonial Agents of the West Indies* [London, 1924], p. 284).

32. Rockingham to the King, March 12, 1766, Fortescue (ed.), *Correspondence of George III*, I, 282; T. 29/37:403, 404; and *Commons Journal*, XXX, 688.

penny per gallon. This statement had no basis in fact; the wholesale price of molasses in New York had gone down in the years 1764–1765. But Kelly scored a point. Brook Watson made another. He testified that the British West Indies could not supply more than 5 per cent of the molasses required by the distilleries of the New England colonies. Nor could the islands possibly consume the output of the New England fisheries.[33] Offering similar evidence, other merchants concluded their testimony on the night of April 7. Resolutions incorporating the new program were to be proposed in the House of Commons a week later. Rockingham's secretary, now a member of Parliament, did not expect much difficulty. The opposition in the Commons was beginning to "evaporate," and even George Grenville began to "slacken in his attendance. . . ."[34] The neophyte in politics and administration was overly confident, for objections soon developed.

Dissension in the cabinet and opposition in the House of Commons soon threatened to block passage of the remedial trade legislation. Rockingham's strategy was to have the cabinet consider the free port project before submitting it to Parliament while Dowdeswell conferred with members of Parliament on the molasses and warehouse scheme. In the cabinet, however, Northington, the Lord Chancellor, the Earl of Egmont, First Lord of the Admiralty, and Grafton, Secretary of State, came out against the free ports while William Pitt, upon whom the administration depended to counteract Grenville in the House of Commons, expressed his disapproval of the project. Burke and several of the merchants, Thomas Walpole, Trecothick, Barclay, and Hanbury, tried to win him over, but on April 30, when Dowdeswell proposed the new regulations in the House of Commons, Alderman William Beckford, Pitt's spokesman, attacked the propositions in a speech lasting more than two hours. Although Townshend spoke "more elegantly" than Beckford, he took an inconclusive stand at this time. As expected, Grenville came

33. T. 1/434:55–56. Kelly's claim had no basis in fact. From January to July, 1764 the wholesale price of molasses in New York City stood at 2.5ˢ. It stood at 2ˢ from August, 1764, to April, 1765 and then dropped to 1.75ˢ in September, 1765. Arthur H. Cole, *Wholesale Commodity Prices in the United States 1700–1861 Statistical Supplement* (Cambridge, Mass., 1938), pp. 52–53.

34. Burke to Charles O'Hara, April 8, 1766, Copeland (ed.), *Correspondence of Edmund Burke*, I, 248.

out strongly against the program, especially the reduction in the duty on molasses. The administration was eliminating one tax after another, he claimed, and listening only to the "ex parte Evidence" of biased witnesses. He condemned the practice of delegating governmental functions to a "Club of North American Merchants at the Kings Arms Tavern who, he hoped, would never be suffered to give Law" to the country. In the face of this opposition the ministry decided to play for time by hearing further evidence, this time from the West Indian planters.[35]

A week later the administration won a complete victory when West Indian spokesmen supported the proposals. Although Pitt seemed to acquiesce to the one-penny duty on molasses, he complained of the British sugar islands being "sacrificed to a speculative project" like the free port, which undermined the carrying provisions of the traditional Navigation Acts. The influential West Indian Rose Fuller supported the administration's proposals on "British Principles," however. The molasses trade was vital to the colonial economy, which in turn meant British prosperity. According to information supplied him by the merchants Hall and Kelly, the reduced tax on molasses would stimulate the importation of West Indian produce and increase revenue. The previous rates of six- and threepence could not be collected and were attended with "bad effects." Using these arguments the administration won a complete victory with the Parliamentary session drawing to a close and the opposition collapsing. In a poorly attended session, with only 70 members present, Townshend played a decisive role. One observer noted that he had "run down Grenville, & done admirably" in arguing the administration's case. The reduction in the duty on molasses and the free port project passed without a division. The business of the American committee was now closed.[36] The Act

35. Rockingham to Newcastle, April 11, 13, 1766, Add. MSS. 32974, ff. 370–371; Newcastle's memorandum to the King, April 16, 1766, Add. MSS. 32974, f. 389; Burke to Charles O'Hara, April 23, 24, 1766, Copeland (ed.), *Correspondence of Edmund Burke*, I, 251; James West to Newcastle, April 30, 1766, Add. MSS. 32975, f. 58; and George Onslow to Newcastle, April 30, 1766, Add. MSS. 32975, f. 56.

36. See the two letters from James West to Newcastle, both dated May 8, 1766, Add. MSS. 32975, ff. 110, 112; George Onslow to Newcastle, May 8, 1766, Add. MSS, 32975, f. 114; Thomas Nuthall to Pitt, May 8, 1766, W. S. Taylor

of 6 Geo. III, c. 49 allowed foreign shipping into the free ports of Dominica and Jamaica. Thus the produce of the foreign islands was more accessible to colonial traders. The reduction of the duty on molasses set by 6 Geo. III, c. 52 to one penny met the figure desired by the North Americans. The money raised by this act was to be used for the same purpose as that provided by the Acts of 1764 and 1765—the defense of the colonies.[37] Ironically there were to be few, if any, constitutional protests by the North Americans against raising revenue by this external tax on trade.

The new legislation passed by the Rockingham administration "Absolutely and totally removed" the grievances of the colonies, so claimed Joseph Sherwood.[38] Other agents were not so easily satisfied. The representatives of the colonies also wanted the administration to curtail the jurisdiction of the vice-admiralty courts, the restrictions on colonial coastal shipping, and the prohibition on issuing paper bills of credit as legal tender. Charles Garth was particularly active in attempting to eliminate restrictions on coastal shipping. In the last months of the Grenville ministry he

and J. H. Pringle (eds.), *Correspondence of William Pitt, Earl of Chatham* (4 vols., London, 1838–1840), II, 417; and Pitt to Nuthall, May 11, 1766, *ibid.*, II, 420–421; Fuller to Newcastle, May 10, 1766, Add. MSS. 32975, f. 147; Fuller's paper on the free port system, Add. MSS. 32975, ff. 149–151. According to James Verchild, president of the Council of the Leeward Islands, the "most sensible Planters" were apprehensive that opening Dominica as a free port would injure their sugar and rum trade. But they felt it their duty to acquiesce in the new law, "especially if the other Colonies *and* the Mother Country are benefited thereby. . . ." Verchild to the Duke of Richmond, Secretary of State for the Southern Department, Sept. 29, 1766, C.O. 152/47:130.

37. The Rockingham Ministry in some instances altered the method of remitting this money. To ensure that the revenue raised by the American duties would not leave the colonies and thus impair the colonial economy, Whately, Grenville's secretary at the Treasury, issued orders for the collectors to remit the money directly to the deputy paymasters of the army in America. But the army did not have a paymaster stationed at every point where a customs collector was located and many collectors did not want to leave their stations in order to deliver the money personally. The Treasury now ordered them to pay over the sums in localities where there were paymasters but to send their collections to the Receiver General in London from those few places where there were no paymasters. See the report of the commissioners of customs to the Treasury, Feb. 27, 1766, T. 1/453:298 and minute of the Treasury Board, April 25, 1766, T. 29/37:426.

38. Sherwood to Governor Samuel Ward, May 15, 1766, Kimball (ed.), *Correspondence of the Colonial Governors of Rhode Island*, II, 384.

had been able to secure immunity for undecked vessels operating off the coast from the cocket provisions of the Revenue Act of 1764. When Rockingham came to power the South Carolina agent pressed for further concessions and submitted a memorial for allowing owners of vessels in the coastal trade to give bond yearly rather than for every voyage that they would not engage in fraudulent traffic. In submitting his proposal to the Treasury he drew up a clause to be inserted in the new trade act. Since Parliament was then preoccupied with other, more urgent American affairs, Dowdeswell, the Chancellor of the Exchequer, asked him to postpone the matter until the next Parliamentary session.[39] By that time the administration had fallen from power and Garth had to begin again.

Ministerial instability also prevented any accommodation during the Rockingham administration on modification of the Currency Act of 1764, which many of the colonies, Pennsylvania, New York,[40]

39. See the two memorials by Garth, Jan. 16, Feb. 18, 1766, T. 1/453:176–177 179; Great Britain, Board of Trade, *Journals of the Lords Commissioners of Trade and Plantations* (14 vols., London, 1920–1938), 1764–1767, pp. 245, 246; Garth to the South Carolina committee of correspondence, June 6, 1766, "Correspondence of Charles Garth," XXVIII (1927), 232–235; Treasury minutes of March 6, 10, 1766, T. 29/37:370, 371, 374; and Grey Cooper to Garth, March 7, 1766, T. 27/29:278.

40. Governor Henry Moore had written the Board of Trade that New York would soon be in dire financial straits from the lack of medium of circulation, since his instructions as governor prevented him from assenting to acts issuing bills of credit as legal tender. After discussing the situation with the agent, Robert Charles, the Commissioners of Trade reported to the King in Council that while the monarch could not suspend the Act of 1764, he could allow the governor to sign provincial laws issuing bills in conformance with the Parliamentary statute. In June, 1766 the Privy Council approved instructions drafted by the Board of Trade allowing New York to issue £260,000 in bills to be backed by sufficient taxes and to be redeemed in five years. But the New York legislature must insert a clause in the bill suspending its operation until approved by the Privy Council. See Moore to the Board of Trade, March 28, 1766, Edmund B. O'Callaghan and Berthold Fernow (eds.), *Documents Relative to the Colonial History of the State of New York* (15 vols., Albany and New York, 1856–1887), VII, 820; Board of Trade, *Journals*, 1764–1767, pp. 279, 281–283; representation and draft of instructions, May 16, 1766, C.O. 5/1130:357–359, 361; James Munroe (ed.), *Acts of the Privy Council, Colonial Series* (6 vols., Edinburgh, 1908–1912), IV, 754, VI, 432; and Board of Trade to Moore, June 11, 1766, C.O. 5/1130:372–375.

and South Carolina in particular, had requested through their agents. Since passage of the act restricting issues of legal tender in 1764, the Board of Trade had collected information from all the American colonies on the paper money then in circulation. Benjamin Franklin, who had submitted a petition from Pennsylvania calling for repeal of the Parliamentary statute, and Thomas Pownall, former Governor of New Jersey and Massachusetts, conferred with Rockingham on the matter. They submitted a scheme for a general currency in the colonies supported by the Bank of England and authorized by act of Parliament. In April, 1766, after consulting with Charles Townshend, the Pennsylvania agent set down his proposal in the form of a bill to be introduced in Parliament. Franklin sought primarily to satisfy British merchants who had suffered by the depreciation of colonial currency in the payments of transatlantic debts. Consequently he included in his plan a clause providing for the payment of sterling debts at the rate of exchange prevailing at the time of payment. But there was little hope for remedial legislation that session, for the Rockingham administration wanted to review thoroughly the paper money question before repealing the Currency Act as requested by the agents. However, spokesmen for the ministry assured the agents that they would consider the matter during the legislative recess in order that they might propose "some general and beneficial" plan for all the North American colonies.[41] Unfortunately the Whigs, who had only been a stopgap for George III until he could form an administration more to his own taste, would not be in office by the next Parliamentary session. Paper money had to wait another day.

Despite their failure at this time on paper money and trade restrictions, the agents and merchants had realized many of the

41. Board of Trade, *Journals*, 1764–1767, pp. 49, 244, 253. The returns from the colonial governors on the paper money circulating in the colonies are in C.O. 323/19. See *Commons Journal*, XXX, 688; Franklin to the Pennsylvania committee of correspondence, April 12, 1766, "Letters of [Benjamin] Franklin . . . ," *Pennsylvania Magazine of History and Biography*, V (1881), 353; Verner W. Crane (ed.), *Benjamin Franklin's Letters to the Press, 1758–1775* (Chapel Hill, 1950), p. 27; Franklin to the Pennsylvania committee of correspondence, April 12, 1766, "Letters of [Benjamin] Franklin . . . ," pp. 353–354; Garth to the South Carolina committee of correspondence, June 6, July 9, 1766, "Correspondence of Charles Garth," XXVIII (1927), 236, XXIX (1928), 41.

aims of their constituents during the winter of 1765–1766. During the brief tenure of the Rockingham Whigs the lobby had enjoyed great success in altering the Grenville program. In part this was due to the nature of the Rockingham ministry as contrasted to the previous Grenville administration. The executive boards staffed by experienced, hard-headed administrators under Grenville had often solicited the agents and merchants on American matters and had allowed them to submit practical alternatives on critical problems, even compromising with them on some issues, particularly the Currency and Mutiny Acts. But basically the professionals under Grenville had carried the day. In contrast the relatively young and inexperienced Rockingham Whigs had formed their program outside regular administration circles, at higher and more informal levels, where the agents and merchants had been more effective. The heads of administration had often reached basic decisions with the agents and merchants at private meetings, and the cooperation between the representatives of the colonies and the British mercantile community, as Franklin pointed out,[42] had been close. Intimidated by the violent reaction in the colonies to the Stamp Act, Rockingham relied heavily on the agents and merchants in formulating his American program, and organized and focused merchant discontent on Parliament to repeal the Stamp Act.

In accommodating the Americans, seemingly under economic pressure, the Rockingham administration had placed American supporters in London and future British ministries in a vulnerable position. Consequently the British merchants and some agents, including Jackson, Sherwood, and Franklin, now warned the colonists against any attempt to challenge the imperial government. Franklin hoped that the colonists in the future would be "so prudent, & grateful . . . that their Friends here will have no reason to be ashamed," for the opposition in Parliament had predicted that the indulgence granted the Americans by the repeal of the Stamp Act would only make them "more insolent & ungovernable. . . ."[43] In a very real sense the fears of those British politicians who

42. Franklin to the Pennsylvania committee of correspondence, April 12, 1766, "Letters of [Benjamin] Franklin . . . ," p. 354.
43. Franklin to Charles Thomson, Feb. 27, 1766, "The Papers of Charles Thomson," New York Historical Society *Collections*, XI (New York, 1878), 13;

opposed the concessions made to the Americans by Rockingham proved justified. The repeal of the Stamp Act convinced many Whig leaders in the colonies that they had coerced the home government by pressure and had thus forced it to acquiesce to colonial demands. They did not realize that Rockingham had used the colonial boycott and the resultant distress of the British merchants as an excuse for repealing the Stamp Act. When future ministries adopted the same tactic the lesson seemed clear to American leaders. Constitutional protests and economic sanction would force the imperial government to retreat. But the lesson was fallacious. Unless supported by government, merchant pressure was of little consequence in altering colonial policy. This the colonists never appreciated, and in the decade 1765 to 1774 a pattern appeared in the American response to British action. Fully expecting that a repetition of constitutional protests and economic boycott would be as effective in 1774–1775 as those measures had been in the 1760's, most Whig leaders in America found themselves in a position they probably had not anticipated and may not have desired. The pattern was initiated in the Stamp Act crisis. The empty declaration of Parliament authority did not end colonial agitation against British legislation. And the ministry formed by William Pitt in 1766 soon found itself in an embarrassing position, for even the Great Commoner's simple formula—Parliament could legislate for the colonies in all cases except internal taxation—was inadequate to meet the continuing challenge to the British government.

Sherwood to Governor Stephen Ward, March 29, 1766, John Russell Bartlett (ed.), *Records of the Colony of Rhode Island and Providence Plantations, in New England* (10 vols., Providence, 1856–1865), VI, 486; Jackson to Governor Francis Bernard, March 15, 1766, Alden Bradford (ed.), *Speeches of the Governors of Massachusetts from 1765 to 1775; and the Answers of the House of Representatives To the Same . . .* (Boston, 1818), p. 73.

CHAPTER IV

The Chatham Ministry, 1766–1768:
The Controversy Renewed

PROSPECTS for a further lessening of tensions between England and America seemed bright in the summer of 1766, when William Pitt, now raised to the peerage as Earl of Chatham, took office as head of a new British administration. Apparently the repeal of the Stamp Act earlier that year had submerged the constitutional crisis in imperial-colonial relations. The duty on molasses had been ·reduced and restrictions on colonial trade alleviated. The moment now seemed opportune for resolving the practical issues still outstanding—paper money and the authority and procedures of the vice-admiralty court. Despite strong efforts by the colonial agents and British merchants, the Chatham administration was not to solve these problems but ironically to renew the basic political controversy by levying new taxes, tightening the administrative procedures for enforcing the authority of Parliament, and collecting taxes imposed by the imperial legislature. Several factors led the new imperial government to take this step. Despite the repeal of the Stamp Act, many colonial assemblies continued to provoke the mother country. Secondly, while the Rockingham ministry may have acceded to colonial demands by reducing and eliminating unpopular taxes, it did nothing to solve the problem of financing the North American defense establishment. This continuing problem, coupled with the renewed American challenge to the

90

British Mutiny Act and trade legislation, precipitated a new crisis early in 1767. Further contributing factors were political instability and lack of cohesion within the new government.

While few British ministries in the eighteenth century were very cohesive, the administration formed by William Pitt in the summer of 1766 was particularly weak. Pitt had formed a government with men who had no common program. Indeed, some ministers had supported measures diametrically opposite to those he favored, particularly on the American question, where he had insisted on the right of Parliament to bind the colonies in all cases except internal taxation. The elevation of Pitt to the peerage as Earl of Chatham had further weakened the administration in the House of Commons, the great scene of business where Pitt had been most effective. Chatham's ability to sway men by his eloquence was of little use in the House of Lords, and Henry Seymour Conway, the administration spokesman in the lower house, was not a strong figure. The inability of Conway to control the Commons and Charles Townshend, the Chancellor of the Exchequer, had decisive consequences for Anglo-colonial relations. In an unstable ministry Townshend was able to push new taxes and procedures for more rigid enforcement of British authority in America through a House of Commons already provoked by the colonial challenge to the Mutiny, Trade, and Navigation Acts.

Few men foresaw this development in the summer of 1766. Ironically, to the colonial agents, fresh from their success with Rockingham, the accession of the new government seemed to auger well for the provinces. Richard Jackson, intimate with most of the highest office holders, was confident that the new ministry "is now such that America can never hope for a better. . . ." The Massachusetts agent reminded his constituents that the new Chancellor of the Exchequer had been "very friendly to the extension of your Trade" during the preceding Parliamentary session. Moreover, Charles Townshend's "liberal notions of Commerce and Consummate knowledge of the State of the Trade and Regulations thereof in all Countries may be of Service," Charles Garth, agent for South Carolina, predicted.[1] In an interview with Dennys DeBerdt,

1. Jackson to Jared Ingersoll, Nov. 13, 1766, Feb. 20, 1767, Franklin B. Dexter (ed.), "A Selection from the Correspondence and miscellaneous papers of Jared

the Earl of Shelburne, the new Secretary of State for the Southern Department, expressed the "highest regard" for America and pledged himself to promote its prosperity. The colonists would enjoy their "just rights & priveleges," he promised, but the "dignity of government must be maint[aine]d as well as due regard to the administration. . . ."² Here was the dilemma which was to plague the Chatham ministry, for the colonists challenged the formula to which both Shelburne and Chatham were committed—the complete authority of Parliament except in cases of internal taxation. The provincial attack ranged from the narrow, specific point of Parliamentary regulation of colonial emissions of paper currency to a broader assault on Parliamentary regulations on commerce, and to the fundamental, constitutional issue of the authority of Parliament to *compel* a colonial legislature to conform to the requirements of the British Mutiny Acts. Disputes on these issues in the early months of 1767 provided the explosive background for new legislation when Parliament again was forced to consider the budget of the military establishment in North America.

The North American assemblies, particularly in the middle and southern colonies, were dissatisfied with imperial regulation of paper money. The Currency Act of 1764 had prohibited legal tender³

Ingersoll," New Haven Colony Historical Society *Papers*, IX (New Haven, 1918), 397, 403; DeBerdt to Thomas Cushing, Sept. 2, 1766, Albert Mathews (ed.), "Letters of Dennys DeBerdt, 1757–1770," Publications of the Colonial Society of Massachusetts *Transactions*, XIII (1910–1911), 325; and Garth to the South Carolina committee of correspondence, Sept. 6, 1766, "Correspondence of Charles Garth," *S.C.H. & G.M.*, XXIX (1928), 47.

2. Johnson to William Pitkin, April 11, 1767, "The Trumbull Papers," Massachusetts Historical Society *Collections* (4 vols., Boston, 1885–1902), 5th Ser., IX, 228; DeBerdt to Thomas Cushing, Sept. 19, 1766, Mathews (ed.), "Letters of Dennys DeBerdt," p. 326.

3. It was possible to circulate non-legal tender as an effective medium. After 1750 the Maryland legislature had been able to build up a reserve fund by buying capital stock with the interest from its land bank loans. By 1766 it had reserves of £35,000, of which £26,000 was invested in the stock of the Bank of England. When the old paper money issued by the colony had expired, the legislature was still able to issue new bills, but not as legal tender. Yet these circulated freely, for the colony's commissioners were able to draw on the reserve in London when the paper currency was presented for redemption. Theodore Thayer, "The Land-Bank System in the American Colonies," *The Journal of Economic History*, XIII (1953), 154–155.

and imposed certain conditions on the issuance of paper money in the colonies. To ensure that colonial laws did not violate the Parliamentary statute, the Crown had prohibited the provincial governors from signing any paper money bill unless it contained a clause suspending its operation until approved by the Privy Council.[4] Dissatisfied with these restrictions, the assemblies ordered their agents to secure remedial legislation.

With the formation of the Chatham ministry, and particularly with the appointments of Shelburne as Secretary of State and of Thomas Nugent, Lord Clare, as president of the Board of Trade, many of the colonial representatives in London were confident that they could secure some relief for their constituents.[5] Charles Garth conferred with Shelburne on the petition of the South Carolina legislature calling for the repeal of the Currency Act of 1764. When the Secretary of State appeared receptive to the idea, Garth and Franklin met with a committee of the London merchants trading to America to concert action. The merchants agreed that

4. The New York assembly would not insert such a clause but in December, 1766 it sent to the Board of Trade a proposal to solve the paper money issue. Apparently this proposal had originated among private individuals in England and had been sent to the colony by the agent, Robert Charles. Hoping to obviate the objections made by British merchants to practices of Virginia in issuing paper money, the New Yorkers proposed to repeal the Currency Act of 1764 and issue currency as legal tender in all cases except for sterling debts owed British residents and for special contracts in the colonies payable in sterling. In these two cases the paper bills would not be legal tender at the nominal value of the bills of credit but at the current cost of bills of exchange in London as set by a provincial court. Governor Henry Moore to the Board of Trade, Nov. 15, Dec. 19, 1766, Edmund B. O'Callaghan and Berthold Fernow (eds.), *Documents Relative to the Colonial History of the State of New York* (15 vols., Albany and New York, 1856–1887), VI, 878, 884; Colden to Amherst [Dec. 26, 1766], "The Letters and Papers of Cadwallader Colden," New York Historical Society *Collections* (11 vols., New York, 1877–1878, 1918–1924, 1935, 1937), X (1877), 126. The sketch of the bill for repealing the Currency Act of 1764 is in C.O. 5/1072:457–460.

5. Joseph Sherwood to Samuel Smith, Nov. 18, 1766, "Letters of Joseph Sherwood . . . 1761–1766," New Jersey Historical Society *Proceedings*, 1st Ser., V (1850–1851), 153; Richard Jackson to William Pitkin (private), Nov. 18, 1766, "The Pitkin Papers . . . 1766–1769," Connecticut Historical Society *Collections*, XIX (Hartford, 1921), 49–50; Garth to the South Carolina committee of correspondence, Sept. 26, 1766, "Correspondence of Charles Garth," XXIX (1928), 45; Samuel Hazard *et al.* (eds.), *Pennsylvania Archives* (9 series, Philadelphia and Harrisburg, 1852–1935), 8th Ser., VII, 5948, 5958, 5964.

it was absolutely necessary to repeal the Parliamentary statute. Moreover, legal-tender currency in America would not be prejudicial to the British merchants if legal tender did not extend to sterling debts contracted with residents in Great Britain.

The merchants then appointed a committee of six to call on Shelburne to solicit his aid in implementing these resolutions. On February 13, 1767, the Secretary of State referred the petitions of the merchants and the several colonial assemblies to the Board of Trade, which in turn requested further information from the merchants. The latter then asked the agents Garth, Franklin, Montague, and Robert Charles to submit their observations. Both groups agreed on a representation to be submitted by the merchants to the Board of Trade. In addition Franklin then outlined a bill for Jackson to bring into Parliament for the repeal of the Act of 1764.[6] All appeared to be going well, but the agents themselves hesitated to take the final step. Some members of the administration, particularly Charles Townshend, had indicated that they would support repeal of the Currency Act and allow the colonial assemblies to issue interest-bearing notes, but only on condition that the interest be appropriated for an imperial revenue fund. Franklin claimed he had suggested such a scheme to Grenville two years before as an alternative

6. Garth to the South Carolina committee of correspondence, Jan. 21, March 12, 1767, "Correspondence of Charles Garth," XXIX (1928), 129–130, 220; Franklin to Jackson, Feb. 13, 1767, Carl Van Doren (ed.), *Letters and Papers of Benjamin Franklin and Richard Jackson, 1753–1785* (Philadelphia, 1947), pp. 196–197; Shelburne to the Board of Trade, Feb. 13, 1767, with enclosures, C.O. 5/378:451–473; Great Britain, Board of Trade, *Journals of the Lords Commissioners of Trade and Plantations* (14 vols., London, 1920–1938), 1764–1767, pp. 367, 370; and John Pownall to Barlow Trecothick, Feb. 26, 1767, C.O. 324/18:87. Ironically, opposition to repeal of the Currency Act of 1764 came from Massachusetts, which enjoyed a sound currency and consequently banned the unstable paper of the neighboring New England colonies. Its government was disturbed over the campaign then going on in England. Since Dennys DeBerdt was agent for the House of Representatives and a member of the committee of London merchants trading to America, his name had appeared in the newspapers as one of the lobbyists soliciting permission for the colonies to issue paper money. The Massachusetts government repudiated DeBerdt's efforts and protested to the Secretary of State against the evils of paper money. Governor Francis Bernard to Shelburne, Aug. 25, 1767, C.O. 5/893:13–16; the minute of the Massachusetts Council on paper money, C.O. 5/893:21–35; and Thomas Cushing to DeBerdt, June 24, 1767, Arthur Lee Papers, Harvard College Library, Cambridge, Mass.

to the stamp bill for raising money in America, but now, after the heated polemic on taxation, the agents and merchants hesitated to commit themselves to such a project for fear of antagonizing the colonial legislatures. Interest-bearing notes would provide the imperial government with an American fund raised independently of the colonial assemblies. Consequently the lobbyists temporarily abandoned the campaign for repeal of the Currency Act of 1764.[7]

The agents and merchants realized that they were also handicapped in the paper money affair by a conflict of authority between the imperial government and the colonial legislatures arising from the provisions of the Mutiny Act of 1765. By specified procedures in this statute Parliament had required the assemblies to provide certain incidental supplies, such as bedding, candles, firewood, and vinegar for troops stationed in or passing through a province. The legislatures of Georgia, South Carolina, and New York, although currently enjoying the protection offered by royal garrisons on their frontiers against the Indians, refused to comply, much to the embarrassment of their agents, who were then asking for repeal of the Currency Act. As Charles Garth remonstrated, the refusal of the colonial assemblies, particularly the legislature of New York, to comply with the Mutiny Act had dampened the enthusiasm of the ministers to repeal the restrictions on paper currency.[8] In New York the civil magistrates would not incur the expense of supplying the British troops unless the assembly made some provision to reimburse them. Although the provincial legislature finally did grant funds to the mayors, recorders, and aldermen of New York City and Albany to issue provisions for the garrisons, it did not follow the requirements of the Parliamentary statute which specified that the governor and council appoint the officials to disperse the money. Dissatisfied by this petty infraction of a technicality the British cabinet initially decided to force the New York legislature to conform exactly to the requirements of the act of Parliament by restraining the governor and council of the colony from assenting

7. Franklin to Joseph Galloway, June 13, 1767, Albert H. Smyth (ed.), *The Writings of Benjamin Franklin with a Life and Introduction* (10 vols., New York, 1907), V, 25–27.

8. Garth to the South Carolina committee of correspondence, March 12, 1767, "Correspondence of Charles Garth," XXIX (1928), 219.

to any bill until the lower house had fulfilled the specifications set by the imperial legislature.[9] The dispute over the Mutiny Act increased the tension with the colonies. Franklin, for one, feared that "imprudencies" on both sides might, "step by step, bring on the most mischievous consequences."[10]

Colonial dissatisfaction with the trade laws further exacerbated Anglo-American relations. The Chatham ministry was particularly sensitive to attempts by the provincial assemblies and their agents to modify the statutes regulating colonial trade. For some time Charles Garth had been active in this respect. Not completely satisfied with the exemptions to coastal shippers from taking out cockets granted in the last year of the Grenville ministry, the South Carolina agent again asked that owners of ships in the intercolonial trade be allowed to take out bond once a year rather than for every voyage. On October 14, 1766, the Treasury referred to the Commissioners of Customs his plea that the colonists be "relieved of the distress" imposed by the restrictions in the trade laws if this could be done without endangering the source of colonial revenue. But the Customs Board argued that sufficient relief had already been granted by the exemptions from cockets, and that waiving bonds would open "a door to continued frauds & abuses," thus leaving the collection of revenue in the colonial trade without the security provided in the acts governing the British coastal trade. Convinced that the Commissioners of Customs had misinterpreted his suggestion, Garth took his case to the Chancellor of the Exchequer, who promised that something might be done to incorporate the agent's suggestion in a new trade law.[11] But by this time the assembly of South Carolina had increased its demands. Why could ships loaded with rice not proceed directly to any European port north of Cape Finisterre without first stopping in Britain, and return directly from northern European ports to the colony? Why not freely import all

9. See the cabinet minute of Aug. 5, 1766, Chatham Papers, P.R.O. 30/8/97:79; and the report of the Board of Trade, March 26, 1767, C.O. 5/1130:389–393.

10. Franklin to Joseph Galloway, June 13, 1767, Smyth (ed.), *Writings of Franklin*, V, 29.

11. Treasury minutes, Oct. 14, Dec. 2, 1766, T. 29/38:150–151, 218; Customs report, Nov. 27, 1766, T. 1/453:174; and Garth to the South Carolina committee of correspondence, Jan. 31, June 6, 1767, "Correspondence of Charles Garth," XXIX (1928), 130, 298.

American produce in "any Bottom merely as Articles of Commerce"? Not content with the favorable modification of the Trade Acts achieved by the agents and merchants during the Rockingham administration, the South Carolina legislature, and other assemblies, advocated a basic revision of the traditional navigation system. The Pennsylvania assembly instructed its agents, Franklin and Richard Jackson, to obtain repeal of those provisions of the Trade Act of 1766 requiring bonds for nonenumerated goods shipped with enumerated produce to European ports north of Cape Finisterre. In addition, the Pennsylvanians also sought permission to import wine, fruit, and oil directly from the Iberian Peninsula and the Azores, Madeira, and the Canary Islands.[12]

The most important challenge to the Navigation and Trade Acts—as measured by the reaction in London—was contained in a petition relating to trade from more than 250 members of the New York mercantile community.[13] In this remonstrance the New Yorkers indiscriminately condemned the trade legislation of the Grenville and Rockingham ministries. *Both* "severely clogged & restricted"

12. South Carolina committee of correspondence to Garth, July 2, 1766, "Correspondence of Charles Garth," XXVIII (1927), 228–229; Pennsylvania committee of correspondence to Franklin and Jackson, Oct. 17, 1767, Benjamin Franklin Papers, Library of Congress, I, 58, 60; Hazard *et al.* (eds.), *Pennsylvania Archives*, 8th Ser., VII, 5946–5947.

13. William Kelly, the New York merchant who had been active in the repeal of the Stamp Act and in the passage of the Trade Act of 1766, circulated this petition in New York. He claimed that he had the support of Charles Townshend for such a memorial. Although Townshend had relied on Kelly for information on American commerce, the New Yorker's claim cannot be verified. Whatever the case, Kelly got nowhere in New York until one of the Crugers—a family connected with the Delancey faction in New York politics—supported his petition. Then he was able to secure almost two hundred and fifty signatures from the New York mercantile community. Without examining the petition, Governor Henry Moore forwarded the explosive document to the Board of Trade. If Charles Townshend deliberately contrived to have the Americans antagonize the administration—and this is improbable—he could not have been more successful, since the program conceived by the agents and merchants and enacted in 1766 was regarded in London as a concession to the colonists. For the background of this petition see Nicholas Varga, "The New York Restraining Act: Its Passage and Some Effects, 1766–1768," *New York History*, XXXVII (1956), 239. On the connection between Kelly and Townshend see Stephen Sayre to Joseph Reed, Sept. 3, 1766, William B. Reed, *Life of Esther Reed* (Philadelphia, 1853), pp. 86–88.

the commerce of North America, the provincial merchants claimed. The New York merchants professed that they were aware that during the last Parliamentary session the necessity of relieving colonial commerce seemed to have been "universally admitted"— indeed, Parliament had shown "Tender Regard" for the Americans —but their experience had convinced them that the commercial laws of 1766 "instead of remedying, have increased, the heavy burthen" under which colonial trade "already laboured." The duty of five shillings per hundredweight on sugar was excessive; the new warehousing provisions were expensive, and the reform regulations hampered the trade in the produce of the West Indies—sugar, rum, molasses, logwood, cotton, and indigo—that was so vital to the economy of the continental colonies.[14] When merchants in Boston adopted and supported the arguments of the New Yorkers, the House of Representatives of the Bay Colony instructed Dennys DeBerdt to protest against the trade legislation of 1766.[15] Ironically DeBerdt, as agent and a member of the committee of London merchants trading to North America, had helped draft the reform trade legislation earlier that same year.

The petition of the New York merchants created a sensation in England and greatly antagonized the administration, supporters of the colonies, and all political factions. According to Shelburne the English merchants and Americans then in London, disavowing the memorial, considered it "the height of imprudence. . . ." It is "likely the talk of the town," the Secretary of State speculated. Grenville in the House of Commons would probably impute it as "rebellion." Chatham, who was willing to concede to the Americans the right to tax themselves internally while upholding the authority

14. Petition of the New York merchants, Nov. 28, 1766, Shelburne Papers, Clements Library, Ann Arbor, 49:524–530; Chatham Papers, P.R.O. 30/8/97: 87–90, printed in [John Almon,] *A Collection of Interesting, Authentic Papers, Relative to the Dispute between Great Britain and America; Shewing the causes and Progress of the Misunderstanding, from 1764 to 1775* (London, 1777), pp. 163–167. Commonly cited as *Prior Documents.*

15. Committee of the Boston merchants to [DeBerdt], Jan. 17, 1767, *Papers Relating to Public Events in Massachusetts Preceding the American Revolution* (Philadelphia, 1856), pp. 28–29. Since the New York petition was so controversial, DeBerdt deferred presenting the Massachusetts counterpart (committee of the Boston merchants to DeBerdt, July 28, 1767, *ibid.*, p. 42). The documents the agent finally did transmit to the Secretary of State are printed in *ibid.*, pp. 44–48.

of the imperial legislature to regulate colonial trade, was furious at the "spirit of infatuation" which seemed to have possessed the New Yorkers. He termed their petition "highly improper," their pretensions, "most excessive," and their reasoning, "most grossly falacious and offensive. . . ." They would draw upon themselves a "torrent of indignation" in Parliament and "resentment" from the nation at large by their "ingratitude." While Shelburne hoped at best that the government would distinguish between the behavior of the New Yorkers and that of the Americans generally, Chatham was less discriminating. "New York has drunk the deepest of the baneful cup of infatuation," he admitted, but none of the Americans "seem to be quite sober and in full possession of reason."[16] In pursuing their course they would deliver themselves into the "hands of their enemies." Chatham's prediction was realized when Lord Clare, president of the Board of Trade, laid the New York merchant petition before the House of Commons on February 16, 1767. As Charles Garth reported, the petition confirmed the Grenville faction in its prediction of the previous year. Nothing would satisfy the colonists "but an absolute Repeal of all Regulations and Restrictions," they argued, and, in the end, "independence" from Great Britain.[17] The Rockingham Whigs were particularly embarrassed. Burke had boasted that the previous administration had "perfectly reconciled" the interests of the North American and West Indian colonies.[18] Now the colonists made a mockery of the boast by condemning the Whig "reform" legislation for having increased the burdens under which the Americans were compelled to carry on their commerce.

In view of the colonial agitation over the Mutiny and Trade Acts, few in the House of Commons—country gentlemen, administration supporters, or the opposition factions under Grenville and Rockingham—listened with sympathy to the arguments of the colonial

16. Chatham to Shelburne, Feb. 3, 1767, Shelburne to Chatham, Feb. 6, 1767, W. S. Taylor and J. H. Pringle (eds.), *Correspondence of William Pitt, Earl of Chatham* (4 vols., London, 1838–1840), III, 188, 191–193.

17. Great Britain, Parliament, *Journals of the House of Commons* (London, 1547—), XXXI, 158; Garth to the South Carolina committee of correspondence, March 12, 1767, "Correspondence of Charles Garth," XXIX (1928), 217.

18. Ross J. S. Hoffman (ed.), *Edmund Burke, New York Agent, with his letters to the New York Assembly and intimate correspondence with Charles O'Hara, 1761–1776* (Philadelphia, 1956), p. 47.

agents when the issue of American expenses further exacerbated the colonial question and triggered a new program for colonial revenue and trade regulation. The taxes imposed by Great Britain on the colonies had never been sufficient to defray the cost of the army in America, and with the repeal of the Grenville revenue program early in 1766 the situation was made even worse. This was evident in Parliament when Viscount Barrington, Secretary at War, submitted to the House of Commons the annual budget and extraordinary expenses of the military establishment in the colonies. The revelation that Britain spent over £700,000 annually led to two explosive debates in January and February and reopened the controversy on American taxation. During these heated sessions, Charles Townshend affirmed his belief in the right of the British Parliament to tax the colonies. At one point as the Chancellor of the Exchequer spoke he glanced up to where some of the colonial agents were seated and added with emotion: "I speak this aloud, that all you who are in the galleries may hear me." When challenged by Grenville, Townshend then pledged to the House of Commons that in the current session he would propose a bill by which Parliament would tax the Americans "conformable to their abilities," and in a "manner that should be least burthensome and most efficacious."[19]

The cabinet was unable to control Townshend, for the administration was leaderless, Chatham having abdicated responsibility and having refused to take part in its deliberations. Consequently Townshend and his rival Shelburne pursued two separate solutions to the problem of reducing the expenses of the military establishment and raising revenue to defray the remaining cost. That spring and summer the Secretary of State developed a program based, in

19. William Samuel Johnson to William Pitkin, Feb. 12, 1767, "The Trumbull Papers," 5th Ser., IX, 215–216; Grenville to the Earl of Buckingham, Jan. 27, 1767, George Grenville Letter Book, Stowe Collection, Huntington Library, San Marino, Calif., St. 7, Vol. II; Lord George Sackville to General John Irwin, Feb. 13, 1767, H.M.C., *Report on the Manuscripts of Mrs. Stopford-Sackville, of Drayton House, Northamptonshire* (2 vols., London, 1904), I, 119; William Rouet to Baron Mure, Jan. 27, 1767, William Mure (ed.), *Caldwell Family Papers* . . . (Maitland Club *Publications* [2 vols., in 3 parts, Glasgow, 1854]), II, ii, 100–101; and Shelburne to Chatham, Feb. 1, 1767, Taylor and Pringle (eds.), *Correspondence of William Pitt, Earl of Chatham*, III, 184–185.

The Earl of Chatham

some measure, on the recommendations of Franklin and Jackson to reduce expenses by withdrawing some army units from the North American interior, where they were expensive to maintain, and returning control—and consequently the cost—of Indian affairs to the separate colonies. Shelburne then had the Board of Trade submit his program, incorporating these provisions among others, to a joint meeting of the London merchants under Barlow Treco-thick and the agents of those colonies most directly concerned in the Indian trade, Franklin, Jackson, Edward Montague, and Fowler Walker, agent for Quebec. They unanimously endorsed Shelburne's proposals.[20] Early the following year the imperial government returned control of Indian relations to the colonies.

Townshend's program in 1767 was more momentous and far reaching. Before his death in September, he was able to capitalize on the adverse sentiment in the House of Commons to put into effect his long-standing desire to have the governors, judges, and other executive officials in the colonies independent of the American legislatures by establishing imperial taxes for their salaries.[21] Under

20. J. M. Sosin, *Whitehall and the Wilderness: The Middle West in British Colonial Policy 1760–1775* (Lincoln, Nebr., 1961), p. 161.

21. As early as 1754 as a Commissioner of Trade he had admitted in the House of Commons that he had been responsible for the instructions to Sir Danvers Osborn requiring that the New York governor obtain a permanent appropriation from the assembly for his salary. By this time others in England agreed with Townshend. In 1765 the Earl of Dartmouth, First Lord of Trade in the Rockingham ministry, had noted that the colonial governors were powerless as long as they depended on the provincial legislations for their salaries. Developments in the colonies during the Stamp Act crisis reinforced this view. In the summer of 1765 Governor Francis Bernard complained to the Board of Trade that the Massachusetts legislature threatened to discontinue his salary. He then recommended that a fixed sum be granted the governor. Shelburne evidently agreed, for it appears that in the spring of 1767 he assured Townshend in the cabinet discussions of his support for independent salaries for the civil officers in North America. See Horace Walpole, *Memoirs of the reign of King George The Second*, ed. by Lord Holland, 2nd revised edn. (3 vols., London, 1847), I, 420; entry for Aug. 18, 1765, Dartmouth Papers, William Salt Library, Stafford, England, Dartmouth memorandum book, V, 221B; Board of Trade, *Journals*, 1764–1767, pp. 205, 209; James Munroe (ed.), *Acts of the Privy Council, Colonial Series* (6 vols., Edinburgh, 1908–1912), IV, 739; Charles Garth to the South Carolina committee of correspondence, March 12, 1767, "Correspondence of Charles Garth," XXIX (1928), 215; and Sir Lewis Namier, *Charles Townshend His Character and Career* . . . (Cambridge, England, 1959), p. 28.

his aegis Parliament was to adopt the recommendations of the Treasury, Customs, and Admiralty Boards for a series of proposals to close the loopholes in the enforcement of trade laws and collection of revenue. Multiple admiralty courts, at Halifax, Boston, Philadelphia, and Charleston, were to replace the sole court in Nova Scotia.[22] Parliament would authorize revenue officials to obtain writs of assistance in the provincial courts[23] and to establish an American Board of Customs in the colonies.[24]

The colonial agents and British merchants apparently had little or no opportunity to influence the administration's decisions until early in May, when a select committee conferred with the Chancellor of the Exchequer. Townshend gave them little satisfaction. He did not doubt the right of Parliament to levy internal taxes on the colonists, for he knew of no distinction between internal and external taxes, as some Americans and Britons advocated. But since the colonists chose to draw such a distinction, he was willing to

22. By the terms of the Stamp Act the vice-admiralty court at Halifax had jurisdiction over all revenue cases, but the repeal of the act in 1766 had confused the jurisdiction of the courts enforcing the collection of revenue. The new vice-admiralty courts would remedy the problem. See Admiralty Board to Conway, Aug. 12, 1766, C.O. 5/66:291–292; Treasury minute, Oct. 14, 1766, T. 29/38:151; and Admiralty Report of April 30, 1767, in William L. Saunders (ed.), *Colonial Records of North Carolina* (10 vols., Raleigh, 1888–1890), VII, 459–460.

23. The Attorney General, William DeGrey, had advised that additional legislation might be necessary to close a loophole in the existing Navigation Acts. Under current law, customs officials in England could secure writs of assistance in a court of exchequer. There were no such courts in America, but by the provisions of the Navigation Act of 1696 customs officials in the colonies could obtain such writs from the higher provincial courts. However, DeGrey questioned the authority of the colonial courts to issue writs under the Act of 7 & 8 William III, c. 22. On the basis of his opinion the Customs Commissioners concluded that their officials in America did not have sufficient authority to execute the Navigation Acts in the colonies. Consequently they recommended increasing those powers by act of Parliament. The Treasury ordered the Customs Board to prepare such legislation as was necessary to arm customs officials in America for enforcing the Navigation, Trade, and Revenue Acts. Customs Commissioners to the Treasury Commissioners, Oct. 31, 1766, T. 1/453:185; Treasury minute, Nov. 4, 1766, T. 29/38:182.

24. Shelburne to Chatham, Feb. 1, 1767, Taylor and Pringle (eds.), *Correspondence of William Pitt, Earl of Chatham*, III, 185; Customs report, April 30, 1767, T. 1/459:84–86; and Treasury minute, May 1, 1767, T. 29/38:366.

"indulge" them by levying only import duties. When the agents and merchants suggested that even these external duties were unnecessary if the army were withdrawn from North America, Townshend flatly refused to consider the proposition. Declaring that a large army was essential in America to frustrate "the designs" of Britain's enemies, he maintained that revenue was essential for the support of the military establishment. Yet he wanted to finance the military establishment "in a manner most easy to the people and for this end would pursue the most moderate measures. . . ."[25]

Townshend's arguments with the agents were specious, as was shown when he broached his program for new American duties in the House of Commons on May 13. Significantly, the American agents were deliberately excluded from the galleries, but Garth, Jackson, and Trecothick as members of Parliament attended. Townshend no longer emphasized revenue for the defense establishment. In view of the events in New York and Massachusetts, he now directed his proposals toward "improving the System of Government" in the colonies so that the "Authority of the executive Power" might carry sufficient respect and weight. In order to restore a mixed government whereby the governors could not be coerced by the assemblies who controlled their salaries, the British Chancellor of the Exchequer meant to raise revenue by taxes on fruit and wine imported directly from southern Europe and the colonies, and on tea, painters' colors, and paper. To enforce collection of the new taxes, Townshend also proposed that Parliament create an American Board of Customs. During the ensuing debate George Grenville objected to the direct importation of produce from southern Europe as a subversion of the Navigation system under the guise of taxing, and he also minimized the revenue to be deprived from the import duties Townshend proposed. Instead Grenville suggested repealing the Currency Act of 1764 and creating a general loan office in America to issue interest-bearing notes. The Crown would then appropriate the interest for the American establishment. In rebuttal Townshend claimed that he had meant to propose such a paper-money plan himself. But it had slipped his mind! Few, particularly the

25. William Samuel Johnson to William Pitkin, May 16, 1767, "The Trumbull Papers," 5th Ser., IX, 229.

British merchants and colonial agents, were anxious to revive this controversial issue, and the matter was dropped.[26]

The entire ministerial program, taxes, the American Customs Board, and the resolution restraining the New York legislature until it complied with the Mutiny Act occupied the House of Commons on the evening of May 17. Again, by express order, the colonial agents were not admitted, although during the course of the debate Grenville, glancing up at the gallery, remarked: "I hope there are no Am[erica]n Agents here, I must hold such Lang[uag]e as I w[oul]d not have them hear." The former minister moved an amendment to the ministerial program to establish a test oath since, he claimed, the colonists persisted in denying the authority of Parliament. Few in the House of Commons were willing to go that far, and Grenville's motion lost by a vote of 141 to 42. Those members of Parliament who were colonial agents then took up the American cause. Charles Garth in conjunction with Rose Fuller moved to recommit the resolution for restraining the New York assembly, arguing that the provincial body had not been "guilty of a *direct* disobedience" to the Mutiny Act. Although Henry Conway, the administration leader in the Commons, favored Garth's motion, Townshend and the Attorney General, William DeGrey, were able to carry against recommitment without a division. The House of Commons now adopted the three resolutions for restraining the New York legislature, levying import taxes, and establishing an American Board of Customs. Not until June 1 did Townshend open his tax proposals before the committee on Ways and Means. In the two-week interval the colonial agents persuaded him to drop salt from the tax list, but the British merchants prevailed on him to delete the provision allowing the direct importation

26. Garth to the South Carolina committee of correspondence, May 17, 1767, "Correspondence of Charles Garth," XXIX (1928), 227-228; William Strahan to David Hall, postscript to a letter of May 9, 1767, "Correspondence between William Strahan and David Hall, 1763-1777," *Pennsylvania Magazine of History and Biography*, X (1886), 322; Thomas Bradshaw to the Duke of Grafton [May 14, 1767], Sir William R. Anson (ed.), *The Autobiography and political correspondence of Augustus Henry, third Duke of Grafton* . . . (London, 1898), p. 177, and Benjamin Franklin to Joseph Galloway, June 13, 1767, Smyth (ed.), *Writings of Franklin*, V, 25-27.

to America of wine, fruit, and oil from the Iberian Peninsula,[27] as the Pennsylvania legislature had requested. The remainder of the ministerial program encountered little difficulty in Parliament. The Act of 7 Geo. III, c. 49 restrained the New York legislature until it had made provision for furnishing the troops according to the British Mutiny Act.[28] By 7 Geo. III, c. 46 Parliament levied duties on painters' colors, paper, glass, and tea imported into the colonies. The revenue was to be used first to defray the cost of the civil establishment where necessary in the royal colonies, and then for the support of the military establishment. Finally, the Act of 7 Geo. III, c. 41 authorized an American Board of Customs[29] to enforce the trade and revenue laws. The five commissioners arrived in Boston early the following year. Not until February, 1768 did the government introduce into Parliament the bill to create district vice-admiralty courts having appellate jurisdiction over the vice-admiralty courts in the respective colonies. When the measure was first introduced many of the colonial agents misunderstood what the bill involved. Alarmed, Garth of South Carolina immediately conferred with Franklin, Robert Charles, Edward Montague, and William Samuel Johnson, special agent for Connecticut. On procuring a copy of the proposed law, they realized, however, that the ministry did not intend to grant new powers, but merely to reduce the territorial jurisdiction of the court at Halifax and establish

27. William Samuel Johnson to Jared Ingersoll, May 16, 1767, Dexter (ed.), "A Selection from the Correspondence . . . of Jared Ingersoll," p. 407; Thomas Bradshaw to Grafton, May 16, 1767, Anson (ed.), *Autobiography . . . of Augustus Henry, third Duke of Grafton,* pp. 179–181; William Samuel Johnson to William Pitkin, May 16, 1767, "The Trumbull Papers," 5th Ser., IX, 232–233; and Franklin to Joseph Galloway, June 13, 1767, Smyth (ed.), *Writings of Franklin,* V, 29.

28. The restraint against the New York legislation was never imposed, as the assembly took action satisfactory to the ministry.

29. Significantly the Treasury and Customs Boards in London had not placed the West Indian colonies under the jurisdiction of the new board at Boston. Due to the influence of Beeston Long, chairman of the London merchants trading to the islands, Rose Fuller, William Beckford, and Richard Maitland, agent for Grenada, the West Indian islands escaped this burden. See the Treasury minute of July 29, 1767, T. 29/38:443; and Richard Maitland to the President and Speaker of Grenada, Oct. 23, 1768, in Lillian M. Penson, *The Colonial Agents of the West Indies . . .* (London, 1924), p. 276.

similar courts with the same powers at Boston, Philadelphia, and Charleston. The administration gave Garth further assurances on this point. The bill became law on March 8, 1768.[30] It would be small consolation to the colonists accused of violating the Trade and Navigation Acts not to have to travel the great distance to Halifax to defend themselves. Richard Jackson saw another benefit to the colonists from the fact that the judges appointed to the new courts were to receive fixed salaries. It was better that they should be "paid a certain Salary, than take a subsistence from fees that arise from Condemnations."[31]

Enforcement and recognition of Parliamentary authority over America were the keys to the legislation of the Chatham ministry, as they had been two years before in the passage of the Stamp Act. Despite the Declaratory Act or Pitt's doctrine that Parliament could legislate in all cases except internal taxation, the repeal of the Stamp Act had seriously undermined Parliamentary authority in the colonies. The resulting challenge to the imperial legislature by the failure of New York and other colonies to comply with the Mutiny Act and the petitions of the assemblies and merchants against the Navigation and Trade laws aggravated British political opinion already concerned over the high cost of the American defense establishment. Why should Britain pay for the defense of colonists

30. Garth to the South Carolina committee of correspondence, Feb. 29, 1768 "Correspondence of Charles Garth," XXX (1929), 215–216. The Act (8 Geo. III, c. 22) is entitled "An Act for the more easy and effectual recovery of the penalties and forfeitures inflicted by Parliament relating to the trade and revenue of the · British colonies in America." By royal letter patent on August 4, 1768, the commission appointing the single court at Halifax with jurisdiction at Halifax was revoked, and an order in council of September 7, fixed four courts, at Halifax, Boston, Philadelphia, and Charleston. Munroe (ed.), *Acts of the Privy Council, Colonial Series*, V, 151–153; order in council, Sept. 7, 1768, T. 1/465:278.

31. Jackson to Jonathan Trumbull, Nov. 7, 1770, Trumbull Papers, Connecticut Archives, Connecticut State Library, Hartford, Vol. III, Pt. i, Doc. 30. By 1770 Jackson had been appointed solicitor to the Board of Trade. He then resigned as agent for Connecticut and Pennsylvania.

No doubt it would have distressed Rhode Island smugglers to know that their agent, Joseph Sherwood, presented a memorial to the Treasury on July 12, 1770, on behalf of Augustus Johnson, judge of the vice-admiralty court in South Carolina, praying for a warrant for payment of the judge's salary out of the sale of old naval stores. Treasury minute, July 12, 1770, T. 29/40:323.

who denied the right of Parliament to tax them? many in Parliament had asked. Townshend had been able to take advantage of this sentiment in the House of Commons and the lack of effective leadership in the cabinet to put through a program designed to buttress Parliamentary authority, correct deficiencies in the machinery for the administration and enforcement of its laws, but unfortunately a program also destined to provoke the colonists to still further resistance. The colonial agents, so hopeful at the onset of the new administration, had been able to accomplish little in the face of the American challenge and the British reaction. Once more the task of the agents and merchants was to bring about an accommodation.

CHAPTER V

"A ground for reconciliation,"
1768–1773

I

THE laws passed by Parliament in 1767 to assert and establish its authority over the colonies evoked as significant, though less violent, a response in America as had the legislation of the Grenville ministry two years previously. Repeating the apparently successful tactics employed in the Stamp Act crisis, the Whig leaders coupled constitutional objections denying the right of Parliament to levy the Townshend duties with economic sanctions, agreements not to import British goods until the imperial legislature repealed the objectionable legislation. The reasoning of the patriot leaders was clear in their correspondence to the agents in Britain. Thomas Cushing, speaker of the Massachusetts House of Representatives, wrote Dennys DeBerdt that as the consumption of British goods in America declined in consequence of the nonimportation agreement, it would "not be long before the merchants on your side of the water will have reason to complain." The British government would then react accordingly. As a London merchant as well as a provincial agent, DeBerdt appreciated the tactic. The "schemes of economy" adopted by the Americans "will doubtless have a good effect," he predicted, but he now warned that the colonists must avoid an "ostentatious parade" in their demands. An overly

108

zealous or overt challenge to the authority of the mother country might be dangerous and defeat the very goal they sought. The special agent from Connecticut issued a comparable warning. Although Britons friendly to the American cause had approved the tactics employed by the colonists in resisting the Townshend Acts, the general publicity given by the extremists to their movement antagonized public sentiment in Britain. And was this notoriety necessary? Why make a parade of it? asked William Samuel Johnson. The Americans could just as well secure repeal of the obnoxious duties by organizing their boycott without undue publicity. By their present course they were merely confirming the claims of those English politicians who argued that the colonists were not objecting to specific acts of Parliament but striving for independence.[1] Despite these warnings by the agents, the Whig leaders persisted in their tactics, especially when it appeared to the Americans that the nonimportation agreements were effective. Early in 1770 the imperial government repealed all but one of the Townshend duties, later compromised on the Mutiny and Currency Acts, and made no serious effort to enforce the remaining Acts of Trade and Navigation. The apparent victory of economic coercion was misleading and was to have serious consequences in 1774–1775.

In the final analysis the nonimportation movement between 1768 and 1770 was not the major cause for the repeal of the Townshend duties. In fact, the colonial boycott was far from effective. Although many British merchants felt the economic pressure, they did not necessarily suffer from a cutback in orders from their American customers. Instead they were already hesitant to enter into any new trade agreements, since they had experienced such difficulty in collecting previous debts, particularly from the southern colonies. According to Henry Eustace McCulloch, sometime agent for North Carolina, the merchants "throughout the Kingdom" had recently entered into a "firm Union, not only not to form any

1. Cushing to DeBerdt, April 18, 1768, "Letters of Thomas Cushing from 1767 to 1775," Massachusetts Historical Society *Collections*, 4th Ser., IV (Boston, 1858), 350; DeBerdt to Samuel Adams, June 27, 1768, Albert Mathews (ed.), "Letters of Dennys DeBerdt, 1757–1770," Publications of the Colonial Society of Massachusetts *Transactions*, XIII (1910–1911), 334; William Samuel Johnson to William Pitkin, Dec. 26, 1767, "The Trumbull Papers," Massachusetts Historical Society *Collections* (4 vols., Boston, 1885–1902), 5th Ser., IX, 249.

new Connections in America, but not to ship to, or Answer the
Orders of their Old Correspondents, while the Sins of the past
times" prevailed.[2] Although the British merchants were not under
as great an economic stress as the Whig leaders in America thought,
in time they did join with the colonial agents to attempt to have the
Townshend duties repealed.

More important than the economic pressure resulting from the
inchoate colonial boycott in securing repeal of the important duties
levied in 1767 were the activities of the lobby of agents and British
merchants—a concert formally organized for the repeal of the Townshend taxes. The impetus for cohesion came from America. On
May 9, 1768, Peyton Randolph, speaker of the Virginia House of
Burgesses, sent a circular letter to the assemblies of the other colonies
urging joint action by their agents in London in contesting the
right of Parliament to tax the provinces. Following this initial
suggestion, the various assemblies ordered their agents to cooperate
in all matters concerning the general interest of North America.[3]
The crisis so impressed the agents in London that they resolved to
meet weekly to consult together and "to Act as Exegencies offer. . . ."
To expedite their work, DeBerdt paid a stipend to a clerk of the

2. H. E. McCulloch to Fanning, Sept. 12, 1767, Henry E. McCulloch-Edmund
Fanning Papers, Southern Historical Collections, University of North Carolina,
Chapel Hill.

3. Randolph's circular letter is printed in Nathaniel Bouton *et al.* (eds.),
Documents and Records Relating to the Province of New Hampshire (40 vols., Concord,
1867–1943), VII, 250. For the action of various assemblies in instructing their
agents, see the resolution of the Commons House of South Carolina, Nov. 19,
1768, C.O. 5/391:157; [John Harvey] to Peyton Randolph, n.d., Miscellaneous
Papers, Colonial Series, North Carolina Department of Archives and History,
Raleigh, Ser. i, Vol. I, 1; Pennsylvania committee of correspondence to Benjamin
Franklin and Richard Jackson, Sept. 22, 1768, Samuel Hazard *et al.* (eds.),
Pennsylvania Archives (9 series, Philadelphia and Harrisburg, 1852–1935), 8th Ser.,
VII, 6278; [Theodore Atkinson?] to Barlow Trecothick, Nov. 17, 1768, Bouton
et al. (eds.), *Documents and Records Relating to the Province of New Hampshire*, VII, 188;
Governor William Pitkin of Connecticut to William Samuel Johnson, June 6,
1767, "The Trumbull Papers," 5th Ser., IX, 277–278; Josias Lydon to Joseph
Sherwood, Sept. 26, 1768, John Russell Bartlett (ed.), *Records of the Colony of Rhode
Island and Providence Plantations, in New England* (10 vols., Providence, 1856–1865),
VI, 564; and Noble Wymberly Jones to Benjamin Franklin, Dec. 24, 1768, "The
Commissions of Georgia to Benjamin Franklin to act as Colonial Agent to the Court
of St. James," *Georgia Historical Quarterly*, II (1918), 151.

House of Commons to keep him fully informed of any matters concerning America which came before the House.[4]

Those colonial assemblies which had not employed the services of an agent at this time now sought to select proper men. Since the dismissal of William Knox during the Stamp Act crisis by the lower house of the Georgia assembly, the two chambers had not been able to agree on a candidate, but in March, 1768, with the new threat, the Commons House resolved that there was "an absolute necessity" of appointing an agent to solicit the affairs of the colony in Great Britain.[5] The legislature then agreed on the nomination of Benjamin Franklin, although the new agent had not asked, and was not too anxious, for the position. At the time, he planned to remain in London for less than a year and would have preferred that Richard Jackson, his associate in the Pennsylvania agency, transact the "common business" of Georgia. As it turned out Franklin remained in London much longer than expected and became regular agent for Georgia as well as New Jersey in 1769, when the assembly

4. Charles Garth to the South Carolina committee of correspondence, Nov. 10, 1768, "Correspondence of Charles Garth," *S.C.H. & G.M.*, XXX (1929), 232. In 1768 DeBerdt proposed retaining the clerks of the House of Commons. See his letter of March 1, 1768, Mathews (ed.), "Letters of Dennys DeBerdt," p. 331. From an extract of his accounts as agent ("The Aspinwall Papers," Massachusetts Historical Society *Collections* [2 vols., Boston, 1871], 4th Ser., X, 717) it is clear that he paid a general retainer to the clerks to keep him informed whenever any important affair concerning the colonies came before the House of Commons.

5. In 1766 the lower house had named Charles Garth as its agent, but both the council and Governor James Wright had contested the right of the assembly to act alone. The council rejected Garth because he was also agent for South Carolina. Since the two colonies were then engaged in a dispute, the council felt that Garth could not represent both. The governor then submitted the name of Richard Cumberland, a clerk at the Board of Trade, but the assembly rejected him. See the action of the council for March 20, 26, 1767, Allen P. Candler (ed.), *The Colonial Records of the State of Georgia* (26 vols., Atlanta, 1904–1916), XVII, 366, 372; the resolutions of the Commons House, March 15, 24, 1768, *ibid.*, XIV, 567, 573; Wright to the Earl of Shelburne (abstract), April 6, 1767, Shelburne Papers, Clements Library, Ann Arbor, 52:219–231; James Habersham to William Knox, May 7, 1768, Georgia Miscellaneous Manuscripts, 1732–1796, Force Transcripts, Library of Congress, Habersham Correspondence, II, 39–1, p. 2; and the Georgia committee of correspondence to Benjamin Franklin, May 19, 1768, Georgia Miscellaneous Manuscripts, correspondence of the committee of correspondence.

nominated him to plead the colony's case for paper money.[6]
Jackson was also the regular agent for Connecticut, but for all
purposes a special agent, William Samuel Johnson, succeeded him
when Jackson in 1770 became solicitor to the Board of Trade and
resigned the agency. Johnson, a member of the provincial council,
was sent to London to defend Connecticut in a suit before the Privy
Council over lands claimed by the Mohegan Indians, and he was
given discretionary powers to act for the colony while in England.[7]
Other colonies employed special agents to secure repeal of the Townshend duties. The three counties on the Delaware River appointed
Dennys DeBerdt. His successor in case of death or disability was to
be David Barclay, Jr., a Quaker merchant of London whose firm
had served as agents to disburse Parliamentary subsidies to the
colony.[8] The lower houses of the Maryland and North Carolina

6. Benjamin Franklin to William Franklin, July 2, 1768, Albert H. Smyth (ed.),
The Writings of Benjamin Franklin with a Life and Introduction (10 vols., New York,
1907), V, 146–147. Franklin had experienced some difficulty with the Pennsylvania
assembly. As agent he should have communicated with the committee of corre-
spondence. Instead he had directed his letters only to his friend and political ally,
Joseph Galloway. As a result the assembly issued a sharp warning to the agent.
See the votes of the assembly for May 7, September 9, 1766, Hazard *et al.* (eds.),
Pennsylvania Archives, 8th Ser., VII, 5870, 5886; and Thomas Wharton to Benjamin
Franklin, March 2, 1766, Benjamin Franklin Papers, American Philosophical
Society Library, Philadelphia, II, 10. For the replacement of Henry Wilmot as
agent for New Jersey by Benjamin Franklin, see the New Jersey committee of
correspondence to Benjamin Franklin, Dec. 7, 1769, Frederick W. Ricord and
William Nelson (eds.), *Archives of the State of New Jersey* (36 vols., Newark, 1881–
1941), 1st Ser., X, 135–139.

7. Resolution of the General Assembly, Oct. 1766, J. H. Trumbull and C. J.
Hoadley (eds.), *Public Records of the Colony of Connecticut (1636–1776)* (15 vols.,
Hartford, 1850–1890), XII, 501; report of the committee of correspondence,
Nov. 3, 1769, Connecticut Archives, War, 1675–1775, Colonial, Vol. X, Pt. 2,
1751–1775, Connecticut State Library, Hartford, Doc. 417; Jackson to Jonathan
Trumbull, Feb. 5, 1770, Trumbull Papers, Connecticut Archives, Connecticut
State Library, Hartford, Vol. III, Pt. i, Doc. 5. For Johnson's connections and
activities in London, see Sir William Johnson to Samuel Johnson, Dec. 2, 1766,
Herbert W. and Carol S. Schneider (eds.), *Samuel Johnson, His Career and Writings*
(4 vols., New York, 1929), I, 375; and the entry for Feb. 9, 1767, Diaries, William
Samuel Johnson Journals and Papers, Connecticut Historical Society, Hartford.

8. Delaware (Colony), *Votes and Proceedings of the House of Representatives of the
Government of the Counties of New-Castle, Kent and Sussex Upon Delaware [1765–1770]*
(Wilmington, 1770, reprinted 1931), pp. 168, 182. Almost two years before,

112

William Samuel Johnson

legislatures, without the concurrence of the councils, named Charles Garth and Henry Eustace McCulloch respectively to act for them.[9] The lobbyists named by the colonial assemblies to secure repeal of the Townshend laws consisted of colonists and Britons, lawyers, merchants, and members of Parliament: Edward Montague (Virginia), Richard Jackson (Pennsylvania and Connecticut), Robert Charles (New York), Barlow Trecothick and John Thomlinson, Jr. (New Hampshire), Joseph Sherwood (Rhode Island), Dennys DeBerdt (Massachusetts and Delaware), Benjamin Franklin (Pennsylvania and Georgia), Charles Garth (Maryland and South Carolina), William Samuel Johnson (Connecticut), Henry Eustace McCulloch (North Carolina), and Henry Wilmot (New Jersey). Jackson, Trecothick, Thomlinson, and Garth were members of Parliament. Trecothick and DeBerdt also served on the committee of London merchants trading to North America. Only Franklin and William Samuel Johnson were Americans.

II

The success or failure of the agents and merchants in securing repeal of the Townshend laws depended, in large measure, on the attitude of the British administration—a reconstructed Chatham ministry, a government nominally headed by the Duke of Grafton but in a continual state of flux until the rise of Frederick, Lord North as First Lord of the Treasury in January, 1770. For a time North served only as administration spokesman in the House of Commons and as Chancellor of the Exchequer, succeeding Charles Townshend, who died in September, 1767. The key figure for colonial affairs was the Earl of Hillsborough, the Secretary of State for the American Department, a post newly created in 1768. The agents received the news of the appointment with mixed reactions. Some

DeBerdt had suffered an apoplectic stroke. His daughter had written to Joseph Reed on Nov. 15, 1766: "We wish my father's indisposition may be kept a secret." William B. Reed, *Life of Esther Reed* (Philadelphia, 1853), p. 106.

9. See McCulloch to Edmund Fanning, July 15, [1767], Sept. 12, 1767, McCulloch-Fanning Papers; McCulloch to Fanning, May 20, 1768, William L. Saunders (ed.), *Colonial Records of North Carolina* (10 vols., Raleigh, 1888–1890), VII, 753; McCulloch to John Harvey, *ibid.*, VII, 755; and the North Carolina committee of correspondence to McCulloch, Dec. 12, 1768, *ibid.*, VII, 877–879.

considered Hillsborough unfriendly to the cause of the colonies; others, including Franklin, who later became his bitter opponent, thought that although the new minister had formerly opposed the agents on the issue of paper money, he was not "in general an enemy to America." In fact, the Pennsylvania agent initially thought Hillsborough's inclinations were "rather favorable," but, he added parenthetically, "as far as he thinks consistent with what he supposes the unquestionable rights of Britain. . . ."[10] Franklin's initial assessment was correct. In the past, although Hillsborough had proved amenable to the colonial position on some specific issues, his Board of Trade during the winter of 1764–1765 had taken up the challenge of the lower houses of the Massachusetts and New York legislatures. The call for intercolonial action against the proposed stamp bill had alerted Hillsborough then. And as Secretary of State in 1768 he reacted in a similar fashion to a comparable challenge from the colonies.

The attitude of Hillsborough, North, and the other ministers was evident when the agents and merchants in the fall of 1768 broached the question of repealing the Townshend laws. Garth and William Samuel Johnson both reported that there was little sentiment in the administration or the House of Commons for repeal that session. Moreover, the ministry would support repeal only after the colonists had submitted to the laws and on the grounds that the new duties were burdensome. The American constitutional position would not be admitted. In an interview with the special agent from Connecticut, Hillsborough made this clear. Although he was willing to repeal the objectionable taxes, the colonists had made this impossible by uniting to dispute the right of Parliament.[11] Other administration spokesmen made the same point in the House of Commons when the

10. For the agents' assessment of Hillsborough, see DeBerdt to Thomas Cushing, Dec. 24, 1768, Mathews (ed.), "Letters of Dennys DeBerdt," p. 330; Franklin to Joseph Galloway, Jan. 9, July 2, 1768, Smyth (ed.), *Writings of Franklin*, V, 91, 149; McCulloch to Edmund Fanning, Jan. 26, 1768, McCulloch-Fanning Papers; Johnson to William Pitkin, Dec. 26, 1767, "The Trumbull Papers," 5th Ser., IX, 252; and Johnson to Colonel Walker, Jan. 23, 1768, "Letters By, 1767–1793," William Samuel Johnson Journals and Papers, No. 30.

11. Johnson to William Pitkin, Oct. 20, Nov. 18, 1768, "The Trumbull Papers," 5th Ser., IX, 296, 305; Garth to the South Carolina committee of correspondence, Nov. 10, 1768, "Correspondence of Charles Garth," XXX (1929), 231.

The Earl of Hillsborough

merchant John Huske attempted to offer a petition from the Pennsylvania assembly complaining against taxation without representation. The petition contained sentiments contrary to the Declaratory Act, the statute affirming the right of the British Parliament to legislate for the colonies in all cases whatsoever. North stated the case for the administration when he declared that there was no distinction between general governmental power and the power to tax. "You must possess the whole of your authority, or no part of it," he told the Commons. He hoped that Parliament would abide by the Declaratory Act and not repeal the Townshend duty because of "any resistance the Americans may give it." This was the only way to hold fast to British rights. He urged the House of Commons "never to give up an iota of the authority of Great Britain. Let us maintain our ground there; but at the same time, do not let there be fresh ground of dispute." He delivered his main point with the plea: "Let us not give way to force."[12] The issue was clear. The Americans denied the right of the British legislature to tax them, while the imperial government maintained the right to legislate for the colonies in all cases and would not submit to force.

Aside from its general position the administration had to propose an immediate concrete program for the Parliamentary session in 1769, inasmuch as Robert Charles could not be prevented from presenting a New York petition to the House of Commons, thus giving the opposition an opportunity to attack the ministry on its American program.[13] Hillsborough took the initiative in drafting

12. House of Commons, Dec. 5, 1768, Jan. 26, 1769, John Wright (ed.), *Sir Henry Cavendish's debates of the House of Commons, during the thirteenth parliament . . . 1768–1774* (2 vols., London, 1841–1843), I, 83–84, 204.

13. The Secretary of State had prevailed on Charles to postpone for some weeks presenting the protest of the New York legislature. He was evidently unsuccessful in persuading Edward Montague not to present a Virginia petition. There is an undated letter written in 1769 from Montague to Hillsborough. "Since I had the Honor of obeying your last Sumons I have given the Occasion of it serious Consideration. By my Instructions, in this very interesting Subject, I am convinced I sho[ul]d incur the Censure of my Constituents, was I to divert the Course of their Complaints And if their humble application sho[ul]d not be received in their several Directions, thro' an officious Interposition on my part, your Lordship may easily guess at the Consequences. Having had the Honor of serving them these ten years with Fidelity, & every Mark of Approbation that my vainest Expectations could suggest, pardon me, my Lord, if I exercise every Precaution not to forfeit

115

a comprehensive plan dealing with the several controversial points then outstanding between Britain and the colonies. At issue were the refusal of the Massachusetts council and the legislature of New York to quarter troops and protect customs officials, the action of Virginia in initiating intercolonial opposition to the Townshend duties, and the general question of Parliamentary taxes as they related to the civil establishment of the colonies. Hillsborough advocated singling out the particular colonies he considered guilty of specific acts against the royal government, New York and Massachusetts, while allowing the other provinces an exemption from Parliamentary legislation if they recognized the authority of the imperial government. Assuming that councilors appointed by the Crown would not be as hesitant in calling for troops to protect the customs officials, Hillsborough favored a bill altering the 1691 charter of Massachusetts, which provided that the House of Representatives elect the upper chamber. To restore the authority of the royal government in Massachusetts, Hillsborough wanted to vest the appointment in the Crown as was the case in other royal colonies. He also recommended an act of Parliament declaring that any measure taken by the Massachusetts assembly denying or questioning the authority of Parliament to bind the colonies in all cases would automatically constitute a forfeiture of the charter. With respect to the challenge of the New York assembly in refusing to accept the British Mutiny Act, Hillsborough advocated enforcing the Restraining law passed in 1767. But he would merely order the governors of the other colonies which had not complied with the Mutiny Act to "call on their Assemblies, with proper exhortations" to comply. Although the Secretary of State favored modifying the Mutiny Act to permit provincial commissaries appointed by the governors to quarter troops in private houses if the assemblies failed to provide public billets, he would not enforce the Mutiny Act in any colony which would pass its own law—a statute confirmed by the British Privy Council. Hillsborough would apply the same condition for the support of the civil establishment in the colonies.

their favourable Opinion on this critical Occasion. Your Lordship will therefore excuse me if I submit to your good Judgment the most effectual Mode of communicating their Grievance to both Houses of Parliament." With a document endorsed "enclosed Mr. Montague Remonstrance & mem." (C.O. 5/114:213).

He favored repealing the Townshend duties, intended to provide money for civil government, as they applied to Virginia and the West Indian colonies, where the legislatures already paid the salaries of judges and governors. The ministry should declare that the Townshend duties would remain in force in the other royal provinces until each should have made permanent provision for its own establishment subject to the approval of the King in Council. Hillsborough's program would permit local exercise of government functions, but under a formula devised by imperial authority, imposed by Parliament, and supervised by the Privy Council. The British government was not to adopt Hillsborough's principle at this time, but it did become the basis of British colonial policy in the crisis of 1774-1775. Yet some facets of his program were used earlier to resolve disputes on the Mutiny Act and colonial paper currency.

In 1769 the decision to implement Hillsborough's suggestions lay immediately with the King, and the monarch at that time did not entirely concur with his minister on the American issue. George III opposed changing the method of appointing councilors for as he put it "the altering of charters is at all times an odious measure." But such a step might be necessary if the Bay Colonists continued to challenge the imperial government. Here was a preview of the legislation to be enacted some years later against Massachusetts in reaction to the Boston Tea Party. For the present the King suggested that the government merely hint that those colonies submitting to the law and properly providing for their own civil establishments might in another year be exempted from any Parliamentary tax "except the Tea Duty."[14] The single impost was to signify the right of Parliament to tax the colonies. There was to be no immediate concession on the Townshend duties in order to save the authority of government, but by 1770 only the symbol would be retained. In 1769 the position of the ministry was clear: the right of Parliament to legislate for America and the power of the Privy Council to superintend colonial laws to ensure that they conformed with

14. See Hillsborough to the King, Feb. 15, 1769, "Measures Proposed by Lord Hillsborough to the Cabinet," and a memorandum by George III, in Sir John Fortescue (ed.), *The Correspondence of King George the Third, from 1760 to December 1783* . . . (6 vols., London, 1927), II, 81-84.

117

Parliamentary statutes. The practical loss in revenue in repealing the duties levied in 1767, less than £40,000 a year, was inconsequential.

III

The agents and merchants who met regularly during the winter of 1768–1769 to concert plans for the repeal of the Townshend Acts were well aware of the position of the administration and recognized that any effort to coerce the home government made their position all the more difficult. Joseph Sherwood for one feared that the behavior of the Boston Whigs "will be so far resented as to prevent any good effects being immediately produced by the endeavors" of those in London friendly to the American cause. The ministers would not think it "consistent with their dignity" to repeal the Townshend duties lest such a step be construed as a "silent acknowledgement" that the government was unable to enforce its laws. Hillsborough confirmed this attitude when he informed a committee of the London merchants trading to America that the ministry would not consent to a repeal of the acts during the early Parliamentary sessions of 1769.[15] Although some merchants were discouraged by this interview, on February 10, 1769, the Livery of London met to instruct its members in Parliament. They were to encourage and promote trade with the colonies. Now that London was acting, Dennys DeBerdt hoped that this "method of instruction will run the greatest part of the kingdom" and have a "good effect" on other politicians in Parliament. At least the example of the City of London demonstrated "the general temper of the people" and their desire to "cultivate a good understanding and trade with America."[16] In any case the merchants did not take the initiative in 1769.

15. Joseph Sherwood to the Governor of Rhode Island, Dec. 8, 1768, Bartlett (ed.), *Records of the Colony of Rhode Island and Providence Plantations*, VI, 511; Garth to the South Carolina committee of correspondence, Nov. 29, 1768, "Correspondence of Charles Garth," XXX (1929), 234; DeBerdt to Richard Cary, n.d., DeBerdt to Thomas Cushing, Feb. 1, 1769, Mathews (ed.), "Letters of Dennys DeBerdt," pp. 349, 355.

16. DeBerdt to the speaker of the Massachusetts House of Representatives (Thomas Cushing), Feb. 11, 1769, Alden Bradford (ed.), *Speeches of the Governors of Massachusetts from 1765 to 1775; and the Answers of the House of Representatives To the Same* . . . (Boston, 1818), p. 194. (Also cited as *Massachusetts State Papers.*)

"A ground for reconciliation," 1768–1773

The colonial agents went ahead, nonetheless, and held a series of meetings during February and March to decide on tactics they would use in calling for repeal of the Townshend laws. At first all agreed to a petition which would not question the right of Parliament. They then commissioned Franklin to draft a document designed to reflect the sentiments of their constituents and yet not arouse resentment in England, a difficult task to say the least. But in the course of their later meetings, agents for some New England colonies objected to this tactic, for all of the petitions from the provinces specifically denied the right of Parliament to tax the colonies. The agents could not take it upon themselves to waive the exemption from Parliamentary taxation or remain silent on the question without express instructions from their constituents. The British government might construe petitions based solely on arguments of expediency as a declaration that the colonies by their agents had, in effect, receded from their claim of exemption from Parliamentary taxation.

But other agents did not agree. Garth of South Carolina thought that a petition based on expediency conceded nothing; rather it "cautiously reserved" to the Americans the exclusive right of taxation. DeBerdt concurred in this judgment. A petition avoiding the question of right and asking for repeal of the Townshend duties on practical considerations would be a "middle way," and would not concede Parliamentary authority to tax. The agents must apply for repeal of the duties this session, the Massachusetts agent urged. On this point Henry Wilmot, agent for New Jersey, added a dissenting note. He assured his colleagues that under no circumstances would the ministry repeal the duties during the present meeting of Parliament. Next year, however, they would remove the taxes of their own volition.[17] Unable to agree among themselves, the agents separately presented to the Secretary of State the memorials their constituents had sent them protesting the Townshend duties. Taking exception even to this procedure, Hillsborough

17. DeBerdt to Thomas Cushing, Feb. 25, March 10, 1769, DeBerdt to Richard Cary, Feb. 25, 1769, DeBerdt to the Delaware committee of correspondence, March 9, 1769, Mathews (ed.), "Letters of Dennys DeBerdt," pp. 364, 365, 366, 367; William Samuel Johnson to William Pitkin, March 23, 1769, "The Trumbull Papers," 5th Ser., IX, 324–326; and Charles Garth to the South Carolina committee of correspondence, March 12, 1769, "Correspondence of Charles Garth," XXXI (1930), 52–54.

complained that any channel of communication from the colonial assemblies to the Crown other than through the governors was irregular. Although he frowned on petitions such as the memorial from New York presented by Robert Charles, which questioned but did not explicitly deny Parliamentary authority, the Secretary of State grudgingly accepted them from the agents. Encountering the same difficulty in presenting a Georgia petition, Franklin concluded that Hillsborough considered agents "unnecessary" or, as he added parenthetically, "perhaps troublesome. . . ."[18]

Since the ministers were proving unsympathetic, some provincial agents and their associates sought to circumvent the administration and lay the ground work for subsequent repeal of the objectionable duties by raising the issue directly in Parliament. Trecothick (chairman of the merchants' committee and agent for New Hampshire) collaborated with Rose Fuller (brother of the agent for Jamaica) and Thomas Pownall (a former governor who aspired to the Massachusetts agency) to bring the question of repeal before the House of Commons. Initially Pownall doubted that he could succeed, but nonetheless on March 12, 1769, he announced to the Commons that he intended the following year to move for a bill repealing the Townshend duties. He then proceeded to abuse the administration "as the most ignorant Blockheads in all American Concerns." For his pains he received a "very severe dressing down" from Lord North, the administration spokesman in the lower house. Undeterred, Pownall pressed on the following month, when he moved for immediate repeal of the duties. Conway, Sir George Savile, and Richard Jackson seconded his motion. According to William Samuel Johnson, special agent from Connecticut, the former governor did not hope to carry the proposal at the current session, but merely to "take from Administration every degree of excuse, and to put them as much as possible in the wrong. . . ."

The debate on the American issue on April 19 afforded the agents and merchants in the House the opportunity to lay the ground-

18. Hillsborough to Moore, March 24, 1769, Edmund B. O'Callaghan and Berthold Fernow (eds.), *Documents Relative to the Colonial History of the State of New York* (15 vols., Albany and New York, 1856–1887), VIII, 156; Franklin to the Speaker of the Georgia Commons House, April 3, 1769, Candler (ed.), *Colonial Records of the State of Georgia*, XV, 26.

work for subsequent repeal and to learn, if indeed it was necessary to repeat the lesson, the conditions on which the administration would be willing to grant concessions to the Americans. Pownall in his speech conceded the supremacy of Parliament over the colonies; it was essential to the security of the empire and ought to be retained. And once passed, the Declaratory Act must "be considered as a kind of hoisting of their colours, which they could never again lower." Consequently he urged repeal of the Townshend duties for commercial reasons only. In seconding Pownall's motion Barlow Trecothick adopted the same argument, emphasizing the commercial motives for repeal and enumerating the steps taken by the Americans to prevent consumption of British manufactures.[19]

Significantly, the supporters of the American cause in the House of Commons did not maintain the right of the colonists exclusively to tax themselves or question the authority of Parliament. In defense of the administration, Lord North emphasized this. No one was more concerned about the differences existing between the mother country and America than he, the Chancellor of the Exchequer professed, but the question was how to eliminate those differences. If Parliament lost its "credit" with the colonists, he told the Commons, "you can never be reconciled" with them. In view of the "combinations going on" in America against Great Britain, the administration refused at this time even to consider repeal of the duties. North even refused to commit himself on some future course. Conway and Alderman William Beckford, the London merchant, now proposed a compromise, a "middle course," at least to consider repeal at the next session of Parliament. But North again objected. Such an agreement might convey to the colonists the impression that the principle of repeal had already been accepted in England.[20] In all probability North adopted this line

19. For the debates of March 1 and April 19, see Edward Sedgwick to Edward Weston, March 14, 1769, H. M. C., *Tenth Report*, App., Pt. I (London, 1885), p. 413; Thomas Pownall to the Rev. Dr. Samuel Cooper, March 19, 1769, Frederick Griffin (ed.), *Junius Discovered* (Boston, 1854), p. 217; William Samuel Johnson to William Pitkin, April 26, 1769, "The Trumbull Papers," 5th Ser., IX, 334–337; Benjamin Franklin to Cooper, April 27, 1769, Smyth (ed.), *Writings of Franklin*, V, 205; and Wright (ed.), *Sir Henry Cavendish's debates of the House of Commons*, I, 391–397.

20. Wright (ed.), *Sir Henry Cavendish's debates of the House of Commons*, I, 397–400.

to protect the administration's political position in case the Whigs in American proved to be intractable. According to Richard Jackson the ministers had expressed themselves publicly so as not to "lay themselves under a Parliamentary obligation," but privately informed some agents that they would support partial repeal of the Townshend duties the next year.[21] Apparently the agent for Pennsylvania was well informed, for after Parliament rose the administration gave concrete assurances of a partial repeal at the next session. In the summer of 1769 Joseph Sherwood, Robert Charles, Franklin, Henry Eustace McCulloch, and DeBerdt among the agents called on the Secretary of State for the American Department. Hillsborough further assured them that the ministry had laid aside "every idea of raising revenue in the colonies, for the service of government," and was resolved to repeal the duties on paper, glass, and painters' colors and to undertake every "reasonable and proper measure" to remove the "jealousies, fears, and apprehensions of the Americans." But the administration was determined to support the dignity of government.[22] Thus it would not repeal all the duties. As George III had insisted earlier that year, the tax on tea would remain as the symbol of Parliamentary authority.

In an effort to exert pressure on the ministry for a total repeal of all the duties, Benjamin Franklin wrote to America, particularly to Charles Thomson—the Samuel Adams of Philadelphia—and to Joseph Galloway, urging that the colonists persist in their nonimportation agreements. Franklin's motive in pursuing this course of action seems to have been oriented toward the political situation in Pennsylvania, for he certainly realized that continued economic pressure would not influence the ministry. And without ministerial support, there was little hope of obtaining full repeal in Parliament.

21. Richard Jackson to William Pitkin, May 16, 1769, "The Pitkin Papers . . . 1766–1769," Connecticut Historical Society *Collections* (Hartford, 1921), XIX, 176. Franklin also referred to "Hints" given by the ministers for a possible repeal the next year. Franklin to the Speaker of the Georgia Commons House, April 3, 1769, Candler (ed.), *Colonial Records of the State of Georgia*, XV, 27.

22. Joseph Sherwood to Governor Joseph Wanton of Rhode Island, July 5, 1769, Bartlett (ed.), *Records of the Colony of Rhode Island and Providence Plantations*, VI, 593; H. E. McCulloch to the North Carolina committee of correspondence, July 14, 1769, Saunders (ed.), *Colonial Records of North Carolina*, VIII, 56; Benjamin Franklin to Noble Wymberly Jones, June 7, 1769, Carl Van Doren (ed.), *Benjamin Franklin's Autobiographical Writings* (New York, 1945), p. 190.

Frederick, Lord North

The previous year he had realistically analyzed the relationship between the ministry and the legislature in London. ". . . nothing is to be done in Parliament that is not a measure adopted by the ministry and supported by their strength, much less anything they are averse to or *indifferent about.*" Whatever the motives behind the agent's letter, it had "wonderful effects" in Philadelphia according to the Pennsylvania merchant Henry Drinker. Through Franklin the patriots and merchants of Philadelphia and Boston then put pressure on the English mercantile community. The provincial traders charged that the London merchants had confined themselves to securing repeal of the duties on paper, glass, and other items while ignoring the tax on tea and other impositions "of a similar Nature, which are equally injurious to us tho' not equally detrimental to you." The Americans would be satisfied with nothing less than total repeal, the Philadelphians claimed. Despite the professions and efforts of the merchants,[23] it was impossible, as their English counterparts well realized, to maintain the nonimportation agreement as an economic sanction to force total repeal of the Townshend duties.

Early in 1770 the agents and merchants in London met to plan common tactics in order to take advantage of the promise made the year before by the administration. Initially they were not in full accord. Jackson, optimistic that the ministry would repeal the duties, realized nonetheless that the ministers would have to act "without Loss of Honour," and consequently would move only for a partial repeal, particularly since the Grenville-Rockingham factions were always ready to reproach them with going too far as well as not far enough. Yet, quieter times might bring further concessions,

23. Franklin to Galloway, Feb. 17, 1768, Smyth (ed.), *Writings of Franklin*, V, 97–99; Henry Drinker to Abel James (extract), May 26, 1770, Henry Drinker, "Effects of the 'Non-Importation Agreement' in Philadelphia, 1769–1770," *Pennsylvania Magazine of History and Biography*, XIV (1890), 45; Franklin to Galloway, July 9, 1769, Smyth (ed.), *Writings of Franklin*, V, 220; the Philadelphia merchants to David Barclay, Jr., Daniel Mildred, Thomas Pownall, Dennys DeBerdt, Richard Neave, and William Neate, June 5, 1769, Benjamin Franklin Papers, Library of Congress, Ser. ii, Vol. I, 71. See also Charles Thomson to Franklin, Nov. 26, 1769, "The Papers of Charles Thomson," New York Historical Society *Collections*, XI (1878), 22; and the committee of Boston merchants to Franklin, Dec. 29, 1769, Franklin Papers, American Philosophical Society Library, II, 210.

even repeal of the tax on tea. Edward Montague, agent for Virginia, objected, however, even to retaining the duty on tea and the "obnoxious" preamble to the Revenue Act. Moreover, the London merchants were extremely "shy, & very unwilling to take the Lead. . . ." Consequently the agents had to prevail on the merchants of Bristol to initiate proceedings. After conferring with the provincial representatives, the Bristol traders urged their members of Parliament to take action. To strengthen their case they sent their members an account of orders from America amounting to £200,000 conditional on the repeal of the Townshend taxes. Whether this stimulated the Londoners is not certain, but on February 1 the merchants of the metropolis held a general meeting attended by several visiting merchants from the colonies. It was apparent that the nonimportation agreements were not effective. One London merchant produced a letter from his correspondent in Boston directing the shipment of goods on condition that only the last of the Townshend Acts be repealed. The Quakers of Philadelphia were also willing to break the nonimportation agreement upon partial repeal. DeBerdt, agent for the Massachusetts House of Representatives, strongly opposed an application for partial repeal, however. The other merchants declared that his decision might be appropriate for him since he was an agent as well as a merchant, but as businessmen there was nothing else for them to do but ship goods agreeable to the orders of their American customers. Still the Massachusetts agent had his way, and the lobby held together when the British merchants agreed to petition for repeal of all the duties imposed in 1767. But in their memorial to the House of Commons, the merchants were careful not to question the right of Parliament to tax the colonists; they complained only of the commercial disadvantages of the taxes.[24]

24. DeBerdt to Thomas Cushing, Feb. 2, 1770; DeBerdt to Edward Sheafe, Feb. 2, 1770; DeBerdt to Thomas McKean, Feb. 15, 1770, Mathews (ed.), "Letters of Dennys DeBerdt," pp. 396, 398, 399; Edward Montague to the Virginia committee of correspondence, Feb. 6, 8, 1770, "Proceedings . . .," *Virginia Magazine of History and Biography*, XII (1904–1905), 164–166; Garth to the South Carolina committee of correspondence, Feb. 5, 1770, "Correspondence of Charles Garth," XXXI (1930), 140; Great Britain, Parliament, *Journals of the House of Commons* (London, 1547—), XXXII, 664–665; and Jackson to Jonathan Trumbull, Jan. 2, Feb. 6, 1770, Trumbull Papers, Connecticut Archives, Vol. III, Pt. 1, Docs. 1c, 6. The petition of the merchants and traders of London is in Chatham Papers, P.R.O. 30/8/73:160.

"A ground for reconciliation," 1768–1773

The stage was set for the debates in Parliament. On March 5, 1770, the day scheduled for the House of Commons to consider the Townshend duties—and ironically the day of the Boston "Massacre"—William Bollan, former agent for Massachusetts, almost upset the carefully concerted plan of the agents and merchants. The lobbyists had planned to request repeal of the duties for reasons of expediency: a measure necessary for British commerce. And to avoid giving the impression that repeal was an American request, they sought to propagate the fiction that it was simply an application from the British merchants. But Bollan "very imprudently," according to Thomas Pownall, presented his own petition questioning the authority of Parliament. Fortunately for the lobbyists, the House of Commons simply tabled Bollan's petition and instead took up the memorial of the London merchants trading to North America. Three distinct views were expressed on the issue of repeal: some favored the Americans, others objected to repealing any of the duties, and a third proposed a partial repeal. Certain members such as Lord Barrington, the Secretary at War, and Welbore Ellis supported rigorous enforcement of the duties. They saw no indication that partial or even total repeal would quiet the Americans. Consequently they favored an absolute execution of the Parliamentary statutes "by all the powers of this nation united."

Governor Thomas Pownall took up the case for the colonies by calling for total repeal. Employing the art of the practiced sophist he informed the Commons that he did not ask for abolition of the duties as a "favour for the Americans—they do not ask the repeal as a favour—they do not ask for it at all." During the current session the colonists had not petitioned Parliament for repeal, they had not directed their agents "even to move in it," they had not "by the most distant hint, applied to any one friend to interpose in the matter." Only the British merchants asked for repeal. This was rhetorical nonsense as most probably realized. But the administration went along with the fiction of repealing the Townshend duties for commercial reasons and at the request of the British merchants. Significantly, North pointed out that in contrast to the coercive tactics employed by the Americans to force repeal, the present petition under consideration was presented by a "very respectable body of merchants" and was couched in "terms most

125

respectful to this House. . . ." Nevertheless the administration spokesman would not go as far as the petitioners, or "several gentlemen"—an obvious reference to the American supporters in the House of Commons—would wish, and repeal all of the duties. The distress of the British merchants, he charged, was due to "illegal combinations" in America which prevented commercial intercourse, but since some of the duties were anticommercial there was no reason why the House of Commons should not give way to the petition of the merchants. North's argument was specious. The duties had been as anticommercial, and the merchants more seriously hurt by the colonial boycott, the previous year, when the ministry had refused even to consider partial repeal. As North demonstrated when touching on the central issue, he was not primarily concerned with the economic benefits of the British merchants. Repealing the tax on tea would mean relinquishing the power of Parliament to tax the colonies. "Let us not desire to be reconciled with the Americans, on account of the demands they are making upon us, by most illegal and unwarrantable means," he pleaded, rather, "let us have a ground of reconciliation . . . without incurring the danger of breaking through rules which are as necessary for them as for us." He concluded by asking permission to introduce a bill repealing only the duties on glass, paper, and painters' colors.[25] North had organized his majority well. The House of Commons rejected Pownall's amendment for total repeal 204 to 142, and four days later the First Lord of the Treasury brought in his bill. It passed the Commons on April 6.

The administration had supported repeal on the grounds that the Townshend duties were inconvenient to British commerce, but as

25. Thomas Pownall to Samuel Cooper, March 8, 1770, Griffin (ed.), *Junius Discovered*, pp. 259–260; *Commons Journal*, XXXII, 745–750; Wright (ed.), *Sir Henry Cavendish's debates of the House of Commons*, I, 483, 484, 489; [John Debrett,] *The History, debates, and proceedings of both houses of Parliament . . . 1743 to 1774* (7 vols., London, 1792), V, 253, 257; William Cobbett (ed.), *The Parliamentary History of England from the Earliest Period to the Year 1803* (36 vols., London, 1813), XVI, 857, 874. The agents for South Carolina and Virginia sent accounts of the speeches to their constituents, however. See Garth to the South Carolina committee of correspondence, March 6, 1770, "Correspondence of Charles Garth," XXXI (1930), 228–232; and Edward Montague to the Virginia committee of correspondence, March 6, 1770, "Proceedings," pp. 168–169.

the King had insisted the previous year, the tax on tea remained as the symbol of the authority of Parliament to tax the colonists. Consequently there was little to justify the hopes of some proponents of the provincial cause, such as Richard Jackson, that even the symbol might go. Nonetheless Barlow Trecothick made one more attempt. On April 9 the chairman of the committee of London merchants trading to America moved for leave to bring in a bill repealing the duty on tea. The ministry blocked the motion by a technicality: it was the rule of the House of Commons that any proposal previously rejected could not be brought up again in the same session and on March 5 the Commons had already voted down a comparable motion by Pownall. Lord Clare now moved the order of the day, a Parliamentary tactic to close debate. The ministry won the ensuing vote, 85 to 52.[26] The bill repealing all except the tea duties passed the House of Lords on April 11 and received the royal assent the next day. The merchants and agents achieved the substance of their goal; they failed to win the principle.

If the colonial agents were aware of political realities they should have realized the futility of further agitation against the symbol of Parliamentary authority to tax the colonies. Apparently most agents recognized the situation, but in June, Franklin wrote to Pennsylvania that although Parliament had adjourned without repealing the duty on tea "it is generally given out & understood that it will be done next Winter." According to the agent's sources, or so he informed his colonial correspondents, the ministers had overruled Lord North and now favored repealing even the last tax. There was nothing to support Franklin's contention. Yet the Pennsylvania agent urged the Americans to continue exerting economic pressure.[27] Franklin's suggestion was pointless, for the

26. Jackson to Jonathan Trumbull, Feb. ?, 1770, Trumbull Papers, Connecticut Archives, Vol. III, Pt. i, Doc. 10; [Debrett,] *The History, debates, and proceedings of both houses of Parliament*, V, 305–306; Cobbett (ed.), *Parliamentary History*, XVI, 928–929; Thomas Pownall to Samuel Cooper, April 11, 1770, Griffin (ed.), *Junius Discovered*, p. 263; Garth to the South Carolina committee of correspondence, April 11, 1770, "Correspondence of Charles Garth," XXXI (1930), 254.

27. Franklin to Galloway, June 11, 1770, Van Doren (ed.), *Franklin's Autobiographical Writings*, p. 193; Gage to Barrington (private), July 6, 1770, Clarence E. Carter (ed.), *Correspondence of General Thomas Gage* (2 vols., New Haven, 1931–1933), II, 546.

nonimportation agreement had collapsed. In May, 1770 the Philadelphia merchants met to consider the situation, and after "much
altercation" they resolved to order duty-free goods from England.
This compromise was meaningless. Even the Boston merchants
receded from the nonimportation agreement. The evidence available
in England indicated that the Virginians "did not keep one article
of" the boycott arrangement even before the partial repeal of the
duties. Now in 1770 the exports of prohibited articles to the Old
Dominion were "never more considerable." There were no complaints that the Virginia boycott had "in the least degree operated
to distress" the manufacturers in Britain. One American in London
confirmed the situation. British merchants were shipping "very considerable quantities of goods" to Virginia and Massachusetts, the
two colonies which led in the movement against the Townshend
duties. According to one colonist in the metropolis, the nonimportation agreement was considered a "mere bagatelle." Even
if the American demand for English goods had slackened, British
trade had not suffered because of the increased demand from
Europe.[28] It is difficult to escape the conclusion that neither the
economic sanctions nor the political arguments of the American
Whigs had been effective, but rather the lobbying of the agents
and merchants and the realization by the administration that it
could retain the symbol of imperial authority and concede an
insignificant sum from the revenue derived from the Townshend
duties.

Many colonial legislatures continued to instruct their agents to
secure repeal of the Parliamentary program of 1767, which still
remained on the statute books: the duty on tea, the legislation
authorizing enforcement of the Trade Acts, and the statute creating
an American Board of Customs.[29] Although Garth, Franklin,

28. Moses Franks to Edmund Burke, June 21, 1770, Burke Correspondence,
Wentworth-Woodhouse Muniments, Sheffield City Library, Sheffield, England;
Samuel Adams to Stephen Sayre, Nov. 16, 1770, Henry A. Cushing (ed.), *Writings
of Samuel Adams* (4 vols., New York, 1904–1908), II, 58; Arthur Lee to Dr. Theo-
dorick Bland, Aug. 21, 1770, Charles Campbell (ed.), *The Bland Papers: Being a
Selection from the Manuscripts of Colonel Theodorick Bland, Jr.* (2 vols., Petersburg, Va.,
1840–1843), I, 28–29; and Joseph Reed to Charles Petit, May 7, 1770, Reed,
Life of Esther Reed, p. 149.

29. See, for example, Henry R. McIlwaine and John P. Kennedy (eds.),

"A ground for reconciliation," 1768–1773

Charles, Montague, and William Samuel Johnson appear to have been alarmed over the attempt in 1768 by the British government to rationalize the vice-admiralty courts in America,[30] the agents and merchants seemingly did not make any particular effort to mitigate the enforcement procedures of the Acts of Trade.

To a great extent, the enforcement statutes were inoperative simply because British officials found it almost impossible to execute them in America. Naval officers in the colonies complained of the difficulties they encountered in seizing smuggled goods. Nor could customs officials in performing their duty find protection in the civil courts of the provinces. Captain George Talbot of H.M.S. *Lively* complained that when an action was laid against him or his officers, justice in the common-law courts of the provinces was out of the question. No one would post bail for them, no lawyer would dare defend them. Although Parliament in 1767 had authorized the superior courts in the colonies to issue writs of assistance, it was clear by 1773 that customs officials in most cases could not obtain them. The chief justices of many colonies simply refused to issue the unpopular general warrants[31] considered unconstitutional by many Americans and Britons. The imperial legislature had also sanctioned an American Board of Customs, but so great was the reaction in Boston against the Customs Commissioners that troops were necessary to protect them. When the two regiments were withdrawn from the city in 1770 following the Boston "Massacre," the

Journals of the House of Burgesses of Virginia (13 vols., Richmond, 1905–1913), 1770–1772, pp. 101–102; votes of the Pennsylvania assembly, Hazard *et al.* (eds.), *Pennsylvania Archives*, 8th Ser., VIII, 6658–6659; and Galloway to Benjamin Franklin, April 5, 1771, Franklin Papers, Library of Congress, Ser. ii, Vol. I, 75. With respect to the protests of the Virginia House of Burgesses, Governor Botetourt charged that they were inspired by the "Patriots of England: The Merchants and Factors resident here having been pressed by Letters from Home to promote Distress to their Mother Country by all possible means." Botetourt to Hillsborough, June 30, 1770, C.O. 5/1372:114.

30. Garth to the South Carolina committee of correspondence, Feb. 29, 1768, "Correspondence of Charles Garth," XXX (1929), 215–216.

31. John Robinson (Secretary to the Treasury) to John Pownall (Undersecretary of State for the American Department) with enclosures from the Admiralty Board, Oct. 26, 1772, Aug. 25, 1773, Joseph Redington and Richard A. Roberts (eds.), *Calendar of Home Office Papers of the reign of George III, 1760–1775* (4 vols., London, 1878–1899), III, 565, IV, 79.

customs officials were rendered impotent. Perhaps the most sensational incident to reveal the futility of enforcing Parliamentary statutes on trade was the burning of the customs ship *Gaspee* by Rhode Islanders in 1772. When the Crown Law Officers, Attorney General Edward Thurlow and Solicitor General Alexander Wedderburn, condemned the destruction of the public ship as an act of treason, Parliament resolved to extend to the colonies an old treason statute of the reign of Henry VIII, and the Privy Council appointed a commission of provincial jurists to investigate.[32] Although it may have been common knowledge in Rhode Island who was responsible for burning the *Gaspee* and scores witnessed the deed, no one would give evidence. The royal government did not prosecute, even under the Tudor statute for treason, since it could not follow normal, accepted due process of law. It did not resort to arbitrary methods to impose its authority. While the *Gaspee* incident illustrated the almost too legalistic, scrupulous mentality of the British ministers, it also demonstrated the futility of attempting to enforce in the colonies the Acts of Trade and Navigation passed by the British Parliament. By 1773 the Townshend program was a dead letter.

IV

The early years of the 1770's also witnessed a more satisfactory resolution of two related controversies which for some time had exacerbated imperial relations: the requirements imposed on the colonial assemblies by Parliament in the Currency and Mutiny Acts of 1764–1765. Both the colonial agents and the British merchants played a significant role in accommodating both sides on these issues.

By the terms of the Mutiny Act of 1765 the British Parliament had required the colonial assemblies by specified procedures to provide certain services in billeting and provisioning troops stationed in, or passing through, a colony. The competing claims of the

32. See the minute of Cabinet, July 30, 1772, S.P. 37/9:235 (also in Dartmouth Papers, William Salt Library, Stafford, England, II, 372); report of the Law Officers, Aug. 10, 1772, Dartmouth Papers, II, 379; and Privy Council minute, Aug. 20, 1772, *ibid.*, II, 386. See also Redington and Roberts (eds.), *Calendar of Home Office Papers of the reign of George III*, Vol. III, 531; and James Munroe (ed.), *Acts of the Privy Council, Colonial Series* (6 vols., Edinburgh, 1908–1912), V, 356–357.

provincial assemblies and the imperial legislature had clashed particularly on the billeting provisions of the Mutiny Act. In the original statute the ministry had attempted to house troops in private homes if necessary, but at that time the agents and British merchants had joined forces with many members of Parliament to have the obnoxious clause deleted, since it was repugnant to what many considered the rights of Englishmen as set forth in the Petition of Right of 1628. But the assemblies of many colonies—notably, New York, Massachusetts, Georgia, and South Carolina—had been dissatisfied even with the statute as passed and through their agents sought to have it modified. The South Carolina committee of correspondence informed its agent that the billeting clause was "highly prejudicial to the rights and Liberties of His Majesty's American Subjects." Both sides evidently agreed on liberty for the subject, but not on its definition. Charles Garth could offer his constituents little hope. From the sentiment expressed in Parliament it was clear to the agent that "Billeting Soldiers in the Colonies by Act of Parliament would never be receded from." Indeed, some had declared that "if the Parliament had no Right to lay Taxes, they had no Right to billet Soldiers, nor to restrain the Freedom of Commerce, nor to pass any law to bind the Colonies. . . ."[33]

Thus the Mutiny Act must be defended as part of the general legislative authority of the imperial legislature. To enforce its jurisdiction Parliament in 1767 had passed a specific law restraining the New York assembly as of October 1, 1767, from passing any bills until the provincial legislature had complied with the Mutiny Act. But by 1768 the ministers were willing to grant the New Yorkers some concessions. Although a subsequent New York law did not exactly follow the procedures specified by Parliament, Hillsborough's Board of Trade and the Crown Law Officers thought it sufficiently satisfied Parliament's intention to obtain money from the provincial legislature to provision the troops in the colony. Accepting this decision, the Privy Council did not enforce the provisions of the Restraining Act against New York.[34]

33. South Carolina committee of correspondence to Garth, April 15, 1768, Garth to the South Carolina committee of correspondence, Nov. 10, 1768, "Correspondence of Charles Garth," XXX (1929), 180, 231.

34. Munroe (ed.), *Acts of the Privy Council, Colonial Series,* V, 137–139.

Agents and Merchants

A practical issue in Boston involving the Mutiny Act gave the colonial agents in Parliament an opportunity to modify the Parliamentary statute and allow the provincial legislatures to escape its more onerous provisions. In 1768 the royal government sent troops into Boston to protect the American Customs Commissioners then attempting to enforce the Trade and Revenue Acts. The garrison itself soon became the center of dispute until removed in March, 1770, following the Boston "Massacre." In the interval the Earl of Hillsborough, wishing to restore royal authority in the Bay Colony, but by employing the troops in a legal manner, proposed that Parliament amend the Mutiny Act. The Secretary of State suggested that if public houses in Boston were insufficient to accommodate the troops, they be housed in private homes unless the colony erected barracks or hired adequate quarters. If provincial commissioners appointed by the governor refused to billet the soldiers, they should be liable to penalties. The Secretary of State further suggested a formula by which the colonies could escape the Parliamentary act and exercise local control. The British Mutiny statute would be in force only in such provinces as did not pass their own laws for billeting the soldiers—laws approved by the King in Council.[35] The cabinet did not accept Hillsborough's proposal, however, and instead directed the Secretary at War, Lord Barrington, to bring in a bill patterned after the last Parliamentary statute passed in 1767. Barrington, perhaps with the support of Hillsborough, then attempted to alter the Mutiny bill and force the colonial assemblies to support the garrisons.

Since the Mutiny law was scheduled for re-enactment by Parliament, the colonial agents had an opportunity again to protect the essential liberties of their constituents. They proposed to prevent if possible the insertion of any clause which might be "disagreeable" to the colonists. Alarmed that the government intended to quarter troops in private houses, the agents "thought themselves bound in duty to prevent so detestable a design from taking effect." Garth gave his colleagues notice on March 13, 1769, when Barrington brought into the House of Commons the bill for continuing the current Mutiny Act. Although none of the agents had received

35. "Measures Proposed by Lord Hillsborough to the Cabinet," Fortescue (ed.), *Correspondence of George III*, II, 84.

instructions from their constituents, they agreed that since it was impossible to delete the billeting clause from the bill, it would be best to follow Garth's lead on the matter and to secure, if possible, an amendment favorable to the Americans.[36] The protagonists in the House of Commons the next day were the Secretary at War and the agent for South Carolina. Convinced that the conduct of the magistrates and council in Massachusetts had demonstrated that the provinces might evade the Mutiny Act, Barrington proposed an amendment stipulating that if the civil authorities in any colony did not comply with the provisions of the Parliamentary statute by providing barracks, the troops could be quartered in private homes. Actually the Secretary at War had no desire to see the troops in private domiciles and offered this drastic amendment only to force the colonists themselves to house the troops. He would demonstrate to the Americans that there were "worse inconveniences" than hiring "empty houses and furnishing Bedding & ca." Fortunately for the colonists, the administration spokesman in the House of Commons, Lord North, did not support the Secretary at War. And when Charles Garth offered a counteramendment he had previously concerted with the other agents, the ministry accepted the agent's clause—the billeting provisions of the Mutiny Act would not apply to any colony which passed laws to provide for the troops—but with an amendment. These laws must have the approval of the Privy Council. Garth felt compelled to accept the ministerial amendment rather than lose his clause altogether.[37]

36. DeBerdt to Thomas Cushing, Feb. 18, March 10, 1769, Mathews (ed.), "Letters of Dennys DeBerdt," pp. 362, 366; William Samuel Johnson to William Pitkin, March 23, 1769, "The Trumbull Papers," 5th Ser., IX, 326; and Garth to the South Carolina committee of correspondence, March 17, 1769, "Correspondence of Charles Garth," XXXI (1930), 35–36.

37. Barrington to Bernard, March 21, 1769, Edward Channing and Archibald Cary Cooledge (eds.), *The Barrington-Bernard Correspondence and Illustrative Matter 1760–1770* ... (Cambridge, Mass., 1912), pp. 185–186; Garth to the South Carolina committee of correspondence, March 17, 1769, "Correspondence of Charles Garth," XXXI (1930), 55–57; Franklin to Galloway, March 21, 1769, Van Doren (ed.), *Franklin's Autobiographical Writings*, p. 189; Franklin to Noble Wymberly Jones, April 3, 1769, Candler (ed.), *Colonial Records of the State of Georgia*, XV, 28; William Bolland to Samuel Danford, March 18, 23, 1769, "The Bowdoin and Temple Papers," Massachusetts Historical Society *Collections* (Boston, 1897), 6th Ser., IX, 131, 134; DeBerdt to Thomas Cushing, March 10, July 20, 1769,

Ironically the billeting clause now conformed to the proposal made by Hillsborough to the King the month before. This provision of the Mutiny Act remained in force until the crisis in Massachusetts in 1774 brought on the need for another alteration in the legislation governing the military forces in America.

The latitude given the colonial governments in the Mutiny Act of 1769 did not entirely resolve the problem of billeting the soldiers. The assemblies of several colonies, particularly New York, South Carolina, and New Jersey, used financial grants for the royal troops as a lever to extract concessions from the imperial government to allow them to issue paper currency as legal tender—a practice prohibited by Parliamentary statute.[38]

V

Parliamentary restrictions on colonial issues of paper bills of credit had long been a sore point. By the Currency Act of 1764 the provincial assemblies could not make them legal tender. They had to vote sufficient taxes to retire them after a fixed period for circulation. To ensure compliance with these conditions by the colonial legislatures, the governors were under instructions not to sign any bill emitting paper currency which did not contain a clause suspending its operation until approved by the Privy Council. The situation became critical by 1768–1769, when the colonies, having retired the bills issued to finance the conflict with the French, now needed a medium of circulation. In London the colonial agents who had concerted a plan with the merchants to introduce remedial legislation in Parliament realized that the support of the ministry

Mathews (ed.), "Letters of Dennys DeBerdt," pp. 366, 376; William Samuel Johnson to William Pitkin, March 23, 1769, "The Trumbull Papers," 5th Ser., IX, 326–327; Thomas Pownall to Samuel Cooper, March 22, 1769, Griffin (ed.), *Junius Discovered*, p. 219; and Arthur Lee to Thomas Ludwell Lee, March 23, 1769, Arthur Lee Papers, Harvard College Library, Cambridge, Mass.

38. See Gage to Barrington (private), July 22, 1769; Gage to Hillsborough, Oct. 7, 1769, Carter (ed.), *Correspondence of General Thomas Gage*, II, 518, I, 239; Lt. Gov. Cadwallader Colden to Hillsborough, Dec. 16, 1769; Gov. Henry Moore to Hillsborough, Oct. 4, 1769, O'Callaghan and Fernow (eds.), *Documents Relative to the Colonial History of the State of New York*, VIII, 194, 189; and Governor William Franklin to Hillsborough, Feb. 12, Sept. 29, 1770, Ricord and Nelson (eds.), *Archives of the State of New Jersey*, 1st Ser., X, 151–152, 200–201.

would be necessary to put through any bill. The agents also felt that they "dare not stir" in the matter without support of the merchants, who were themselves optimistic since the Earl of Hillsborough, now Secretary of State, had previously listened to them on other matters. The tactic adopted by the lobbyists was to propose repeal of the Currency Act of 1764 as a favor to the British merchants, asked by them, and not by the agents as "a favour to America."[39]

The difficulty stemmed from the fact that Hillsborough, whatever his personal reaction to paper money, was primarily concerned with maintaining the authority of the imperial government: the Parliamentary restriction against legal tender and the superintending authority of the Privy Council over colonial legislation. In reacting to the various proposals submitted by the colonial assemblies through their agents and governors, he made this evident. Pennsylvania for one wanted outright repeal of the Currency Act of 1764,[40] while the Virginia House of Burgesses presented a plan comparable to that employed by Maryland to issue money at 5 per cent interest to be invested in some public fund in England.[41] In the plan proposed by the North Carolina House of Representatives there was

39. Garth to the South Carolina committee of correspondence, Jan. 27, 1768, "Correspondence of Charles Garth," XXX (1929), 183; Franklin to Galloway, Feb. 17, 1768, Smyth (ed.), *Writings of Franklin*, V, 97–99.

40. Franklin to the Pennsylvania committee of correspondence, April 16, 1768, Smyth (ed.), *Writings of Franklin*, V, 120; Georgia committee of correspondence to Franklin, May 19, 1768, Lila M. Hawes (ed.), "Letters to the Georgia Colonial Agent, July 1762, to January, 1771," *Georgia Historical Quarterly*, XXXVI (1952), 275–276; William Franklin to Hillsborough, Aug. 24, 1768, Ricord and Nelson (eds.), *Archives of the State of New Jersey*, 1st Ser., X, 49–50; William Franklin to Benjamin Franklin, May 10, 1768, Franklin Papers, American Philosophical Society Library, II, 126; petition of the North Carolina legislature to the King, Saunders (ed.), *Colonial Records of North Carolina*, VII, 681; Governor William Tryon to Shelburne, March 5, 1768, *ibid.*, VII, 693; Great Britain, Board of Trade, *Journals of the Lords Commissioners of Trade and Plantations* (14 vols., London, 1920–1938), 1768–1775, p. 29; and Governor Henry Moore to Shelburne, Jan. 3, 1768, O'Callaghan and Fernow (eds.), *Documents Relative to the Colonial History of the State of New York*, VII, 1.

41. Board of Trade, *Journals*, 1768–1775, pp. 29, 30, 31–32; petition of the burgesses, C.O. 5/1372:16; the proposal for paper money, C.O. 5/1372:20–22; Board of Trade report, June 10, 1768, in C.O. 5/1372:35 and C.O. 5/1368:356–359.

no clause suspending operation of the paper money until approved by the Privy Council.[42] The most bitter and protracted dispute, however, came in the years 1768–1770 on almost identical proposals by New York and New Jersey to issue paper money which would not be legal tender in all cases but accepted only at the provincial loan office issuing the paper and the colonial treasury in lieu of taxes. This plan, drafted in England and sent to New York by Robert Charles, would satisfy the British merchants since the money would not be legal tender in the payment of transatlantic debts. But would it satisfy the requirements of the Currency Act of 1764 and subsequent royal instructions to the governors?

These were the central issues when the Privy Council in November, 1769 took under consideration a proposed New York statute to issue £120,000 in paper bills. The Privy Council referred the matter to the Board of Trade, and in turn the board called for the opinion of the Crown Law Officers on two questions. Was the paper money proposed under the New York law legal tender within the meaning of the Currency Act of 1764? Could the King, consistent with the provisions of the Parliamentary statute, authorize the governor of the colony to assent to the provincial bill? The report of Attorney General William DeGrey and Solicitor General John Dunning was inconclusive. The notes of credit to be issued by the New York bill were *not* legal tender within the "true meaning and intention" of the Currency Act of 1764, for as the Law Officers interpreted the preamble of that act, Parliament intended prohibiting the practice of making bills legal tender in the discharge of *private* contracts. The New York law now under consideration made the bills legal tender *only* at the public loan office and the treasury of the colony. Consequently, if the paper money should depreciate, the loss would then fall only on the province. If this reading was correct, DeGrey and Dunning continued, then the King could assent to the New York law; but if the prohibition against legal tender came within the general meaning of the words "Due and

42. Hillsborough to Tryon, April 16, 1768, Saunders (ed.), *Colonial Records of North Carolina*, VII, 709; Hillsborough to Tryon, March 1, June 7, July 15, 1769; McCulloch to the North Carolina committee of correspondence, July 14, 1769; and McCulloch to John Harvey, July 24, 1769, Jan. 26, 1770, *ibid.*, VII, 17–18, 51, 62, 59, 55–56, 172.

Demands whatsoever," contained in the Currency Act of 1764, the monarch could not assent to the provincial law without violating an act of Parliament. In accepting this inconclusive opinion the Commissioners of Trade refused to go beyond the observations on the general question of paper money as legal tender made by the Board of Trade six years before.[43] While the imperial government was acting on the question the New York assembly passed another law embodying the same provisions for paper money and threatened that there would be no money issued to billet royal troops in the province if the governor did not sign the act. This threat had no effect. Inasmuch as this new bill did not differ from the earlier one and did not contain a suspending clause as required by the royal instructions to the governor, the Commissioners of Trade recommended that the Privy Council disallow it.[44]

Direct action in Parliament by the New York agent resolved the impasse and paved the way for a later general solution of the paper money question. On April 24, 1770, Robert Charles petitioned the House of Commons to allow the New York legislature to emit £120,000 in paper bills of credit to be legal tender only at the colonial loan office and treasury. That same day the House appointed Jeremiah Dyson, a Commissioner of Trade, and Richard Jackson (soon to be solicitor of the Board of Trade) to bring in a bill pursuant to the petition of the agent. The bill passed the House of Commons on May 7 and received the royal assent twelve days later.[45] The New

43. Colden to Hillsborough, Oct. 4, 1769; Hillsborough to Colden, Nov. 4, Dec. 9, 1769, O'Callaghan and Fernow (eds.), *Documents Relative to the Colonial History of the State of New York*, VIII, 189, 190, 193; John Pownall to the Solicitor General, Nov. 17, 1769, C.O. 5/1130:455–456; order in council, Nov. 10, 1769, C.O. 5/1074:321–323; report of the Law Officers, Dec. 4, 1769, C.O. 5/1074:371–376; report of the Board of Trade, Dec. 20, 1769, C.O. 5/1131:34–38; and Board of Trade, *Journals*, 1768–1775, p. 116.

44. Colden to Hillsborough, Dec. 16, 1769, Jan. 6, 1770; Colden to the Board of Trade, Jan. 6, 1770; Colden to Hillsborough, Feb. 21, 1770, O'Callaghan and Fernow (eds.), *Documents Relative to the Colonial History of the State of New York*, VIII, 194, 198, 199, 206; Board of Trade report, Feb. 8, 1770, C.O. 5/1131:42–45; order in council, Feb. 9, 1770, "The Letters and Papers of Cadwallader Colden," New York Historical Society *Collections* (11 vols., New York, 1877–1878, 1918–1924, 1935, 1937), LVI (1923), 166.

45. *Commons Journal*, XXXII, 899, 916. The Act is 10 Geo. III, c. 35. Charles did not live to see the final passage of his measure, for he died on May 14. Franklin,

Agents and Merchants

Yorkers had obtained paper money by appealing to the authority of Parliament and giving up a principle: the authority of the colonial assembly vis à vis the British Parliament. But they had bartered the point in exchange for money for the British troops under the terms of the English Mutiny statutes.[46]

The permission granted New York to issue paper money opened the way for the agents to lobby for a bill granting similar permission to the other provinces. With this in mind Charles Garth in 1770

who had unsuccessfully attempted to secure permission for his New Jersey constituents to pass similar acts, claimed that Charles was distraught because of the amendments to the bill and feared that it would not be approved. He was "so bewilder'd and distress'd with the Affair, that he finally put an End to his Perplexities—by a Razor!" Franklin to Galloway, June 11, 1770, Van Doren (ed.), *Franklin's Autobiographical Writings*, p. 194. Franklin's story seems doubtful. There is no other evidence that Charles committed suicide. His death on May 14 was noted without comment in the *Gentlemen's Magazine*, XL (1770), 239. Why should Charles have committed suicide for fear the bill would not be approved 'when it had passed the House of Commons—the decisive chamber—the week before?

46. The extremists in the colony appreciated the situation. The patriot press condemned the assembly when it voted to supply provisions for the troops in return for the governor's assent to a paper money bill. A "Son of Liberty" accused the assemblymen of betraying the inhabitants and abandoning the liberty of the people. In turn, the "representatives of the people" unanimously condemned his broadside as a "false, seditious and infamous Libel." C.O. 5/1219:48, "Journal of the Votes and Proceedings of the General Assembly of the Colony of New-York," November 21, 1769–January 27, 1770. See also Leonard W. Levy, "Did the Zenger Case Really Matter? Freedom of the Press in Colonial New York," *William and Mary Quarterly* 3rd Ser., XVII (1960), 44–45. By acting with the *permission* of Parliament to pass bills emitting paper money the New York assembly tacitly recognized the authority of the British legislature. Governor Thomas Hutchinson, then engaged in a bitter struggle with the General Court of Massachusetts, appreciated the point. Reflecting the loyalist position, he wrote privately to Hillsborough: "Every Act of Parliament carried into Execution in the Colonies tends to strengthen Government there. A firm persuasion that Parliament is determined at all events to maintain its supreme authority is all we want." The Act of 1770 permitting the New York legislature to issue paper money "was extremely well adapted to maint[ain]ing the authority of Parliament. . . ." The speaker of the New York assembly himself later observed to the new agent for the colony, Edmund Burke, that a subsequent New York act "was Neither Contrary to the Spirit nor Letter of the Act of Parliament Restraining the Issuing of paper curr[enc]y." Hutchinson to Hillsborough (private), Jan. 22, 1771, C.O. 5/246: 5–6; John Cruger to Edmund Burke, April 6, 1773, Wentworth-Woodhouse Muniments, Burke Correspondence, BK264.

prepared a clause for a general dispensation for the other colonies to be passed as an amendment to the Currency Act of 1764. The ministry would not allow it at this time, however, speciously claiming that there was nothing before the House of Commons to indicate that the other American provinces desired permission to issue paper money. This was mere sophistry, for many provinces had petitioned the King. The point was that they would have to come to Parliament with requests to emit currency and thus explicitly recognize its authority.

Possibly the ministers did have one valid argument in rejecting the proposal of the South Carolina agent in 1770. They would need time to learn the effects of the paper money experiment in New York before extending a general dispensation to the other provinces. Garth now suggested to his constituents that if the other colonies were to apply by their agents, the ministers might listen at some future date. A general resolution of the paper money issue came in the spring of 1773, when Garth informed the South Carolina committee of correspondence that the new Secretary of State for the American Department, the Earl of Dartmouth, was considering a "Relaxation" of the Currency Act of 1764. While the administration would not press for a repeal of the law as the provincial agents desired, it would allow the assemblies to adopt the system used by New York and issue certificates, notes, or bills, backed by taxes, to be legal tender at the public treasury in discharge of any taxes or debts due the colony.[47]

By the Act of 1764 Parliament had intended to prevent paper money being made legal tender for private debts. Since the colonies were perpetually short of specie, some other medium of circulation was necessary for a viable economy. But the legality of paper notes payable at the colonial treasuries was questionable under a strict interpretation of the Parliamentary statute which prohibited all bills of credit or notes "whatsoever" being legal tender.[48] To remove any doubt the Board of Trade, acting through one of its Commissioners and its solicitor, Bamber Gascoyne and Richard

47. Garth to the South Carolina committee of correspondence, May 14, 1770, "Correspondence of Charles Garth," XXXI (1930), 285-286; Garth to the South Carolina committee of correspondence, April 3, 1773, Charles Garth–South Carolina committee of correspondence Letter Book, South Carolina Archives, Columbia, f. 150.
48. "Paper Money in the Colonies," Dartmouth Papers, II, 775.

Jackson, in the spring of 1773 put through a bill.[49] The Act of 13 Geo. III, c. 57 amending the previous Currency statute allowed the colonial assemblies to issue notes deemed legal tender at the colonial treasuries for duties and taxes. Since this paper could be redeemed at the provincial treasuries it would circulate at face value as a *bona fide* medium of exchange.

After nine years the colonial agents with the support of the British merchants had secured a paper currency for the colonies. But in the process the Americans had explicitly acknowledged the authority of Parliament. In this sense the adjustment had followed the other accommodations in colonial policy won by the agents and merchants since 1768: modification of the territorial jurisdiction of the vice-admiralty courts, amendment of the Mutiny Act, and repeal of all but one of the Townshend duties. The tax on tea remained: a symbol of the power of Parliament to tax the Americans. Still the tax was merely symbolic. And the vice-admiralty courts could not enforce the laws of trade and navigation enacted by Parliament. It is difficult to find another practical goal the agents could have won for their constituents.

Ironically, in the few short years before the final crisis leading to the American Revolution, tension between the colonies and the mother country seemed to have subsided. True, the destruction of the *Gaspee* marred the apparent successful reconciliation, but the Mutiny Act passed in 1771 and 1772 without incident. The times seemed indeed uneventful. North told the House of Commons: "the American disputes are settled. . . ."[50] The calm was more apparent than real, however. This was merely the lull before the crisis of 1774–1775—a crisis when the Empire would need the full potential of the colonial spokesmen in London. But at this crucial point the effectiveness of the agents was to be seriously impaired and their position in British government circles jeopardized by political

49. Board of Trade, *Journals*, 1768–1775, p. 353; *Commons Journal*, XXXIV, 288, 302; and Charles Garth to the South Carolina committee of correspondence, May 4, 1773, Charles Garth–South Carolina committee of correspondence Letter Book, f. 157.

50. As reported in Garth to the South Carolina committee of correspondence, March 27, 1771, April 4, 1772, "Correspondence of Charles Garth," XXXIII (1932), 129, 235; Cobbett (ed.), *Parliamentary History*, XVII, 165.

animosities in the colonies. These in turn were linked with the developing revolutionary challenge to imperial authority. With the approach of the final crisis many colonies were to find themselves with no agent, or with representatives identified with the revolutionary movement.

CHAPTER VI

Franklin and the Crisis in the Agencies

IN the few years immediately preceding the outbreak of the American Revolution the ability of the concert of colonial agents to influence British policy sharply declined as a result of losses in key personnel and the close identification of some provincial representatives with the Revolutionary movement. Richard Jackson had become solicitor to the Board of Trade, while palsy incapacitated another important agent and liaison with the merchants of the imperial metropolis, Barlow Trecothick. Dennys DeBerdt and Robert Charles died in 1770. When the temporary agents William Samuel Johnson[1] and Henry Marchant[2] returned to their native colonies, the general courts of Connecticut and Rhode Island failed to appoint replacements. Factions within the governments of the Delaware counties and Maryland had never been able to agree on agents after the Stamp Act crisis. The inability of three parties within the House of Burgesses, each supporting a separate candidate— Arthur Lee, Edward Montague, and Thomas Adams, a Virginia

1. Johnson left England after completion of the Mohegan land affair. On him, see George C. Groce, *William Samuel Johnson* (New York, 1937).

2. Henry Marchant, the Attorney General of Rhode Island, resided in Great Britain for only a short time. See his "Journal of Voyage from Newport in the Colony of Rhode Island to London, Travels thro' many parts of England & Scotland began July 8th 1771 . . .," microfilm copy, Rhode Island Historical Society, Providence.

142

merchant living in London—to agree meant that Virginia also did without an agent after 1770.[3] The provincial governments did not fill all these vacancies with new men, while the total number of agents further declined as Franklin assumed the post for four colonies, Pennsylvania, Georgia, New Jersey, and Massachusetts. The prominence of Franklin in the agencies was highly significant.

Well before the outbreak of the Revolution, Franklin in the minds of the British administrators became identified with a revolutionary junta in Massachusetts Bay. By insisting that the lower house of the legislature had the unilateral power to appoint and instruct the representative for the colony in England, this faction jeopardized the legal standing and the effectiveness of the agent in London. Moreover, the struggle over the appointment of agents in Boston specifically linked the agency with the Revolutionary movement, since Franklin joined the patriots in an unsavory attack on the royal governor in Massachusetts and in propounding a revolutionary theory of the imperial constitution—a doctrine strongly implying the independence of the colonies and freedom from Parliamentary control. Since Franklin was agent for four colonies at the time, the entire institution came into question.

The method of appointing regular agents to represent the provinces had caused difficulty throughout the eighteenth century, but in the pre-Revolutionary decade it received special urgency due to the heightening of imperial tensions and the particular need for an agent to speak for the colonies in London. Various British administrations had recognized the pre-eminence of the representative lower house of the legislatures in appointing agents, but they had insisted that if he was to act authoritatively, an agent must represent the colony in its full, legal, or corporate sense. An agent invested by the authority of all branches of the provincial government greatly facilitated the functioning of the Empire. In the few,

3. For the patronage dispute on the Virginia agency, see Arthur Lee to Richard Henry Lee, Aug. 17, 1772, Arthur Lee Papers, American Philosophical Society Library, Philadelphia; Richard Bland to Thomas Adams, Aug. 1, 1771, "Virginia in 1771," *Virginia Magazine of History and Biography*, VI (1898–1899), 133–134; Richard Adams to Thomas Adams, March 24, 1772, "Letters of Richard Adams to Thomas Adams," *ibid.*, XXII (1914), 389–390; and Arthur Lee to [Richard Henry Lee], Feb. 14, 1773, Arthur Lee Papers, Harvard College Library, Cambridge, Mass.

critical years before the Revolution, the British ministry, in re-affirming a century-old principle, also stressed that the agent should not represent one faction, interest, or governmental body. Recognizing the special, representative quality of the lower chambers in the assemblies, the Board of Trade as early as 1761 emphasized that while all three branches of government must join in any appointment, the governor and council should play only a negative role and merely exercise a veto on the choice of the popularly elected house. The positive power of naming the agent belonged to the people's representatives. But the imperial government strongly objected to any implication that an agent named by an assembly should have a role roughly analogous to the minister of an independent nation or foreign power at an alien court.[4] In the disputes on appointing agents the lower houses sometimes used such terminology with its implication of independence.

In many colonies, such as Massachusetts, North Carolina, New York, New Jersey, and Maryland, the various branches of government waged a hot political struggle over the agency, but nowhere did the contest assume such proportions or significance as in the Bay Colony, where Governor Francis Bernard and his successor challenged the attempt of the House of Representatives unilaterally to control the agent. In taking his case to the imperial government in 1767 Bernard charged that the assembly was seeking to undermine the balance of governmental authority. There could be no more certain test of the intention of the faction in the lower house under Samuel Adams and James Otis to acquire for the assembly "the Chief management" of the government. Moreover, the representatives, by designating their appointee as agent for the assembly *"at the Court of Great Britain"* had introduced "a kind of Revolution" in the government of the Bay Colony.[5] To deny this pretentious claim and restore a balance the public offices in London could

4. See the Commissioners of Trade to Governor Arthur Dobbs, April 4, 1761, Feb. 17, 1762, William L. Saunders (ed.), *Colonial Records of North Carolina* (10 vols., Raleigh, 1888–1890), VI, 539, 702; and Great Britain, Board of Trade, *Journals of the Lords Commissioners of Trade and Plantations* (14 vols., London, 1920–1938), 1759–1763, p. 249. See also above, pp. 11–12, 16.

5. Bernard to Shelburne, March 28, but with postscript of April 13, 1767, C.O. 5/892:494–501 (abstract in C.O. 5/766:34–39).

reject the appointment of a "partial" agent simply by refusing to recognize any person as the representative of the colony unless named by all branches of the provincial government.[6]

Indeed, the problem was not new and in 1768 the administration sought to regularize the procedure for recognizing agents. Several years before, the Board of Trade had specified in the case of New Jersey and North Carolina agents that while all three branches must join in any appointment, the governor must restrict his role merely to approving or rejecting any candidate named by the assembly. When the agency dispute in Massachusetts was referred to the Board of Trade after the Stamp Act crisis the commissioners now reaffirmed this principle. The lower houses of the colonial legislatures could not unilaterally appoint the agent; nor would the British government receive in a public capacity any person so invested. As precedent the Board of Trade cited an opinion of 1709 respecting the Jamaica agency.[7] Hereafter the ministry seems to have made some effort to adopt a standard procedure for the agencies. The rule was clearly set down in a commonplace entry book of a secretary at the Plantation Office, under the entry, "Note relative to American agent":

It having been represented to His Majesty that the Admission in the several public offices of Persons to act as Agents for the several Colonies and Islands in America under appointments from the lower House of Assembly only, without the Concurrence of the other Branches of legislature, had been attended with great Prejudice & Inconvenience; It is His Majesty's pleasure that for the future, no Person shall be received in any of the said public offices in the character of Agent for any Colony or Island; but such only as shall have been regularly appointed for that purpose by an Act or concurrent Vote of the whole Legislature of such Colony or Island.[8]

6. Bernard to Shelburne, June 22, 1767, C.O. 5/892:537–540 (abstracts in C.O. 5/766:48–51 and Shelburne Papers, Clements Library, Ann Arbor, 51:587–590).

7. Shelburne to the Commissioners of Trade, Dec. 7, 1767, Shelburne Papers, 62:229–230; C.O. 5/893:41–42; Shelburne to Bernard, Sept. 17, 1767, Shelburne Papers, 54:37, 41; Commissioners of Trade to Hillsborough, Feb. 4, 1768, and Board of Trade report, Feb. 4, 1768, C.O. 5/757:17, 15–16. The reports of 1768 and 1709 are in C.O. 325/1:141–148. See also Hillsborough to Bernard, Feb. 16, 1768, C.O. 5/757:31–32.

8. Secretary's Commonplace book for 1761–1769, C.O. 5/216:67.

By adopting this procedure in 1768 the administration did not intend to control the appointments, impair the choice of agents, or curtail the rights of lower houses in the selection of an agent. An episode relating to the New Hampshire agency demonstrates this point. In November, 1768, the Secretary of State for the American Department notified Governor John Wentworth that inasmuch as the royal government desired that the affairs of the provinces should be dispatched with "every possible facility," the colonists should have as in the past an agent in London "to answer for the Colony on all Occasions in which Its Interest may be concerned. . . ." Consequently the chief executive was empowered to sign any "proper Law" for an agent providing he was appointed by concurrent act of the governor, council, and House of Representatives as was then the practice in the West Indian Islands, Virginia, South Carolina, and Georgia. In response to this suggestion from London the lower house then replied that the agent, Barlow Trecothick, had already been appointed according to the procedure specified by the Secretary of State. The London merchant was perfectly acceptable to them, and until he resigned there was no need further to pursue the matter. Since Trecothick had not entered his appointment at the Plantation Office as was usual, the Earl of Hillsborough had been "entirely Ignorant" of his nomination. While the form of Trecothick's commission did not correspond "exactly" with what the Secretary of State had recommended, the concurrence of three branches of government was "certainly sufficient authority" for Trecothick to act as agent in any business relating to the colony. Hillsborough promised that the imperial government would receive him accordingly.[9]

In the ensuing years difficulties stemmed not so much from the procedure of appointing and receiving agents as with two specific agents, Franklin and Edmund Burke, who opposed Hillsborough

9. Hillsborough to Wentworth, Nov. 15, 1768, C.O. 5/935:234–235; message of the assembly to Wentworth, April 28, 1769, C.O. 5/936:41; Wentworth to Hillsborough, May 1, 1769, C.O. 5/936:38–39; and Hillsborough to Wentworth, July 15, 1769, C.O. 5/936:57–58. Trecothick was received as agent. On July 20, 1769, the Treasury Board read his memorial requesting reimbursement to New Hampshire for wartime requisitions (T. 29/40:73). Two years later the House of Commons received his petition as agent for the province. Great Britain, Parliament, *Journals of the House of Commons* (London, 1547—), XXXIII, 333.

for personal and political motives. As a follower of the Marquis of Rockingham, Burke was opposed almost as a matter of course to practically every measure of the North administration. On learning of the death of Robert Charles, the New York assembly, perhaps under the impression that they were appointing a prominent London politician who shared their views,[10] named Burke to be agent of the colony "to the Court of Great Britain."[11] Misled by inaccurate newspaper reports of Burke's speeches in the House of Commons and their own preconceived ideas of what the Irish politician represented, the New Yorkers formed an "idea of Burke's sentiments and conduct that did not correspond perfectly with reality." They understood neither his aristocratic conservatism, his belief in the supremacy of Parliament, nor the fact that many of his speeches from·1766 to 1770 and after were based merely on factional opposition to whatever government happened to be in power.[12]

Burke's position as a partisan politician in opposition also largely influenced his attitude on the agency, particularly when John Pownall, Undersecretary of State for the American Department, in 1771 objected to the appointment by the lower house of the legislature only in violation of the principle reasserted three years before that all branches must concur in the agency. Again, the attitude of the administration was that while the representatives positively named the agents, the governor and council had the right to negate

10. James Delancey wrote the Marquis of Rockingham that he and his friends would derive "great Pleasure in having one of your Lordships Party for their Agent as I consider you as the only real Friends of the Colonies and know that while in Opposition You have always shewn yourselves our Friends and when in Administration rendered us real Service in the Repeal of the Stamp Act." Delancey to Rockingham [Dec. 1770–Jan. 1771?], Wentworth-Woodhouse Muniments, Sheffield City Library, Sheffield, England, R1–1343.

11. Ross J. S. Hoffman (ed.), *Edmund Burke, New York Agent, with his letters to the New York Assembly and intimate correspondence with Charles O'Hara 1761–1776* (Philadelphia, 1956), p. 99; Hugh Wallace to Sir William Johnson, Jan. 7, 1771, James Sullivan *et al.* (eds.), *The Papers of Sir William Johnson* (12 vols., Albany and New York, 1921–1957), VII, 1072–1073; entry for Feb. 9, 1771, William H. W. Sabine (ed.), *Historical Memoirs From 16 March to 9 July 1776 of William Smith . . .* (New York, 1956), p. 99.

12. Carl B. Cone, *Burke and the Nature of Politics. The Age of the American Revolution* (Lexington, Ky., 1957), pp. 58–59; Hoffman (ed.), *Edmund Burke, New York Agent*, p. 191.

their choice. Since the officer was agent for the colony and not for the elected house only, the consent of all elements was necessary to invest the agent with complete authority to represent the corporate body of the province. Contesting this view, Burke argued that the agent for the colony, no matter what his title, was *"in effect agent for the House of Representatives only"* and was appointed by the lower chamber to "take care of the interests of *the people*" of the province as distinct from its "executive government." The formula proposed by the Board of Trade for appointing agents Burke considered "destructive of one of the most necessary mediums of communication" between the colonies and the mother country, for the Americans should have some person to present their sentiments freely and directly to the administration and Parliament. The "intervention" of the royal governor in the nomination of such an officer would "totally frustrate" the purpose of an agent. How this deduction necessarily followed was not clear, but Burke's next maxim was even more tenuous. If the agent did not "depend totally on the Colony for his election" he would be useless to the Americans and "to all intents and purposes an officer of the Crown." The agency would be an "appointment of the Ministry. . . ." As a loyal member of an opposition faction in Parliament, Burke, of course, could not hold such a position. Consequently if the ministry insisted on the "new plan" for agents, as Burke erroneously termed it, he could not serve.[13]

Although the controversy between Burke and the Plantation Office dragged on for some time, the Whig politician did not have to resign or become a ministerial "tool," for the Board of Trade never insisted that the colony of New York follow the full procedure in naming the agents. Even so, Burke's fears were unjustified, for it is difficult to see how a royal governor with a mere negative vote over the nomination of the representatives could play a positive role in his selection. Whether Burke's conclusion was justified or not, Benjamin Franklin adopted the same attitude when the administration disputed his appointment as agent for

13. Burke to James Delancey, Dec. 4, 1771; Burke to the New York committee of correspondence, Dec. 4, 1771, Lucy S. Sutherland (ed.), *The Correspondence of Edmund Burke Volume II July 1768–June 1774* (Cambridge and Chicago, 1960), pp. 289–292, 292–293.

Edmund Burke

Franklin and the Crisis in the Agencies

New Jersey by resolution of the House of Representatives.[14] The determination of the Commissioners of Trade to admit as agents only those appointed by concurrent act of the entire government would put an end to the agencies, Franklin predicted, for the colonial assemblies "will think agents, under the ministerial influence that must rise from such appointments, cannot be of much use to their colony affairs."[15] Franklin's analysis was not necessarily correct, as perhaps he knew. Such agents as Garth, Trecothick, and the good Doctor himself as agent for Georgia were not under the "ministerial influence" because the royal governors of Georgia, New Hampshire, and South Carolina had concurred in their appointments. In a particular sense Franklin's prediction did come true, but not for the reason he expected. For practical purposes the agents did become almost useless in the last year before the final imperial crisis, but not because the representatives' assemblies refused to appoint them with the concurrence of the governor. An important factor was the disrepute in London of Franklin himself. Franklin's role as agent for the House of Representatives of Massachusetts—more accurately, agent for a revolutionary faction in the lower chamber—helped to discredit the agency with the British administration.

Franklin won the Massachusetts agency in 1770 after the death of Dennys DeBerdt by virtue of his professing a constitutional doctrine acceptable to the colonial Whigs and by outdistancing several rivals. William Bollan, named agent by the provincial council for his conspicuous role in opposing Governor Francis Bernard, was one possible candidate. Some representatives favored Stephen Sayre, then in London and the first choice of Samuel Adams. But since Sayre was known only to a few members, the assembly did not

14. For the dispute over the New Jersey appointment, see the resolution of the provincial council, Dec. 11, 1771, Frederick W. Ricord and William Nelson (eds.), *Archives of the State of New Jersey* (36 vols., Newark, 1881–1941), 1st Ser., XVIII, 235; Commissioners of Trade to Governor William Franklin, June 21, Oct. 21, Dec. 26, 1771, *ibid.*, X, 317–320; William Franklin to Benjamin Franklin, Jan. 6, 1772, Benjamin Franklin Papers, American Philosophical Society Library, Philadelphia, III, 84; and the copy of the resolution appointing Franklin, Dec. 11/20, 1771, *ibid.*, LIII, 8.

15. Benjamin Franklin to William Franklin, Jan. 20, 1772, Ricord and Nelson (eds.), *Archives of the State of New Jersey*, 1st Ser., X, 330.

149

Agents and Merchants

select him. Sayre himself and Joseph Reed, who might have received the post had he remained in London, both recommended a Virginian, Dr. Arthur Lee. From an influential Westmoreland County family, Lee had moved to the British Isles, where he studied medicine and then law. In the opinion of William Samuel Johnson, who had known him in London, Lee, who delighted in the "fire and fury of a Party," was well adapted to please the Bostonians. The Virginian now narrowly missed the Massachusetts agency. Indeed, the representatives might have chosen him, had they but only "known his Christian name." Such were the standards of the Whigs of Massachusetts! Instead they selected Lee as associate agent and Franklin as the official representative.[16] Franklin's victory was due in no small measure to his revolutionary sentiments on the constitutional relationship between the colonies and Great Britain—sentiments expressed in a letter to Samuel Cooper, minister of the West Church

16. Cooper to Pownall, Oct. 12, 1770, "Letters of Samuel Cooper to Thomas Pownall, 1769–1777," *American Historical Review*, VIII (1901), 321; Thomas Cushing to Stephen Sayre, Nov. 6, 1770, "Letters of Thomas Cushing from 1767 to 1775," Massachusetts Historical Society *Collections* (Boston, 1858), 4th Ser., IV, 357; Samuel Adams to Sayre, Nov. 16, 23, 1770, Henry A. Cushing (ed.), *Writings of Samuel Adams* (4 vols., New York, 1904–1908), II, 58–59, 66; and Esther DeBerdt to Dennis DeBerdt (the younger), Dec. 12, 1770, William B. Reed, *Life of Esther Reed* (Philadelphia, 1853), pp. 161–162. Lee had achieved some fame, if not notoriety. In 1768 he had published "The Monitor's Letters" in William Rind's *Virginia Gazette* to aid John Dickinson's more famous "Farmer's Letters" protesting against the Townshend duties. Under the name of *Junius Americanus* he continued to defend the American cause while in London by issuing a series of articles almost monthly. Controversial, paranoid, a man who "loved troubled waters and was expert in creating them," Lee was "constantly haunted by the most fantastic suspicions of the people around him. . . ." To him, the British were engaged in the most horrible conspiracies against America. In a letter to his brother in Virginia, he charged that the majority of the American agents "are unknown, . . . of no abilities, no rank & if of any of a bad character. . . ." Some were "menial placemen, all . . . servile expectants." In England Lee was connected with the opposition, particularly the Earl of Shelburne, and at least on one occasion, the "Jesuit of Berkeley Square," as he was known, invited the Virginian for a week at his country seat. Helen Auger, *The Secret War of Independence* (New York, 1955), p. 9; Arthur Lee to Richard Henry Lee, Sept. 18, Aug. 15, 1769, Arthur Lee Papers, American Philosophical Society Library, Philadelphia; William Samuel Johnson to Jared Ingersoll, June 15, 1772, Franklin B. Dexter (ed.), "A Selection from the Correspondence and miscellaneous papers of Jared Ingersoll," New Haven Colony Historical Society *Papers* (New Haven, 1918), IX, 436.

Arthur Lee

in Boston. A member of the patriot faction, Cooper had circulated Franklin's views among the leading members of the party.

America was independent of the mother country, Franklin declared in effect, for the colonies and England were "distinct and separate States," connected only by the same "head, or Sovereign, the King. . . ." Moreover, the several American "States" had "equal Rights and Liberties . . . being connected as England and Scotland were before the Union" of Great Britain in 1707. Consequently Parliament had no jurisdiction over these separate states in the New World and had indeed "usurp'd an Authority" when it legislated in the past.[17] Perhaps Franklin was simply misreading history, but he was propounding a revolutionary doctrine—a statement of colonial independence which could justify the apprehensions of the British ministry. The imperial government soon became aware of Franklin's doctrine when the Massachusetts legislature adopted his theory in a constitutional dispute with the royal governor in 1772–1773. Governor Thomas Hutchinson fully appreciated the implication in the claim of the assembly when it contended, as Franklin had, that the colonial charters had created American states separate from Great Britain, and that the provincial assemblies, not the British Parliament, had exclusive jurisdiction in the New World. It was impossible to have "two independent Legislatures in one and the same state," for this would result in "two governments as distinct as the kingdoms of England and Scotland before the Union." With masterly understatement the House of Representatives replied: "Very true, may it please your Excellency. . . ."[18] As far as Franklin and the Massachusetts Whigs were concerned the Declaration of Independence three and a half years later merely proclaimed the separate "kingdom" of Massachusetts a republic.

17. See Franklin to Cooper, June 8, 1770, Albert H. Smyth (ed.), *The Writings of Benjamin Franklin with a Life and Introduction* (10 vols., New York, 1907), V, 259–261. It should be noted that the colonists accepted the Revolutionary Settlement of 1688–1689 and by its terms under the Coronation Oath Act, the monarch swore to rule the dominions by the laws of Parliament.

18. Hutchinson's message, Jan. 26, 1773, and the reply of the assembly, Jan. 26, 1773, Alden Bradford (ed.), *Speeches of the Governors of Massachusetts from 1765 to 1775; and the Answers of the House of Representatives To the Same* . . . (Boston, 1818), p. 340–363. (Also cited as *Massachusetts State Papers*.)

Franklin's doctrine of independence was soon known in England. Moreover, it was directly involved in the dispute over the appointment of the provincial agent when Hutchinson refused to recognize a sole agent for the lower house and successfully solicited an instruction from the Privy Council prohibiting the governor from approving such an agent. Hutchinson had warned the home government: "This Doctrine of Independence must sooner or later become a serious Affair," for the same "spirit which denied the Authority of Parliament" to legislate for the colonies now "denies the Authority of the King" to instruct his governors on bills concerning among other matters, the appointment of agents.[19]

In London, the Secretary of State for the American Department supported the governor. In a conference with Franklin the Earl of Hillsborough would not admit the power of the assembly to appoint a unilateral representative. Unmoved, Franklin terminated the interview by observing that it was of no great importance whether or not the ministry recognized his appointment, since under the present circumstances the agents were of no use to the colonists. If the agent were appointed in the manner insisted upon by the administration, Franklin speculated in a letter to the speaker of the Massachusetts House of Representatives, Hillsborough would be able to appoint the officer or at least negate any nomination. However, when the colonies "come to be considered in the light of *distinct states*, as I conceive they really are," Franklin suggested, "possibly their ministers," that is their agents, "may be treated with more respect, and considered more as public ministers." But for the present Hillsborough, regarding them with "an evil eye, as obstructors of ministerial measures," would be pleased "to get rid of them," Franklin fancied.[20] The resignation of the agent's nemesis in the summer of 1772 temporarily eased the situation. But in an interview with the new Secretary of State, the Earl of Dartmouth,

19. Hutchinson to Hillsborough, July 18, Aug. ?, 1771, C.O. 5/894:306; C.O. 5/246:25–26.

20. See Franklin's minutes of his conference with Hillsborough, Franklin to Cushing, Feb. 5, 1771, Smyth (ed.), *Writings of Franklin*, V, 292–295; Leonard W. Labaree (ed.), *Royal Instructions to British Colonial Governors, 1670–1776* (2 vols., New York, 1935), I, 387, No. 543; and Hutchinson to Hillsborough, May ?, 1771, C.O. 5/894:277–278.

Franklin took the opportunity to point out that the colonies now questioned the authority of Parliament and that the king appeared to be the "only Connection between the two Countries. . . ."[21] The basic issue still had not been resolved. And the imperial government was to resist any implication of independence or any attempt to further autonomy by combinations in the colonies it considered illegal.

As agent for the Massachusetts House of Representatives, Franklin lent support to a movement for colonial unity to resist purported imperial transgressions. In April, 1773, Speaker Thomas Cushing, who had corresponded privately with Franklin on behalf of the patriot faction within the assembly, sent the agent a pamphlet on the hotly debated dispute with Governor Thomas Hutchinson in which the House of Representatives had adopted Franklin's thesis that the American provinces were separate and distinct states. Fearing that the public expression of the doctrine might provoke the British, Cushing hoped the colonies would undertake joint action should the ministry resort to "high measures" against the Bay Colony. Indeed the Virginia House of Burgesses had already called for intercolonial committees of correspondence. Perhaps a congress of delegates from the various colonies might later develop from this organization.[22] Franklin approved of the resolutions the Virginia burgesses had adopted. "It is natural to suppose" that if the "Oppressions" of the British government continued, an intercolonial congress might evolve from the committees of correspondence.

21. Franklin to Cushing, Dec. 2, 1722, Smyth (ed.), *Writings of Franklin*, V, 449–450.

22. Cushing to Franklin, April 20, 1773, Benjamin Franklin Papers, Library of Congress, Ser. ii, II, 158–161. It was clear that Cushing did not speak for the entire assembly, for he warned Franklin that when the agent wrote to the speaker "upon any affairs which it may be necessary to communicate to the House, it would be best to direct to me as Speaker and in my public Character and when you write in Confidence what is to be Communicated only to a few in such Case to write to me in my private Character."

Franklin's correspondence with Cushing—particularly a letter describing an interview with Dartmouth—proved embarrassing. As the agent had requested, Cushing had not revealed its contents to the members of the House, but only to a select few, the patriot party, with the request that they not divulge its contents. One had inadvertently mentioned the letter, however, and Cushing was forced to make extracts available. This seemed to satisfy the assembly.

"Nothing would more alarm our Ministers," Franklin predicted. Through such a congress or even the committees of correspondence the Americans could best draw up a full declaration of their rights and pledge not to grant any aids to the Crown until both houses of Parliament and the King acknowledged their rights. "Such a Step," the agent prophesied, "will bring the Dispute to a Crisis. . . ."[23] This prognostication was all too correct, for in 1764 the call for intercolonial action had confirmed the decision to pass the Stamp Act. In 1768 the attempt by Massachusetts and Virginia to unite the colonies against the Townshend duties had further aroused the British ministry. Moreover, Hillsborough had specifically objected to colonial attempts in 1770–1771 to regulate the Indian trade by congressional action.[24] Any further proposals for an intercolonial congress to resist British measures could not fail to alienate the ministry, which had always proved sensitive on this point.

The imperial administration soon learned of the agent's close involvement in the activities of the Whigs in Boston. Despite the fact that Franklin's correspondence with Cushing was private, his letters, as well as those of Arthur Lee, the associate agent, were known to Governor Hutchinson, for Cushing, who should have known better, lent them to some person in Boston who made a copy for the governor. In October, 1773, Hutchinson wrote privately to the Secretary of State that Franklin had proposed a general congress of delegates from all the colonies, a step which in the governor's opinion would be an effective bar to reconciliation.[25] The governor's revelation was not without effect in Britain. George III himself felt that Franklin's correspondence with the Whigs of the Bay Colony

23. Franklin to Cushing (private), July 7, 1773, C.O. 5/118:126–127. See also his public letter of the same date, Smyth (ed.), *Writings of Franklin*, VI, 73–81.

24. On Hillsborough's opposition to a colonial Congress to regulate the Indian trade see J. M. Sosin, *Whitehall and the Wilderness: The Middle West in British Colonial Policy, 1760–1775* (Lincoln, Nebr., 1961), p. 214.

25. Hutchinson to Dartmouth (private), Oct. 19, 1773, Dartmouth Papers, William Salt Library, Stafford, England, I, ii, 897. For Hutchinson's account as to how he obtained copies of the letters of Franklin and Lee, see Hutchinson to Dartmouth, March 20, 1774, H.M.C., *Eleventh Report, The Manuscripts of the Earl of Dartmouth*, App., Pt. V (London, 1887), p. 350. See also Thomas Hutchinson, *The History of the Colony and Province of Massachusetts Bay*, ed. Lawrence Shaw Mayo (3 vols., Cambridge, Mass., 1936), III, 281.

was "too Characteristick" of his sentiments.[26] One might wish the King had been more explicit, but there was little doubt as to the sentiment in the administration. Evidently the ministers considered the views of both Franklin and Lee as contained in their letters to Cushing as treasonable. A few months later, the Secretary of State informed General Thomas Gage that "proofs of this dangerous and unwarrantable Correspondence" had come to him by a "confidential communication" from Boston. Two letters from the regular and associate agent publicly read in the House of Representatives were "expressed in such terms as makes it very much to be wished that such Evidence could be obtained of the Authenticity of them as might be the grounds of a proper Proceeding thereupon." With whatever secrecy and caution Gage considered necessary, he was to procure either the original letters or attested copies and as soon as possible transmit them to England.[27] There is little doubt that the administration considered Franklin, by this time the agent for four colonies, involved in a revolutionary movement contesting the authority of the imperial government.

Franklin's role in the sordid efforts of the Boston patriots to discredit the royal governor of Massachusetts also damaged the agent's standing with the British ministry. Some aspects of Franklin's involvement in the affair of the Hutchinson-Oliver letters are well known, but what needs to be emphasized is its relation to the agency.

26. George III to Dartmouth, Nov. 19, 1773, H.M.C., *Thirteenth Report*, App., Pt. IV (London, 1892), p. 499.
27. Dartmouth to Gage (separate and secret), June 3, 1774, Clarence E. Carter (ed.), *Correspondence of General Thomas Gage* (2 vols., New Haven, 1931–1933), II, 167. Neither Franklin nor Lee were in immediate danger of prosecution, since it was impossible for Gage to obtain the letters, which Cushing kept in his private possession. Not until the fall of 1775 after the outbreak of hostilities in Boston was the general able to procure the correspondence of Franklin and Lee with the patriot faction. In October he transmitted to England a packet of letters from a number of papers found scattered about Cushing's home, but Franklin had already left England some months before. See Gage to Dartmouth, Oct. 15, 1775 (private), Carter (ed.), *Correspondence of General Thomas Gage*, I, 422–423. The captured Lee and Franklin letters are in C.O. 5/118. In 1774 Franklin had got wind of the rumor that the ministry considered his letters objectionable and wrote to Cushing on April 16: "I am not conscious of any treasonable Intention, and I know that much violence must be us'd with my Letters before they can be construed into Treason. . . ." Smyth (ed.), *Writings of Franklin*, VI, 229.

Agents and Merchants

Moreover, Franklin's position as agent for four colonies was critical to the entire institution. The episode further reveals the extent to which Franklin was emotionally involved, and how his emotions warped his judgment.

For years the opponents of Thomas Hutchinson in the Bay Colony had sought to damage the reputation of the most influential and successful politician in Massachusetts,[28] a man who had gone far in the political world as councilor, lieutenant governor and finally chief executive of his native province. In 1765 they had so convinced the Boston mob that Hutchinson had had a share in the Stamp Act that it destroyed his home. Although Hutchinson had protested against the measure before and after passage of the revenue bill, he had been shocked, as other American leaders had been, by the violence of the subsequent colonial reactions. In a private correspondence with friends in England, among them Thomas Whately, Hutchinson, and Andrew Oliver, secretary and later lieutenant governor of Massachusetts, had concluded that some measures were needed in the colony to curb liberties degenerated into licentiousness.[29] In some manner never satisfactorily explained, Franklin after the death of Whately obtained a few of the letters sent by Oliver and Hutchinson from some individual in London whose identity was never disclosed.[30]

28. On the partisan opposition to Hutchinson and the royal administration, see Merrill Jensen, "Democracy and the American Revolution," *Huntington Library Quarterly*, XX (August 1957), 326; and Leslie Joseph Thomas, "Partisan Politics in Massachusetts During Governor Bernard's Administration, 1760–1770" (Ph.D. dissertation, University of Wisconsin, 1960).

29. It is difficult to attach great significance to this correspondence with Thomas Whately begun in 1766. Whately and his patron George Grenville were not in office, and they were in no position to implement any suggestion by Hutchinson. If the lieutenant governor sought to influence British policy he could write directly to the ministry. It was useless to write to Grenville's associates until 1771, for it was only after the death of Grenville in October, 1770, that Whately joined the North ministry as a Commissioner of Trade. In any case he soon followed his original patron to his final reward.

30. The agent refused to disclose the identity of the person who had given him the letters. See Charles A. W. Pownall, *Thomas Pownall, Governor of the Colony of Massachusetts Bay; author of the Letters of Junius, etc.* (London, 1908), p. 255; and William Whately to Andrew Oliver, March 19, 1774, Massachusetts Historical Society *Proceedings*, LVIII (Boston, 1924–1925), 89–91. In a letter of Aug. 2, 1773,

When Franklin transmitted these documents to the patriot leaders in Boston, the Whigs used the purloined correspondence in a sensational manner. The governor later claimed that it was his refusal to sanction Franklin as agent which "probably excited" him to procure and send to Boston the letters which were then "perverted to set the province in a flame."[31]

Franklin initiated the new attack on the chief executive by transmitting to Cushing the pilfered letters that Hutchinson and Oliver had sent to Whately. They proved, the agent concluded in a long and impassioned letter, that the measures of the British government designed to coerce the colonists and subvert their liberties were the result of the private ambitions of the now governor and lieutenant governor. In order that this "truth" be known, Cushing was to allow the members of the provincial committee of correspondence and the leaders of the popular party, and only these men, to examine the documents. But by the conditions stipulated by the agent's anonymous source they were not to copy the letters, merely to examine and then return them to London.[32] Read dispassionately, the letters of Hutchinson and Oliver fall far short of Franklin's allegations. Moreover, it is doubtful if they were originally sent to England to produce public measures.[33]

When returned to Boston, however, this correspondence had great consequences. On receiving the potent package, Thomas Cushing informed the agent that the Boston junta thought the letters "ought to be retained on this side of the Water to be hereafter improved [*sic*] as the Exigency of our Affairs may require or at least that authenticated copies ought to be taken before they are Returned."[34] In the spring of 1773, with no authorization from Franklin

an anonymous writer informed Dartmouth that Temple (who he erroneously thought was governor of New Hampshire) obtained the letters and sent them to America. Dartmouth Papers, II, 672. Despite the public statement by Franklin, Temple afterwards claimed the credit for obtaining the documents.

31. Thomas Hutchinson, *The History of the Colony and Province of Massachusetts Bay*, III, 176n.

32. Benjamin Franklin to Thomas Cushing, Dec. 2, 1772, C.O. 5/118:85–87.

33. Verner W. Crane, *Benjamin Franklin and a Rising People* (Boston, 1954), pp. 142–143.

34. Cushing to Franklin, April 20, 1773, Benjamin Franklin Papers, Library of Congress, Ser. ii, II, 158. The word "improved" in Cushing's letter is, of

in London, and with John Hancock cooperating in a prefabrication about a second set of Hutchinson's letters being found in Boston, Samuel Adams published the documents. In editing the correspondence, he claimed, and it was originally the thesis of the agent, that the "plan for the ruin of American Liberty" was laid in England by Hutchinson and Oliver, who were "governed by Avarice and a Lust for Power." In the ensuing debate in the House of Representatives some members pointed out that even Adams' printed version of the letters did not substantiate his charges. The Whig leader blandly declined to explain or even discuss the differences between the two.[35] Emotion and partisanship prevailed and on June 23, 1773, the Massachusetts assembly adopted petitions to the King requesting the removal of Hutchinson and Oliver. As agent Franklin was to present the requests to the Secretary of State.[36]

Franklin as agent was now more directly involved than ever with the patriot faction against the royal governor and administration. On August 21, 1773, he presented to Dartmouth the address of the Massachusetts assembly calling for the removal of the governor and lieutenant governor on the grounds that they had conspired to

course, critical. It might shed some light on the question Malcolm Freiberg raised in "Missing: One Hutchinson Autograph Letter," *Manuscripts*, VIII (1956), 179–184, as to who altered the copies of Hutchinson's letters retained by the governor in his home and which later fell into the hands of the Massachusetts Provincial Committee of Safety at the outbreak of the Revolution. Is it possible that the retained copies were identical to those actually sent by Hutchinson and that they were altered by William Gordon, the patriot historian of the Revolution who prepared selections for publication in the provincial press in 1775? Did Gordon alter these drafts to make them conform to the versions earlier printed by the anti-Hutchinson faction? A further question arises. Why is "improved" changed to "employed" in the extract of Cushing's letter of April 20, 1773, that Franklin prepared in attempting to vindicate himself in this affair? See Carl Van Doren (ed.), *Benjamin Franklin's Autobiographical Writings* (New York, 1945), p. 313.

35. Clifford K. Shipton, *Biographical Sketches of Those Who Attended Harvard College in the Classes 1736–1740 with Biographical and Other Notes; Sibley's Harvard Graduates*, X (Boston, 1958), 442.

36. See the letter of the two houses of the Massachusetts legislature to Dartmouth, June 29, 1773, Bradford (ed.), *Massachusetts State Papers*, pp. 398–400; and Cushing to Franklin, Aug. 26, 1773, Benjamin Franklin Papers, Library of Congress, Ser. ii, II, 186–187.

annihilate the rights and liberties of their fellow Americans. The machinery for deciding the issue was now set in motion. On December 3, 1773, John Pownall, Undersecretary of State for the American Department, forwarded the Massachusetts petition and Franklin's covering letter to the clerk of the Privy Council.[37] The Lords of the Committee for Trade and Plantations were scheduled to hear the petition against Hutchinson and Oliver on January 11, 1774, but in the interval Hutchinson had written to London charging that the plot against him had originated in London. Obviously referring to Franklin, he informed the administration that the leaders of the Boston faction "give out that they take no step without Advice or Direction from England."[38] Moreover, in London, when William Whately accused John Temple of pilfering his deceased brother's effects, the two men fought a duel over the affair. To Franklin's credit he now publicly admitted that he, and not Temple, had transmitted to Boston the letters on which the Massachusetts assembly based its demand for the removal of Hutchinson and Oliver. In making the admission, however, Franklin lent credence to the governor's accusation that the agent had been instrumental in the affair.

The famous hearing on the Massachusetts petition occurred in the Cockpit at Whitehall on January 29, 1774. Before thirty-five spectators and members of the Committee of Trade and Plantations of the Privy Council, Alexander Wedderburn, the Solicitor General and close personal friend of the deceased Thomas Whately, delivered his famous philippic. Significantly he charged the faction in the Massachusetts legislature with fomenting rebellion and specifically linked Franklin as a unilateral agent for this revolutionary junta. Franklin may have been "so long possessed with the idea of a great American Republic," Wedderburn speculated, "that he may easily slide into the language of the minister of a foreign independent state." One suspects that the Solicitor General was familiar with the

---

37. Franklin to Dartmouth, Aug. 21, 1773, in "Proceedings of his Majesty's Privy Council, upon an address to remove Governor Hutchinson, with an Address of Lord Loughborough [Alexander Wedderburn] upon that occasion; collected by Israel Mauduit, Esq.," [John Debrett,] *A Collection of Scarce And Interesting Tracts* (4 vols., London, 1788), II, 222; the petition of the assembly in *ibid.*, pp. 223–226; and Pownall to the Clerk of the Privy Council, Dec. 3, 1773, C.O. 5/133:191.

38. Hutchinson to [John Pownall?], July 3, 1773, C.O. 5/246:61.

agent's letters to Thomas Cushing and Samuel Cooper on the constitutional relations between England and the provinces, and on the role of the colonial agents. But Franklin's position was not even that of a provincial agent, Wedderburn continued—"he moves in a very inferior orbit." A proper provincial agent, appointed by all three branches of the colonial government, would consider it his duty to consult the "joint services of all three" and contribute to the "general welfare and prosperity of the province." But Franklin, on the contrary, served to furnish the party leaders in Boston with "materials for dissentions, to set at variance the different branches of the legislature, and to irritate and incense the minds of the kings subjects against the King's Governor."[39]

From the smiling approval registered by the committee—representing almost the entire administration—there was little doubt that they agreed with the Solicitor General and that Franklin had lost most of his standing.

Wedderburn had exaggerated in his violent attack on the agent, but regardless of the violence of his manner and tone, Franklin had little to support him when it came to the immediate issue of the petition of the Massachusetts legislature demanding the dismissal of Hutchinson and Oliver. The assembly of the Bay Colony had based its case on the letters Franklin had sent to Boston, questionable evidence to say the least. Since neither the agent nor his constituents had produced other, valid proofs against the royal officials, the administration dismissed the charges against Hutchinson as "groundless, vexations, and scandalous," calculated only for the "seditious purpose of keeping up a Spirit of clamour and discontent" in Massachusetts Bay.[40]

39. Wedderburn's speech is printed in [Debrett,] *A Collection of Scarce and Interesting Tracts*, II, 234–248; and in Israel Mauduit, *The Letters of Governor Hutchinson, and Lieut. Governor Oliver, &c. Printed at Boston, and Remarks Thereon with the Assembly's Addresses, and the Proceedings of the Lords Committee of Council.* . . . (2nd edn., London, 1774), pp. 90–108. For Franklin's version of the hearing at the Cockpit see his letter to Thomas Cushing, Feb. 15, 1774, Massachusetts Historical Society *Collections*, 1st Ser., III (Boston, 1794, 1800), 109–116.

40. The reports of the Committee and the Privy Council of January 29 and February 7, 1774, are printed in [Debrett,] *A Collection of Scarce and Interesting Tracts*, II, 258–262, 263. See also James Munroe (ed.), *Acts of the Privy Council, Colonial Series* (6 vols., Edinburgh, 1908–1912), V, 385–388.

Franklin and the Crisis in the Agencies

The episode is significant for an understanding of the failure of the spokesmen of the colonies in London to lessen the tension between America and the mother country then developing over the Boston Tea Party, which had occurred just over a month before. It further contributed to discrediting the man who was agent for four colonies. The ministers now linked Franklin with what they regarded as a revolutionary junta seeking independence. While Alexander Wedderburn may have represented an extreme group in administration, even a moderate such as the Earl of Dartmouth now confessed that whatever respect he may have had for Franklin on other accounts, he could "not applaud his conduct on the occasion of Mr. Hutchinson's letters."[41] The British administration associated the attempt of Franklin and the Boston patriots to discredit Hutchinson with the doctrine inspired by the agent and adopted by the provincial assembly that Parliament had no authority over the "separate" and "distinct" country of America. In addition the ministers were aware that the agent and the Whigs in Boston favored an intercolonial congress to further the claims of the colonies. These developments, associated in one way or another with Franklin, all received notoriety when the Boston Tea Party brought on an imperial crisis in 1774. North, Wedderburn, and Thurlow, the administration spokesmen, stressed these points during the debate in Parliament on the "coercive" or "intolerable" bills proposed in reaction to the challenge from Massachusetts. After almost a decade of half-hearted attempts, the British administration faced a decision. More than ever before an effective concert of colonial agents and British merchants was needed to present the American case, but provincial politics and Franklin's association with the revolutionary movement in Massachusetts had seriously reduced its effectiveness.

41. Dartmouth to Joseph Reed, July 11, 1774, William B. Reed, *Life and Correspondence of Joseph Reed* (2 vols., Philadelphia, 1847), I, 74.

CHAPTER VII

The Massachusetts Acts, 1774

BY 1774 the crucial issue dividing Great Britain and America was the sovereignty of Parliament—whether the British legislature had any authority over the colonies, or whether the assemblies in America had sole jurisdiction. Although both sides had taken a stand as early as 1764 over the impending stamp bill, they had never satisfactorily resolved this question in the ensuing decade. Colonial agents and British merchants had aided in bringing about accommodations and adjustments such as the repeal of the Stamp Act and all but one of the Townshend duties, but in 1770 Parliament had retained the tax on tea as the symbol of its authority. In America the Whig leaders had attempted to further their cause by establishing a network of committees of correspondence, a movement the British administration considered an illegal combination against the mother country. It was but a short step to the formation of an intercolonial congress to defend American rights. Benjamin Franklin in 1773 predicted that such an eventuality would precipitate an imperial crisis and force the home government to a decision. Although there were few specific points at issue from 1770 to 1773, the imperial government and the Whig leaders in the colonies were further apart than ever before. Initially the Whigs had claimed freedom merely from Parliamentary laws for the purpose of raising revenue, then freedom from all Parliamentary taxation, and finally, by 1773, many were claiming complete immunity, that Parliament had no

162

authority in the colonies. Some in the home government attributed this increase in colonial "pretentions" to the leniency of the imperial administration in repealing the Trade and Revenue Acts. Concessions by Parliament had merely encouraged the Americans. Now with the outbreak of further resistance to Great Britain, the home government concluded that it must come to grips with a revolutionary situation in the provinces, particularly Massachusetts Bay, considered the ringleader in the anti-British movement in America. Unfortunately the concert of colonial agents and British merchants never fully appreciated what they faced in attempting to prevent the passage of the legislation relating to the Bay Colony. Indeed several of the key agents were connected with the very revolutionary leaders against whom the "Intolerable" acts were directed. The British merchants, primarily concerned with a possible interruption of their trade, failed to understand that the government was principally concerned with a basic political crisis which threatened British rule over North America. For the first time in a decade, the agents and merchants were to make no impression.

The crisis of 1774 originated out of a bizarre coincidence of two seemingly unrelated developments. In 1770 the British Parliament had repealed all but one of the Townshend duties but had retained the tax on tea as the symbol of its authority. In time the duty might be more than symbolic, a real factor in imperial administration, for the home government used the revenue to defray the salaries of executive and judicial officials in those provinces where the assemblies attempted to upset the balance in government by not making permanent or adequate provision for the civil establishment. In Massachusetts, where Thomas Hutchinson was embroiled in a dispute with the assembly, the governor received his stipend from the revenue raised by the tax on tea.

Although Hutchinson was a stockholder in the British East India Company, material gain does not seem to have motivated him to write the British government when he pointed out that it could considerably increase this fund by stimulating the consumption of British tea and eliminating the illicit trade in the smuggled Dutch product. If the price of British East India Company tea were lowered, it would render the profit from smuggling not worth the

163

risk involved in breaking the law.[1] Hutchinson made his suggestion at a time when the home government was particularly concerned with the financial and political state of the East India Company, whose internal affairs for some time had been mismanaged. To dispose of a tremendous surplus in its warehouses by stimulating consumption in the colonies, in March, 1773 the company petitioned the House of Commons that it be allowed to export tea duty-free to America. If Parliament granted permission, it would have thereby eliminated the tax imposed in 1767 and deliberately retained three years later.

Presented with an opportunity finally to remove the last of the objectionable Townshend duties, the colonial agents as a group seemed strangely apathetic. William Bollan, agent for the Massachusetts council, did take advantage of the request of the East India Company, however, by conferring with an English merchant familiar with the tea trade. Bollan's "expert" drew up a statement favoring repeal of the tax which the agent then presented to the First Lord of the Treasury. But the administration dashed his hopes by deciding to continue the tax on tea as a "badge of sovereignty" over the colonies. In the House of Commons, Lord North made a counterproposal to the plan of the East India Company designed to retain the symbolic tax but still provide relief for the company. When the merchant Anthony Bacon reported the resolutions of the committee appointed to consider the company's suggestion to repeal the provincial tax, North moved that Parliament vote to allow a drawback on the original taxes paid on the importation of the tea into England when it was exported to the colonies. By rebating the duty collected in England the ministry would lower the price on tea but retain the symbolic tax in America.

Barlow Trecothick, agent for New Hampshire and chairman of the London merchants trading to America, took up the case for the colonies. The most effective method to increase the consumption of tea and reduce the company's surplus would be to remove the import duty of threepence per pound in the colonies. Once relieved of this import duty, the Americans would buy more of the British

1. Hutchinson to [Hillsborough], Aug. 25, Sept. 10, 1771, Joseph Redington and Richard A. Roberts (eds.), *Calendar of Home Office Papers of the reign of George III, 1760–1775* (4 vols., London, 1878–1899), III, 290, 294.

tea. The resulting loss in revenue to the imperial administration would be inconsequential, since the revenue hitherto raised had been minimal. But if the government still desired to raise money, it could repeal the colonial tax and grant only a partial, not a full, rebate of the tax levied in Great Britain. The administration spokesmen refused, however, to alter their plan. While declining to enter into any political argument on the right of Parliament to impose taxes on the Americans, they were convinced that it would be sufficient to rebate the English duty so that the colonists would be able to purchase tea at a lower rate from the merchants designated to represent the East India Company in the provinces. "Men will always go to the Cheapest Market," they told the House of Commons.[2]

In the summer of 1773 the East India Company concluded arrangements with selected merchants in America who were designated consignees to receive and sell the tea. The British product would now be able to compete with smuggled Dutch tea if the colonists were willing to pay the three-penny duty, symbolic of Parliamentary authority. If they were unwilling, they could demonstrate their principles by purchasing from the Dutch. Benjamin Franklin felt confident that they would prefer the latter course. The British ministers "have not Idea that any People can act from any other Principle but of [material] Interest," he wrote sarcastically to the Boston leaders. The English believed that the lower price of East India Company tea would be "sufficient to overcome all the Patriotism of an American."[3]

Generally the colonial agents in London were not too concerned, or they failed to see any particular constitutional significance in the

2. Petition of the East India Company, March 2, 1773, William Cobbett (ed.), *The Parliamentary History of England from the Earliest Period to the Year 1803* (36 vols., London, 1813), XVII, 800; *ibid.*, XVII, 841; Great Britain, Parliament, *Journals of the House of Commons* (London, 1547—), XXXIV, 286; Bollan to the Massachusetts council, Sept. 1, 1773, "The Bowdoin and Temple Papers," Massachusetts Historical Society *Collections* (Boston, 1897), 6th Ser. IX, 309; Charles Garth to the South Carolina committee of correspondence, May 4, 1773, Charles Garth–South Carolina committee of correspondence Letter Book, South Carolina Archives, Columbia, f. 157.

3. Franklin to Thomas Cushing, June 4, 1773, Albert H. Smyth (ed.), *The Writings of Benjamin Franklin with a Life and Introduction* (10 vols., New York, 1907), VI, 57.

statute retaining the duty imposed six years before but making it more probable that the colonists would now pay this tax to a greater extent than ever. Evidently Franklin and the Whig leaders in America feared to put the patriotism of their countrymen to the test, for they attempted to prevent the landing and sale of the tea. The agent now suggested to his American correspondents a course of action comparable to the tactics used with apparent success in the past. If the colonists rejected the tea, the British would undoubtedly repeal the act. The Philadelphia patriots circulated the agent's advice in a garbled form. One Quaker merchant reported that Franklin had written his political ally in Pennsylvania, Joseph Galloway, that if the Americans refused to accept the tea and sent it back, "it will more over-sett the ministry than any thing that could happen, but if they tamely receive the same and thereby submit to the duty, it is only the beginning of their trouble & c."[4] Undoubtedly the advice of the agent in London confirmed and supported the Whig leaders in their resistance.

Opposition to the landing of the tea and payment of the three-pence duty was widespread in such urban centers as Boston, New York, Philadelphia, and Charleston, and this opposition convinced the British government that a significant challenge to its authority existed in America—a challenge comparable to the Stamp Act crisis which necessitated some measures to secure the dependence of the colonies. Some officials in the provinces who had been vociferous in defense of American rights *within* the Empire now agreed. William Smith, Jr. of the New York council observed that "A New Flame is apparently kindling in America." Setting up the "cry of liberty," the local smugglers and Sons of Liberty condemned the tea consignees as "another Species of Stamp Masters. . . ." Their design, so Smith charged, was to inspire "terror" and "animate the Populace. . . ." "Virtue and Vice being thus united," he speculated, "all the confusions" of the stamp riots would be repeated.[5]

4. Franklin to Galloway, Nov. 3, 1773, Smyth (ed.), *Writings of Franklin*, VI, 152; Thomas Wharton to Samuel Wharton, Jan. 1, 1774, "Selections from the Letterbook of Thomas Wharton, of Philadelphia, 1773–1783," *Pennsylvania Magazine of History and Biography*, XXXIII (1909), 325.

5. Entry for Oct. 13, 1773, William H. W. Sabine (ed.), *Historical Memoirs from 16 March to 9 July 1776 of William Smith . . .* (New York, 1956), p. 156.

The Massachusetts Acts, 1774

The most marked and overt challenge to the British government occurred in Boston. The particular events there, culminating in the destruction of the tea on the night of December 16, 1773, were most significant. They led directly to legislation by the British authorities to restore balanced government in a colony where the normal law-enforcement procedures and governmental processes seemed to have failed. To understand fully the purpose of this legislation and why the concert of colonial agents and merchants in London failed to prevent passage of these measures, it is essential to note certain events which occurred in the Bay Colony during the fall of 1773. In the name of the Boston town meeting, the patriots had attempted to force the local merchants to send the tea back to England. In the face of this coercion the consignees then sought aid from the magistrates and council. But the provincial officials refused. And as had been the case elsewhere during the Stamp Act riots, the military and naval forces in Boston Harbor had not been able to interfere, since they could act legally only on the call of the civil authorities. For some time the Massachusetts council—elected by the House of Representatives—had sided with the patriots.[6] Since Governor Thomas Hutchinson, the *bête noir* of the local Whigs, showed no desire to call out the military[7]—he had no authority to do so—the tea consignees and the royal customs commissioners fled to the protection of the royal garrison at Castle William.

Through the Boston town meeting the patriots now organized in defense of American liberties.[8] On the night of December 16, Samuel Adams' "Mohawks" boarded the ships of the East India Company and dumped three cargoes of Bohea tea into the harbor.

6. See Frances G. Walett, "The Massachusetts Council, 1766–1774: The Transformation of a Conservative Institution," *William and Mary Quarterly*, 3rd Ser., VI (1949), 605–627.

7. Malcolm Freiberg writes: ". . . it may be (although this is a point I am not yet prepared to argue) that [Hutchinson's] intransigeancy as governor in 1773 that precipitated the Boston tea party derived from the fact that he had a financial interest in the East India Company." "How To Become A Colonial Governor: Thomas Hutchinson of Massachusetts," *Review of Politics*, XXI (1959), 647. It may also be argued that the "intransigeancy" of the patriots precipitated the Tea Party.

8. For the "Minutes of the Tea Meetings, 1773," in the hand of the Boston town clerk, William Cooper, see Massachusetts Historical Society *Proceedings*, XX (1882–1883), 10–17.

Agents and Merchants

This "most magnificent movement of all" stirred the impressionable John Adams to write: "There is a dignity, a majesty, a sublimity, in this last effort of the patriots, that I greatly admire. The people should never rise without doing something to be remembered, something notable and striking."[9] But the Boston patriots had carried out this memorable blow only because local government had broken down. Controlled or intimidated by the Whigs, the magistrates and councilors had refused to aid the consignees or call for troops to protect them. In despair, Hutchinson had written to the Secretary of State. The royal governor, he complained, "is without the least support in measures for maintaining the authority of the Crown."[10] The failure of legally constituted authority indicated to the British administration that the balance of power in the colony had fallen to the Revolutionary leaders in the town meetings. This analysis determined the specific content of the acts passed by Parliament in 1774. In seeking to stem the reaction against Massachusetts, the colonial agents, particularly those representing the Bay Colony, never appreciated the fact that this legislation sought merely to prevent a revolutionary challenge and to restore a balanced government.

The agents themselves were involved in the resulting crisis within a week following the destruction of the tea in Boston Harbor. A committee of the House of Representatives consisting of Thomas Cushing, Samuel Adams, John Hancock, and William Phillips sent its account of the episode to Franklin, their agent in London. The destruction of the tea, they charged, was due to the "obstinacy" of the consignees in refusing to send the cargoes back to England. By law the customs officials would confiscate the tea twenty days after it arrived in Boston in order to secure payment of the duties. Since there were "just grounds" to think that the customs officers would take this step and attempt to land the tea "by force, and overbearing any opposition," the patriots claimed—the evidence to the contrary—a "number of persons unknown and in disguise" had destroyed the obnoxious weed. But this extreme step was justified.

9. Entry for Dec. 17, 1773, Adams' diary in Charles Francis Adams (ed.), *The Works of John Adams* (10 vols., Boston, 1850–1856), II, 323.

10. Hutchinson to Dartmouth (private), Dec. 2, H.M.C., *Eleventh Report*, App., Pt. V (London, 1887), p. 343.

The colonists considered that the East India Company Act was contrary to their interests, "introductive of monopolies" that were "forever dangerous to public liberty," paved the way for further impositions, and was "pregnant with new grievances." Furthermore, it threatened the "final destruction of liberties." Truly a formidable statute.

This was the patriot interpretation of the Boston Tea Party as sent to Franklin in London. The committee did not doubt that the agent would make "such an improvement of this intelligence as shall be most for the Interest" of Massachusetts Bay in particular, and the colonies in general.[11] Still the committee for the lower house of the Massachusetts legislature had not acted quickly enough. The morning after the destruction of the tea, a man-of-war left Boston Harbor for England. Franklin would have his work cut out for him. After being berated by Wedderburn in the Cockpit in January, 1774 over the Hutchinson-Oliver letters, he had left London for a "Month or two's Ramble" in Ireland and Scotland.[12] On his return he found himself once more involved in a crisis precipitated by the revolutionary leaders in Boston. It was doubtful if he could influence the ministry by any "improvement" of the intelligence sent him from Massachusetts.

The agent for the House of Representatives was less than enthusiastic over the position the patriots had placed him in, and he agreed to some extent with the ministers who were to insist that the town of Boston make restitution for the property which had been destroyed in its name. He wrote privately to Thomas Cushing that the violent destruction of the tea "seems to have united all Parties" in London against the Bay Colony. Consequently Franklin hoped that the Massachusetts assembly would, by this time, have proposed to compensate the East India Company. Such a gesture would "remove much of the Prejudice now entertain'd against us," he

11. Samuel Adams, Thomas Cushing, William Phillips, and John Hancock to Franklin, Dec. 21, 1773, Benjamin Franklin Papers, Library of Congress, Ser. ii, Vol. I, 208–210 (also in Arthur Lee Papers, Harvard College Library, Cambridge, Mass.).

12. Michael Collinson to Cadwallader Colden, March 11, 1774, "The Letters and Papers of Cadwallader Colden," New York Historical Society *Collections* (11 vols., New York, 1877–1878, 1918–1924, 1935, 1937), LVI (1923), 218.

speculated. Franklin took the same position with the Massachusetts committee which had written him of the Boston Tea Party in an attempt to justify the acts of the patriots. He was "truly concern'd" that any person should see the necessity for carrying matters to such an extreme as "to destroy private Property" in a dispute over public rights. It was impossible to justify such behavior to Britons who were already so "prejudiced in favour of the Power of Parliament" to tax America. As the tea had been destroyed by "persons unknown" who would probably not be "found or brought to answer for it," Franklin conjectured, "there seems to be some reasonable Claim on the Society at large in which it happened."[13]

Evidently Franklin seemed to agree with the ministry on the justice of closing the port of Boston until the town had paid compensation for the destruction of the tea. But much more was involved as far as the administration was concerned—a basic political challenge to the authority of the mother country. Neither the colonial agents nor the British merchants appreciated this sentiment within the imperial government. Yet as the administration received the earliest reports of the disturbances in the colonies, it hesitated to use extreme measures. The Secretary of State cautioned the governors that the civil magistrates should not requisition the army "upon a Slight Ground but only in Cases of absolute Necessity when every other Effort has failed."[14] But the news arriving in London from the Bay Colony[15] was particularly disturbing. The King expressed himself as "much hurt that the instigation of bad men hath again drawn the people of Boston to take such unjustifiable steps. . . ."[16] To the leading figures within the administration the conclusion seemed clear: the compromises of the past had merely encouraged further disobedience. Lord Chancellor Apsley was not alone in thinking that "It has been the giving into palliative measures that

13. Franklin to Cushing, March 22, 1774, C.O. 5/118:147; and Franklin to Cushing, Samuel Adams, John Hancock, and William Phillips, Feb. 2, 1774, Smyth (ed.), *Writings of Franklin*, VI, 179.

14. Dartmouth to Governor William Tryon of New York, Jan. 8, 1774, "The Letters and Papers of Cadwallader Colden," LVI (1923), 202.

15. These accounts from the East India Company may be found in T. 1/505.

16. George III to Dartmouth, Jan. 19, 1774, H.M.C., *Thirteenth Report*, App., Pt. IV (London, 1892), p. 499.

has brought us to the present Scituation."[17] Perhaps George III best summarized opinion within the government. Everyone now agreed that the "fatal compliance" in 1766, the repeal of the Stamp Act, had encouraged the Americans "annually to encrease their pretensions" of independence. General Thomas Gage, the commander-in-chief in America, then in England on consultations, urged prompt, decisive action. The Americans will be "Lyons, whilst we are Lambs," he warned, but if the government acted resolutely the colonists "will undoubtedly prove very meek." Four regiments of troops garrisoned in Boston and four stationed throughout the other provinces would be sufficient to control the situation.[18]

After a decade of compromise the British government came to a crucial decision: since colonial demands had merely been encouraged by past concessions, prompt action was now essential to arrest further challenges to legally constituted government. As early as January 29, 1774, the cabinet, consisting of the Lord Chancellor, Lord President Gower, North, the First Lord of the Admiralty (the Earl of Sandwich), and the Earls of Rochford, Dartmouth, and Suffolk (the Secretaries of State), agreed that as a result of the disorders in America, the home government must take effective steps "to secure the Dependence of the Colonies on the Mother Country." The reports from Governor Thomas Hutchinson had been decisive in convincing the cabinet that it should take action against the revolutionary leaders in Massachusetts Bay.[19] The specific policy adopted by the cabinet depended on its assessment of the situation and the legal means available to implement its course of action. Both the Attorney General and the Solicitor General, Edward Thurlow and Alexander Wedderburn, agreed that the acts in Boston constituted high treason, "namely levying War against His Majesty." The proceedings òf the Boston patriots were a deliberate, concerted attempt pursued with open force to

17. Apsley to Dartmouth [March 6, 1774], Dartmouth Papers, William Salt Library, Stafford, England, II, 849.

18. George III to Lord North, Feb. 4, 1774, Sir John Fortescue (ed.), *The Correspondence of King George the Third from 1760 to December 1783* . . . (6 vols., London, 1927), III, 59.

19. Minutes of cabinet meetings, Jan. 29, Feb. 5, 1774, Dartmouth Papers, II, 799, 819.

obstruct the execution of an act of Parliament and restrain lawful trade as if that Parliamentary statute were a public grievance.[20]

Initially the cabinet considered only two measures: closing the port of Boston so as to compel the town to compensate the East India Company for the destruction of the tea, and prosecuting the Boston leaders heading the anti-British movement. But the evidence on which the cabinet could legally act through the courts, according to Wedderburn and Thurlow, was insufficient to warrant prosecution.[21] The ministers now resorted to action by Parliament for a more limited objective, the suppression by legal means of any future challenge to the home government and a restoration of the political balance in the Bay Colony. The administration's program was contained in four bills brought into Parliament between March and May, 1774: the Boston Port Act, the Massachusetts Government Act, the Act for the Impartial Administration of Justice, and the Quartering Act.

The ineffectiveness of local, traditional government in Massachusetts had been decisive. Events in the Bay Colony demonstrated that the executive had insufficient power, or at least that the patriots so controlled the legislative branches and the extralegal bodies that they could nullify any act of the governor and intimidate judicial officials. By the legislation now proposed in Parliament the

20. Report of the Crown Law Officers, Feb. 11, 1774, C.O. 5/160:79.

21. Thurlow and Wedderburn may have had another motive. They may not have wanted to take sole responsibility for warrants to apprehend and transport the patriot leaders to England. William Knox left the following amusing account. He and John Pownall were waiting in the outer room when the Law Officers came out of the session with the ministers. "'Well,' cried Pownall [referring to the signing of the warrants], 'is it done?' 'No,' answered Thurlow, 'nothing is done. Don't you see,' added he, 'that they [the ministers] want to throw the whole responsibility of the business upon the Solicitor-General and me, and who would be such damned fools as to risk themselves for such —— fellows as these. Now if it was George Grenville, who was so damned obstinate that he would go to hell with you before he would desert you, there would be some sense in it.'" H.M.C., *Report on Manuscripts in Various Collections*, VI (London, 1919), 270. On this point see also the entries for July 5 and August 14, 1774, Peter Orlando Hutchinson (ed.), *The Diary and Letters of Thomas Hutchinson* (2 vols., London, 1883–1886), I, 183, 219, for the purported influence of William Murray, Lord Mansfield. The minute of the cabinet of Feb. 28, 1774, by Dartmouth does not indicate that Mansfield was present.

chief executive in Massachusetts could rely on a royally appointed council and magistrates subject to his removal. Consequently the civil government could requisition the army, as it had not been able to do in the crisis during the last months of 1773. To ensure proper facilities for the troops, the Quartering statute allowed the commander-in-chief to requisition quarters independently of the civil magistrates, if need be, under procedures specified within the current Mutiny Act. To eliminate the center of the revolutionary movement all town meetings except those held with the sanction of the governor or those for the purpose of electing representatives would be prohibited.

The ministry did not intend to subvert local, democratic government as such, but only to check the revolutionary movement. Town meetings for the purpose of electing members to the colonial General Court and local officials were still allowed, and the Massachusetts House of Representatives was not disturbed. As the method of appointing the council was to be altered, the army could now be called out to enforce order and support the government. The danger in meeting force with force to execute Parliamentary legislation was that royal officials, both civil and military, might be indicted and tried before prejudiced or inflamed local juries. To provide for the more impartial administration of justice in such cases, trials would be held in some other colony or in England.[22] These were the goals behind the four acts relating to Massachusetts presented to Parliament in the spring of 1774 and labeled "intolerable" and "coercive" by the Whig leaders in America.

Lord North openly explained the ministry's intention in the House of Commons in two speeches on March 21 and March 28. He stressed that the issue was of the highest political consequence. In the first of his addresses he emphasized that the question no longer concerned the "degrees of freedom or restraint" in which the

22. This analysis is based on the following documents: minutes of the cabinet of Jan. 29, Feb. 5, 19, 28, and March 1, 1774, Dartmouth Papers, II, 799, 819, 834, 839, and 842; the "Narrative Case," C.O. 5/7: 1, 25; Dartmouth to the Treasury Board, Feb. 11, 1774, C.O. 5/160:91–92; Dartmouth to Wedderburn and Thurlow, Feb. 5, 1774, C.O. 5/160: 1, 25; and the report of Wedderburn and Thurlow, Feb. 11, 1774, C.O. 5/160: 79–86 (and C.O. 5/247: 192–193). For a fuller discussion of the Massachusetts Acts, the motives behind them and their relation to the crisis in Boston in the fall of 1773, see my article, "The Massachusetts Acts of 1774: Coercive or Preventive?" *Huntington Library Quarterly*, XXVI (1963), 235–252.

colonies were to be held, but whether they should be "totally separated" from the mother country. In Boston, he commented, England and America are "considered as two independent States"— not an inappropriate conclusion to draw from the position previously adopted by Franklin and the Massachusetts Whigs. Boston had been the "ring-leader in all riots," North charged, and had "at all times shewn a desire" to frustrate the laws of Great Britain. The question was no longer whether Parliament had any power to legislate or tax, but whether "we have any authority" in the colonies. Parliament must "punish, controul, or yield to them."[23]

The solution for preserving the authority of the imperial government lay in restoring the balance of government in the colonies, North informed the House of Commons a week later. Events for the past several years in the Bay Colony had demonstrated that "an executive power was wanting" in Massachusetts, and that it was necessary to strengthen the powers of the magistracy and the governor. Apparently there was a "total defect" in the constitutional power of government, for if the "democratic part shews that contempt for obedience to the laws," he asked, "how is the governor to execute any authority vested in him?" The administration called only for regulation of the "irregular assemblies," the town meetings, unless they were held for the annual election of "certain officers, which it is their province to chuse." North claimed to be open to any suggestion, but he stressed that until a balance in government was restored, and the executive free to act, "our regulations here are of no import. . . ."[24]

Never before in the previous decade had the administration taken so firm a position, never before had it been so united at the highest policy level, and never before had the colonial agents and British merchants faced such an obstacle. The ministry demonstrated no willingness to compromise with the lobbyists, and little even to

23. Burke to the New York committee of correspondence, April 6, 1774, Ross J. S. Hoffman (ed.), *Edmund Burke, New York Agent, with his letters to the New York Assembly and intimate correspondence with Charles O'Hara 1761–1776* (Philadelphia, 1956), pp. 245–246; [John Debrett,] *The History, debates, and proceedings of both houses of Parliament . . . 1743 to 1774* (7 vols., London, 1792), VII, 70–72.

24. [Debrett,] *The History, debates, and proceedings of both houses of Parliament*, VII, 104–105.

hear them out. This was clearly demonstrated when the London merchants attempted to prevent the restraining legislation against the Bay Colony from being passed. Fearing the economic consequences of another nonimportation agreement by the colonists, the manufacturers and merchants in the principal cities and towns were alarmed. A few who visited London conferred with Franklin on the course of action to be concerted with the provincial agents.[25] Also apprehensive since the British islands in the Caribbean were dependent on the mainland provinces for foodstuffs, the merchants trading to the West Indies proposed to meet with William Bollan, agent for the council of Massachusetts. They agreed with him that this was "one common cause of all the Colon[ie]s."[26]

But the time was past and the political issue too important for the ministry to listen to the discontented merchants as it had in 1766 and 1770. The British merchants trading to New England were most concerned with restitution to the East India Company, if only because their trade would suffer if the ministry closed the port of Boston, as it proposed to do when Lord North put the finishing touches to the Boston Port bill on March 16. As soon as the merchants trading to the northern provinces learned of the contents of the proposed statute, "the most considerable" among them went in a body to call on the First Lord of the Treasury. They were prepared to go far. The merchants offered "to [be] answerable" to the East India Company for over £16,000—double the value of the tea destroyed—"by way of Compensation. . . ." The Lord Mayor of London himself "repeatedly & publicly declared that he would be Security to the amount of £20,000 for the People of Boston" if only the administration would not introduce the punitive act. The merchants requested six months to come to a settlement with the town of Boston or the assembly of the Bay Colony "confiding in their dispositions" to reimburse or refund the money. But Lord North would "proceed on no other ground" than that the British

25. William Bollan to the committee of correspondence of the Massachusetts Council, April ?, 1774, Peter Force (ed.), *American Archives* (4th and 5th Ser., 9 vols., Washington, D.C., 1837–1853), 4th Ser., I, 234–235; Franklin to Cushing, April 2, 1774, C.O. 5/118:148–149.

26. Bollan to the committee of correspondence of the Massachusetts Council, March 11, 1774, "Bowdoin and Temple Papers," p. 356.

merchants should be "answerable for the future peaceable conduct & entire acquiescence" of the Bay Colonists in receiving British tea. This the merchants "utterly refused as absurd and impossible," as the First Lord of the Treasury probably knew they would. Yet he professed that he meant "nothing inimical" to the trade of Boston or to the "Liberties" of America. Consequently he advised the merchants to "return & set quietly at their Compting Houses & leave their Affairs to his Direction for that their Property should henceforth be better secured than heretofore. . . ."[27]

No longer would the administration tacitly or explicitly as in the past use economic discontent as a political weapon. As North told one official some months later, he knew full well that "all the stir made by the manufacturers" at the time of the repeal of the Stamp Act was made by the "contrivance of the then Ministry" under the Marquis of Rockingham.[28] Indeed, North himself had utilized the economic discontent of the merchants to justify repeal of the Townshend duties in 1770. Now in the face of the seemingly critical challenge from Massachusetts Bay the political issue was paramount. But would the agents, merchants, and most important the Whig leaders in America now realize the futility of economic pressure?

Rebuffed by North, the British merchants as a group did not persevere against the administration. At best a few merchants such as Rose Fuller, William Baker, and David Barclay, Jr. continued the struggle when the ministry presented its program to Parliament.

There remained the lobby of colonial agents to attempt to mitigate the preventive legislation resulting from the Boston Tea Party. But measured by its strength and influence during the preceding decade, the concert of provincial representatives had reached its nadir. Maryland, the Delaware counties, Virginia, and North Carolina still had no agents. Rhode Island had appointed no replacement when Joseph Sherwood died in 1773 and the special agent, Henry Marchant, returned to his native province. Neither had Connecticut filled the vacancy created when Richard Jackson

27. See the undated, unsigned account of this meeting in the Chatham Papers, P.R.O. 30/8/97:260–261. The writer was hostile to North, accusing him of "extreme duplicity."

28. Hutchinson to ?, July 8, 1774, Hutchinson (ed.), *Diary and Letters of Thomas Hutchinson*, I, 182.

became solicitor to the Board of Trade. The colony had not fully empowered Thomas Life to act. For several months palsy incapacitated Barlow Trecothick, agent for New Hampshire.[29] Burke was to conduct himself more as an opposition Member in Parliament than as an agent for the assembly of New York. Charles Garth, also a Member of Parliament and agent for South Carolina, does not seem to have been very active.[30] Perhaps he realized as early as 1774 the seriousness of the political crisis. Within a year he was to support the administration on the American issue.[31] Only three agents remained to protest against the ministerial program: Franklin, agent for Georgia, New Jersey, Pennsylvania, and the Massachusetts House of Representatives; and Arthur Lee and William Bollan, alternative agents, for the lower house and council of the Bay Colony respectively. None of these three men stood highly with the administration, with both Franklin and Lee having been positively associated with the same revolutionary Whigs in Boston against whom the ministry was directing its program.[32] Moreover,

29. See William Lee to Richard Henry Lee, Sept. 10, 1774, Worthington C. Ford (ed.), *Letters of William Lee, sheriff and alderman of London; commercial agent of the Continental Congress in France; and minister to the courts of Vienna and Berlin, 1766–1783* (3 vols., Brooklyn, 1891), I, 96–97.

30. In December, 1773 Garth submitted a petition to the Privy Council, but I have not been able to learn its contents. See John Pownall to the clerk of the council, Dec. 17, 1773, C.O. 5/133:193.

31. See the entries for February 11, and February 26, 1775, Hutchinson (ed.), *Diary and Letters of Thomas Hutchinson*, I, 376, 396.

32. Early in 1774 the Earl of Dartmouth received an account of an incriminating letter Lee had sent Thomas Cushing in Boston. Lee approved of the intercolonial committees of correspondence proposed by the Virginia House of Burgesses in 1773. The associate agent was "clearly of the Opinion, that the Declaratory Act is a mere Nullity," so that if the Americans obtained repeal of all the Revenue Acts passed since 1764, "with all their pernicious appendages, it will be enough." If the British were obliged to "retract from the exercise of their assumed power now, when will they be able to resume it?" Lee had asked. He suggested that the Whigs remain quiet for the present, but only until the "gentle Course of Nature shall bring us to maturity and Independence. . . ." After this letter had been read at the Boston town meeting, Governor Hutchinson had obtained a rough transcript from an informer and sent it to Dartmouth in England with the admonition that although Lee had warned the Americans against denying the supremacy of Parliament until the colonists were better prepared, the "plan for a confederacy" against Great Britain "was highly criminal, and this correspondence has had a

after the treatment Franklin had received from Wedderburn in the Cockpit early that year on the hearing concerning the Massachusetts petition calling for the removal of Hutchinson and Oliver, he had decided that it was pointless for him to act any longer as agent for the Massachusetts House of Representatives. This left Arthur Lee to act as associate agent, but the Virginian chose this of all times to "go abroad for a few Months." The departure of Lee determined Franklin to remain in London to act unofficially with other Americans then resident in the imperial capital.[33] He realized, perhaps, that there was little to be done to counteract the government's program in Parliament. Some years earlier he had pointed out to an American correspondent that little could be achieved in the imperial legislature if not supported by the administration. There was no hope for any measure the ministry actively opposed.[34]

All efforts to block or delay the administration's program revolved about the attempts of William Bollan, agent for the Massachusetts council, and a group of colonists then in London to petition against the government's proposals. After an unsuccessful attempt in January to appeal directly to the monarch,[35] Bollan asked Henry Seymour Conway to present a petition to the House of Commons. While agreeing to support the Massachusetts remonstrance, the former Secretary of State refused to present it. Bollan then approached Alderman Richard Oliver, but to little avail. Finally, at the request of the Lord Mayor of London, Sir Joseph Mawbrey agreed to present Bollan's petition on March 14, when the administration asked permission of the Commons to bring in the Boston Port bill. After all of Bollan's efforts, however, the House of Commons refused to hear him. Evidently "Governor" Thomas Pownall, now

most mischievous effect" in Massachusetts. See A[rthur] L[ee] to [Thomas Cushing], n.d., Dartmouth Papers, I, ii, 922; and Hutchinson to Dartmouth (private), March 30, 1774, Dartmouth Papers, I, ii, 964. This letter, in addition to others by Lee and Franklin, led the ministry to consider the possibility of instituting charges of treason against the two agents.

33. Franklin to Cushing, April 2, 1774, C.O. 5/118:148; Franklin to Cushing, April 16, 1774, Smyth (ed.), *Writings of Franklin*, VI, 229.

34. Franklin to Joseph Galloway, Feb. 17, 1768, *ibid.*, V, 98.

35. The petition of William Bollan to the King dated Jan. 26, 1774, Dartmouth Papers, II, 796.

siding with the administration, persuaded the members to reject Bollan, since he was not the "proper" agent for Massachusetts.[36] The major effort on behalf of the Bostonians came on March 25 with the third reading of the bill closing the port. Brass Crosby of the London mercantile community offered a petition from Bollan, who "stiled himself agent for the Council of Massachusetts Bay," but again the House of Commons would not accept this office. Bollan did not have "due Authority to act or appear in that Capacity." The agent for the council was not agent for the colony. Nor would the House of Commons receive any agent unless chosen by the constituent parts of the corporation. Many members with whom Franklin had conferred expected a petition from him as agent for the House of Representatives, but the Pennsylvanian, now considering himself only a private individual after the treatment he had received from Wedderburn in the Cockpit, chose only to act with other Americans then residing in London, including Stephen Sayre and William Lee, in presenting their own petition against the Boston Port bill.

Drawn up by the merchant Lee and presented by the Lord Mayor of London, this petition was intended to allow the colonists to register a protest. Although read to the Commons it did little good. Neither did the verbal efforts of the West Indian merchant, Rose Fuller, or Burke, the agent for the lower house of the New York assembly, who charged that the ministry was hurrying through the bill. The members of Parliament had refused to hear Bollan on the grounds that he was not the properly authorized agent. ". . . you have not now one left in England," Burke maintained, "to be heard on behalf of any of the Colonies. . . ." The Whig politician was conveniently forgetting himself and another member of Parliament, Charles Garth, the agent for South Carolina. But whether or not the Commons heard the American view mattered little. Determined to act, the administration had the bulk of opinion with it. The House of Commons rejected Bollan's petition, 170 to 40, and then passed the Boston Port bill without a division. In commenting on the day's events, George III wondered how forty members

36. Bollan to the committee of correspondence of the Massachusetts council, March 11, 15, 1774, "Bowdoin and Temple Papers," pp. 355–356, 360–361; Force (ed.), *American Archives*, 4th Ser., I, 35; and *Commons Journal*, XXXIV, 561.

could be found ready to admit Bollan in an "unacknowledged Office" of agent for the Massachusetts council.[37] So far had the controversies in the provincial governments on the appointment of agents damaged the office!

Bollan and the London merchants persisted against the Boston Port bill in the House of Lords. On March 28, Lord Wycombe and the Earl of Stair presented petitions from the Massachusetts agent and the Americans resident in London. David Barclay, Jr., a Quaker merchant who was to replace Barlow Trecothick as chairman of the London merchants trading to America, also presented a memorial. They accomplished nothing, as the Lords passed the Boston Port bill on March 30 without a dissenting vote. On April 8, the Treasury dispatched orders to close the Massachusetts port.[38]

The American lobby had made no showing against the ministry. Sentiment in Parliament against the town was overwhelming and the imperial legislature was willing to support whatever punitive measure the administration considered necessary. But two agents, Franklin and Bollan, still carried on the fight. Bollan hoped that the merchants of the East India Company would assist the colonies; possibly the British manufacturers, now "alarmed and stirring," might also support the colonial spokesmen. Immediately following the passage of the Boston Port Act, several of the principal manufacturers from the towns traveled to London and arranged to dine with Franklin in order to concert a plan against the government's program.[39]

37. Franklin to Cushing, April 2, 1774, C.O. 5/118:148; Charles Garth to the South Carolina committee of correspondence, March 31, 1774, Charles Garth–South Carolina committee of correspondence Letter Book, ff. 168–169; Force (ed.), *American Archives*, 4th Ser., I, 46, 50; *Commons Journal*, XXXIV, 595, 596; [Debrett,] *History, debates, and proceedings of both houses of Parliament*, VII, 83, 97; and George III to North, March 25, 1774, Fortescue (ed.), *Correspondence of George III*, III, 86.

38. Great Britain, Parliament, *Journals of the House of Lords* (London, 1558—), XXXIV, 98, 612; Force (ed.), *American Archives*, 4th Ser., I, 59–60; Bollan to the committee of the Massachusetts council, April ?, 1774, *ibid.*, 4th Ser., I, 234–235; and John Robinson (Secretary to the Treasury) to John Pownall, April 8, 1774, C.O. 5/145:241. See also the minute of the Treasury Board, C.O. 5/145:243–246.

39. Burke to the New York committee of correspondence, April 6, 1774, Hoffman (ed.), *Edmund Burke, New York Agent*, pp. 246–247; Bollan to the committee of the Massachusetts council, April ?, 1774, Force (ed.), *American Archives*, 4th Ser., I, 234–235; Franklin to Cushing, April 2, 1774, C.O. 5/118:148–149; Franklin to Cushing, April 16, 1774, Smyth (ed.), *Writings of Franklin*, VI, 229.

The Massachusetts Acts, 1774

Undeterred, the administration introduced two further bills relating to Massachusetts. On April 21 the opposition again interjected the agency question during the debate on the bill for revising the charter of the Bay Colony. They contended that the Americans where not allowed to speak. It was extraordinary, Sir George Savile charged, that the House of Lords admitted William Bollan as an American agent but that the House of Commons refused him permission to testify. Information by Bollan was vital since the administration was founding its bills on insufficient evidence. Henry Conway took the same line, adding that Parliament could not "break into a [charter] right without hearing the parties." Whether or not Bollan was fully authorized as an agent to speak for the colony of Massachusetts mattered little. Conway could see "no harm upon this occasion, in stretching a point." He would rather hear Bollan as agent of America, "though he is a little irregular in his appointment," than have it said that the bill altering the government of the Bay Colony passed without a full hearing of the interested parties.

The politicians of the Rockingham faction persisted in opposing the administration through the agents. Four days later, Willam Dowdeswell announced that he meant to present a petition from Bollan, "the Agent of America," before the third reading of the bill for the impartial administration of justice. Dowdeswell was giving Bollan an even grander title! On April 28, Rockingham's Chancellor of the Exchequer moved for leave to present a petition from the agent of the Massachusetts council requesting that Parliament postpone the Massachusetts bills until Bollan had received instructions from his constituents. This time the Commons heard the agent's memorial and the arguments of Savile, Burke, and Thomas Townshend that it was unjust to pass laws without hearing from the Americans. Their pleas made little difference. The Commons rejected the petition, 95 to 32 and then voted down a motion to defer the bills for another four months.[40] According to Charles Garth, the House of Commons refused to acknowledge the right of one branch of the Massachusetts legislature to appoint "an agent Generally. . . ." Burke interpreted this stand, or so he informed

40. *Commons Journal,* XXXIV, 667; [Debrett,] *History, debates, and proceedings of both houses of Parliament,* VII, 215, 218–219, 228; Cobbett (ed.), *Parliamentary History,* XVII, 1290–1291, 1297; and North to George III, Fortescue (ed.), *Correspondence of George III,* Vol. III, 99.

his New York constituents, as a declaration by the spokesmen of the administration in the House of Commons that the few colonies, and New York in particular, had "no agent properly authorized to communicate your desires in that character to Parliament."[41] The factional disputes in the colonial governments had had their effect; and the Massachusetts agents were involved with the patriot movement. But it made little difference whether the agents of the Bay Colony were fully authorized or not, for the administration was determined to act.

Since the Commons had rejected Bollan merely as an agent for the Massachusetts council, and not the full government of the colony, four days later on May 2, Savile attempted to present a petition against the Massachusetts bills from the Americans resident in London. William Lee, Franklin, and Stephen Sayre headed this group. They charged that the bills for administering justice and altering the government of the Bay Colony constituted destruction of charter rights without hearing the parties concerned and consequently was a "dangerous system of judicial tyranny." Their petition made no difference, indeed, if they had intended that it should. By substantial margins the House of Commons passed the regulation bill on May 2 and the bill for impartial administration of justice four days later. The Americans made one more effort in the House of Lords, but both measures easily went through the upper chamber.[42]

The spokesmen for the colonies had made no impression during the passage of the four Massachusetts bills, but they were able at least to modify one Parliamentary statute. Regardless of the interpretation of the Americans and Britons such as the agent Burke or the merchant William Baker, who advised them, the final measure dealing with America enacted by Parliament in 1774, the Quebec Act, was not related to the crisis in the Bay Colony. Unfortunately

41. Garth to the South Carolina committee of correspondence April 32 [*sic*], 1774, Charles Garth–South Carolina committee of correspondence Letter Book, f. 171; Burke to the New York committee of correspondence, May 4, 1774, Hoffman (ed.), *Edmund Burke, New York Agent*, p. 251.

42. *Commons Journal*, XXXIV, 696, 702, 712; Cobbett (ed.), *Parliamentary History*, XVII, 1296–1300; *Lords Journal*, XXXIV, 182; and [Debrett,] *History, debates, and proceedings of both houses of Parliament*, VII, 234, 251–252.

it followed so closely that many considered it one of the "coercive" laws and demanded its repeal along with the Massachusetts Acts. By the summer of 1773, after more than a decade of discussions and false starts, the North ministry resolved to settle more equitably the affairs of Quebec,[43] a province whose boundaries and civil-religious establishment had been temporarily fixed by the Proclamation of 1763. The Quebec Act provided for an appointed governor and council possessing full legislative powers, combined English criminal and French civil law, allowed complete toleration and full legal rights to Roman Catholics, and extended the boundaries of the province, previously restricted by the Proclamation of 1763, to include the area north and west of the Ohio River.

The Quebec Act did not establish "absolute" rule and was not designed, as Jefferson charged in the Declaration of Independence, "to render it at once an example and fit instrument for introducing the same absolute rule" into the other British colonies to the south.[44] The governmental and ecclesiastic provisions of the act followed the wishes of the French Canadians who comprised the vast majority of the population, while the extension of the boundaries of the

43. For evidence that the government was contemplating the program later incorporated into the Quebec Act before the crisis over the tea incidents, see Dartmouth to Daniel Blouin, Dec. 1, 1773, C.O. 5/74:361–362; Dartmouth to Hector Cramahé, Dec. 1, 1773, C.O. 42/32:93–94, transcript, Public Archives of Canada; James Marriot to the Earl of Suffolk, Nov. 27, 1773, and Suffolk to Marriot, Nov. 28, 1773, S.P. 37/10:182–183; Francis Maseres to Dartmouth, Aug. 26, 1773, Arthur S. Doughty and Adam Shortt (eds.), *Documents relating to the constitutional history of Canada, 1759–1791* (Ottawa, 1907), p. 375; and Apsley to Dartmouth, *ibid.*, p. 374n3.

44. This was not mere propagandistic rhetoric, but reflected an erroneous view held by many colonists. Gurdon Saltonstall, for one, saw an even greater plot. The Quebec Act presaged the overthrow of the constitution in England! He wrote Silas Deane on August 29, 1774: "The Quebeck Act is the finishing Stroke for the Ministry. That the Roman Catholic Religion is there establish'd does not surprize me; you well know that it has been my opinion for many years, that [it] was at the bottom of the Ministerial System; and that it should make its appearance at this juncture is most fortunate for America and G. Britain also.

"This will make Britains [*sic*] see, the Acts to abridge American Liberty were preparatory to the alteration of the British Constitutions at home and abroad, and therefore they will throw their interest into the American scale." "The [Silas] Deane Papers," New York Historical Society *Collections*, XIX (New York, 1886), 4.

province represented the practical culmination of a decade of British policy for the North American interior. Although such agents as Franklin and Richard Jackson had been certain in 1767 that the colonial assemblies would adequately regulate the frontier and Indian affairs, the provinces had not effectively dealt with these problems when control was returned to them in 1768.[45]

Despite the obvious need for the Quebec bill, the measure met opposition in London by some agents and merchants. Perhaps because the London merchants feared that under French civil law they would be unable to collect debts owed them, those trading to Quebec petitioned the House of Commons against the proposed statute. Even after it was passed they persisted in their opposition. The Lord Mayor, Council, and Aldermen of London assembled formally at Saint James's to ask the King not to sign the measure.[46] Nonetheless, the monarch gave his assent on June 22. At best the opposition in Parliament led by Burke and William Baker had been able to amend the bill so that the boundary of Quebec would not be constructively defined in terms of the boundaries of the other colonies. Burke had been particularly active in securing a precise line. As Baker put it, this set a "defined bound to despotism" by drawing a line to protect New York and Pennsylvania.[47] But the British

45. The North administration had arrived at this solution by a process of elimination after every other expedient to ensure the lands reserved for the Indians and to conduct the trade with the natives under proper regulations had failed. These goals were considered essential to the stability and security of the frontier and hinterland of North America. Direct imperial control had proved impractical because of the difficulty of financing and maintaining royal garrisons and an imperial system of Indian affairs. The British colonists had not acknowledged the need for either imperial control or taxes to finance the system. When given the opportunity as early as 1768, they had failed to assume responsibility for, or exercise effective control of, Indian relations and frontier conditions. In the resulting chaos, a general Indian war seemed imminent. Only the Canadians had demonstrated the willingness and ability to deal satisfactorily with the tribes. For the background to the Quebec Act, see J. M. Sosin, *Whitehall and the Wilderness: The Middle West in British Colonial Policy, 1760–1775* (Lincoln, Nebr., 1961), pp. 211–255.

46. *Commons Journal*, XXXIV, 795. The petition and the address of the City of London are in S.P. 37/10:231.

47. See Baker to Charles Lee, Sept. 3, 1774, "The [Charles] Lee Papers," New York Historical Society *Collections* (4 vols., New York, 1871–1874), IV (1871), 132;

government intended neither despotism nor tyranny in passing the Quebec Act or the four previous measures called "intolerable" by the American colonists. This partly explains the failure of the agents and merchants.

The gravity of the situation in America, the weakness of the lobby itself, the unity within the ministry, and the attitude in Parliament that a firm position was necessary to counteract a revolutionary movement which had merely been encouraged by former British concessions, all further account for the failure of the agents and merchants. It is doubtful if they would have been able appreciably to alter the result, even if the agents had been recognized as fully accredited spokesmen for the Bay Colony.

Although the colonial agents had failed to prevent the passage of these laws they still had an important role to play. If the Empire was to survive the crisis of 1774, it was essential that both sides fully understand the position of the other. Here the agents would be decisive, for the American assessment of the Massachusetts Acts would depend, in great measure, on the evaluation of Franklin, the Lees, and Burke. It was soon evident that they did not agree with the administration.

The ministers did not consider the acts passed in 1774 as harsh. They had sought by legal means to put down what they considered an unjustifiable revolutionary movement aimed at nullifying imperial authority. To the imperial officials events in the Bay Colony had demonstrated that the executive had insufficient power, or at least that the patriots so controlled the extralegal bodies that they could nullify any action of the governor and intimidate judicial officers. By the legislation enacted in 1774 the ministry did not intend to limit the democratic or representative elements in the Massachusetts government as such, but only to restrict the town meetings in so far as the revolutionary patriots used them to further the anti-British movement. As Lord North put it in the House of Commons on March 28, 1774, the administration merely sought to "remedy a defect" in the constitutional power of the governor to execute the authority vested in him.[48] It sought to restore that balance in

---

and Burke to the New York committee of correspondence, Aug. 2, 1774, Hoffman (ed.), *Edmund Burke, New York Agent*, pp. 256–258.

48. [Debrett,] *History, debates, and proceedings of both houses of Parliament*, VII, 104.

Agents and Merchants

government embodied in the Glorious Revolution, a mixed or blended form in which the executive balanced the representative assembly. Many of the colonists themselves shared this concept of an ideal government.[49]

The position of the administration on the crisis of 1773–1774 was best stated in a letter the Secretary of State sent to Joseph Reed in Philadelphia, the scene shortly of the first Continental Congress. A "little time" would convince all men who can think with "coolness and temper, that the liberties of America are not so much in danger from anything that Parliament had done, or is likely to do here, as from the violence and misconduct of America itself." The idea prevalent in the colonies that the imperial government intended to "enslave" the Americans was an "absurdity." On the contrary, it wished the colonists to "enjoy all the freedom and rights which belong to British subjects," without exception save those arising from their connection with the mother country. What was the crucial issue, then? The colonists, particularly the Bostonians, had resisted the authority of Parliament and opposed the execution of its laws "in a manner clearly treasonable." Consequently the home government, although unwilling to resort to extreme measures,

49. As one writer has noted, Americans in the eighteenth century did not consider democracy or any other form of government, monarchy or aristocracy, as practical or desirable in its pure form. To them the ideal was a combination, a blend of government types. Not only did most colonists "regard the English constitution as the ideal mixed government," but they "believed that their own colonial governments were copies, or imitations, of the English." Roy N. Lokken, "The Concept of Democracy in Colonial Political Thought," *William and Mary Quarterly*, 3rd Ser., XVI (1959), 570, 573, 574. And after all, the alteration of the Massachusetts government merely imposed on that colony a system which had existed for some time in the other royal provinces. One may be struck by the common appeal to the principles of popular sovereignty and rule of the people in the arguments the American patriots used against British measures, but this appeal may have been an aberration. It did not constitute the basis of American government as established in the federal Constitution of 1787, when the Founding Fathers returned to the principle of mixed government although in a less obvious form than had existed during the colonial period. Despite the recent attacks on particular economic interpretations of the Constitution—valid as they may be—the delegates to the Constitutional Convention did not create a democratic government, for they deliberately set bounds on legislative authority and checks on the power of majorities. Not until the rise of organized political parties in the nineteenth century, both in England and America, were impediments to popular government removed.

had exercised the undisputed right of every government to punish the most flagrant offenders, reform abuses, and prevent "like extremeties" in the future. Would the colonists submit to this legislation? If they did not, in effect, they were declaring themselves no longer a part of the British Empire. They were then altering the basis of the controversy, for no longer would they be contending that Parliament did not have the right to pass legislation in particular fields, but that it had no right to legislate for any.[50]

In 1774 the British ministry was not culpable of attempting to subvert representative government in the colonies or depriving individuals of rights, but of trying to maintain its authority and in failing to make clear to the Americans what it was attempting to do and why. It was further at fault in underestimating the strength of the American reaction, but this, in turn, was conditioned by the estimate of the situation the provincial agents sent back to the Whig leaders in the colonies.

The most influential agents and their associates in London misrepresented to their constituents in America the nature and intent of the Massachusetts Acts, the political situation in England, and the course of action most likely to force the imperial government to accommodate the colonists. Burke and William Baker informed their correspondents that the recent legislation was tyrannical. The New York agent went even further in his messages to the provincial committee of correspondence. The administration had passed the late acts not only to bring "refractory" Boston and Massachusetts to heel, but also to hold out an "example of terror" to the other provinces. This was pure fantasy. Partisan politics had warped Burke's judgment, but his letters had their effect.

The contents of Burke's correspondence were common knowledge, for inasmuch as he had not enjoined the provincial committee of correspondence to secrecy, they had thought it proper to communicate his sentiments to their friends. Since the agent's correspondence was "pretty generally known," the delegates from Massachusetts passing through New York on their way to the meeting of the first Continental Congress at Philadelphia were

---

50. Dartmouth to Joseph Reed, July 11, 1774, William B. Reed, *Life and Correspondence of Joseph Reed* (2 vols., Philadelphia, 1847), I, 73 (draft in Dartmouth Papers, I, ii, 991).

soon "enlightened" on the situation in London.[51] Other delegates received similar intelligence from London. Arthur Lee,
the associate agent for the Massachusetts House of Representatives,
wrote to his brother in Virginia, Richard Henry Lee, on the best
course of action. A general resolution by the colonists "to break
off all commercial intercourse" with Great Britain until the
Americans were secure in their liberties was the only advisable
mode of defense. This might be "irksome" initially, but the
colonists would be amply compensated not only by saving
money and becoming "independent of these petty tyrants," the
British merchants, but also by securing their "general liberties."

Both the Lee brothers in London suffered from paranoid men-
talities. The merchant William Lee also advised their relations in
Virginia, and he too painted a distorted, if not altogether false,
picture, not an uncommon practice among the Lees. The British
merchants and manufacturers concerned in the American trade
"are almost universally your enemies," he informed Richard Henry.
They had been "forwarding the late iniquitious measures with all
their force. . . ." Only William Lee himself, Barlow Trecothick,
and a few others had been friendly to the American cause. Consequently the colonists must support only those merchants who had
"avowedly" espoused the American position and apply economic
sanctions against all others.[52]

Benjamin Franklin advised the Whig leaders to follow the same
course recommended by the Lees to force repeal of the Massachusetts Acts. The agent had reason to believe, he informed Thomas
Cushing, that a "strong Push" would be made at the beginning

51. Burke to the New York committee of correspondence, May 4, 1774, Lucy
S. Sutherland (ed.), *The Correspondence of Edmund Burke Volume II July 1768–June
1774* (Cambridge and Chicago, 1960), p. 534; Burke to the New York committee
of correspondence, Aug. 2, 1774, Hoffman (ed.), *Edmund Burke, New York Agent*,
p. 254; John Adams' diary, entry for Aug. 22, 1774, in Adams (ed.), *Works of
John Adams*, II, 350–351; and the New York committee of correspondence to
Burke, May 31, 1774, Burke Correspondence, Wentworth-Woodhouse Muniments,
Sheffield City Library, Sheffield, England.

52. Arthur Lee to Richard Henry Lee, March 18, 1774, Force (ed.), *American
Archives*, 4th Ser., I, 229; Ralph Izard to Henry Laurens, Aug. 22, 1774, Anne
Izard Dees (ed.), *Correspondence of Mr. Ralph Izard, of South Carolina, from the Year
1774 to 1804, with a Short Memoir* (2 vols., New York, 1844), I, 14; and William Lee
to Richard Henry Lee, Sept. 10, 1774, Ford (ed.), *Letters of William Lee*, I, 95–97.

of the next Parliamentary session to have all the late statutes "revers'd, and a solemn Assurance given America that no future Attempts shall be made to tax us without our consent." Much would depend on the proceedings of the congress at Philadelphia. "Unanimity and Firmness" by the delegates "will have great Weight here" and, he speculated, "probably [will] unhorse the present wild riders." In further letters to Cushing and Joseph Galloway, a Pennsylvania delegate to the congress, he repeated this argument. "If you declare & resolve your rights, and confederate not to use British Manufactures till they are acknowledged & confirmed here," he wrote Galloway, "you will certainly carry your Point." The ministry "must be disbanded & their late Acts repeal'd."[53]

Franklin had been correct in his previous prognostication that the calling of an intercolonial congress would bring on the final crisis. In view of the relations he had enjoyed with the Rockingham ministry in 1766 and with North later, he should have realized that economic coercion had had an artificial effect then and would be pointless now. Complaints in the past by the merchants had been effective only when supported, sustained, and encouraged by the administration. In the summer of 1774 the ministry would contend for restitution to the East India Company and a "state of quiet" in Boston.[54] There would be no tax imposed on the Americans except the symbolic duty on tea. The determination of the British government was reflected in the attitude of George III: "the dye is now cast, the Colonies must either submit or triumph." If the British unremittingly pursued the measures already adopted, the King was certain that the colonists would submit.[55] As George III penned these words, the delegates to the first Continental Congress were meeting at Philadelphia. They must now decide.

53. Franklin to Cushing, June 1, 1774, C.O. 5/118:160; Franklin to Cushing, Sept. 15, 1774, C.O. 5/118:167–168; Franklin to Galloway, Sept. 7, 1774, Benjamin Franklin Papers, American Philosophical Society Library, Philadelphia, XLV, 92; and Franklin to Cushing, Oct. 6, 1774, Smyth (ed.), *Writings of Franklin*, VI, 249–250.

54. Governor William Tryon to Cadwallader Colden, Aug. 18, 1774, "Letters and Papers of Cadwallader Colden," LVI (1923), 243; Bollan to Dartmouth, Sept. 29, 1774, Dartmouth Papers, I, ii, 1030.

55. George III to Lord North, Sept. 11, 1774, Fortescue (ed.), *Correspondence of George III*, Vol. III, 131.

CHAPTER VIII

Failure of a Lobby, 1774–1775

I

IN the spring of 1774 ships westward bound across the Atlantic brought to America news of the recent laws the British government had enacted for Massachusetts. They also carried advice from the few remaining colonial agents in London to their constituents on the best course the Americans should adopt: economic sanctions to intimidate the British merchants and, in turn, the imperial government. The counsel of the agents and their associates such as William Lee merely confirmed the apparent success of past tactics in meeting similar crises. During the controversies over the stamp and Townshend duties, the colonists had buttressed statements of their constitutional and political rights with economic pressure. Hitherto the refusal to purchase British goods until colonial grievances had been redressed had appeared successful. Why abandon the formula now? Past experience and the recommendations of their trusted advisers in London indicated the course the Whig leaders would follow in 1774.[1]

1. Evidently British merchants knew what to expect. Following the passage of the Massachusetts Acts, Dennis DeBerdt, son of the deceased Massachusetts agent, wrote to his brother-in-law in Philadelphia inquiring if there would be any more business for the British merchants. Joseph Reed thought not. He predicted that they would be ruined; one-half the debts owed them would never be paid "unless there should be an immediate repeal of all the obnoxious laws..." Joseph Reed to Dennis DeBerdt, Sept. 26, 1774, William B. Reed, *Life and Correspondence of Joseph Reed* (2 vols., Philadelphia, 1847), I, 80.

Failure of a Lobby, 1774–1775

Yet the counsel of such agents as Franklin and Arthur Lee was misleading, for the situation in 1774 was not at all comparable to the previous crises in the past decade. Moreover, economic pressure alone had never been successful in the past, and there was no chance now that sanctions would cause the overthrow of the North administration and a repeal of the "intolerable" acts. In operating on these assumptions to achieve a limited goal, repeal of objectionable legislation passed since 1763, the delegates to the Continental Congress were to find themselves committed to a position—independence—they had not anticipated and, perhaps, had not initially desired. Only Edmund Burke, biased as he was in his analysis of the motives of the ministers, accurately informed his constituents of the strength of the government and the basic political goal behind the recent legislation. The North administration, stronger and more firmly entrenched than ever, seemed determined to enforce obedience to the British revenue laws. Moreover, the imperial government had legislated on the assumption that the Whig leaders in America sought independence. The New York committee of correspondence, for its part, was distressed that this issue should have been raised at all. "A Desire of dissolving our Connection with the Parent Country," it protested to the agent, "is an Idea to which every good American is a Stranger, however difficult it may be with Precision to state the true Extent of their Dependence."[2] This was the crux of the matter.

In the winter of 1774, colonial agents, British merchants, and members of the administration were to attempt to solve the problem, to formulate a more precise, yet more liberal, constitution allowing greater home rule for the Americans within the Empire. The success of their efforts depended on each side understanding the views of the other. Here the agents could play a singular role.

2. Burke to the New York committee of correspondence, May 4, 1774, Lucy S. Sutherland (ed.), *The Correspondence of Edmund Burke Volume II July 1768–June 1774* (Cambridge and Chicago, 1960), p. 534; Burke to the New York committee of correspondence, Aug. 2, 1774, Ross J. S. Hoffman (ed.), *Edmund Burke, New York Agent, with his letters to the New York Assembly and intimate correspondence with Charles O'Hara 1761–1776* (Philadelphia, 1956), p. 254; and the New York committee of correspondence to Burke, May 31, 1774, Burke Correspondence, Wentworth-Woodhouse Muniments, Sheffield City Library, Sheffield, England.

II

When the congress met in Philadelphia in September, 1774, Joseph Galloway presented a plan of union for the colonies within the British Empire. He had already sent an outline of his proposal to Richard Jackson, former agent for Pennsylvania and now solicitor to the Board of Trade, to be transmitted to the Secretary of State. Galloway had speculated that the congress would employ emissaries or agents in England to propose some plan of reconciliation. When the delegates began to assemble in Philadelphia the Whig leader pursued this line, arguing that it was necessary to send "Commissioners fully authorized" to the British court to present any plan of accommodation the congress might adopt. By having commissioners in London the delegates would no longer be "misled by News paper Accounts and private Letters," but could proceed instead on "solid Information and Principles of Safety. . . ." Otherwise the petitions and plans of the congress would have little effect.[3]

Rather than adopting Galloway's plan of union within the Empire or his proposal to send authorized commissioners to England, the Continental Congress followed the advice of Franklin and Arthur Lee. On October 20 the delegates drew up articles of association to exert economic pressure, and five days later they ordered an address drawn up enunciating the rights and grievances of America, to be delivered by the standing agents then in London. In a covering letter drafted by Richard Henry Lee and John Jay, the delegates gave the agents the "strongest proof of our reliance on your zeal and attachment to the happiness of America and the cause of liberty. . . ." Yet the congress failed to give the agents discretionary powers; rather it restricted them to a fixed course of action. There was no room for negotiation or compromise. The agents were to deliver the address to the King, publish the colonial grievances in the English press, furnish copies of the congressional memorial to the people of Great Britain in the great trading towns, and obtain support for the colonial cause from the English merchants. If the British government did not satisfy the grievances of the colonists,

3. Jackson to Dartmouth, Dec. 21, 1774, enclosing Galloway to Jackson, Aug. 10, 1774, Dartmouth Papers, William Salt Library, Stafford, England, II, 1031; and Galloway to Franklin, Sept. 3, 1774, Edmund C. Burnett (ed.), *Letters of the Members of the Continental Congress* (8 vols., Washington, D.C., 1921–1938), I, 6.

the agents were then to send to the speakers of the respective provincial assemblies the "earliest information of the most authentick accounts" they could collect of all "such conduct and designs of the Ministry, or Parliament, as it may concern America to know."[4] On October 26 Charles Thomson, secretary of the congress, sent the agents their instructions. Six days later he sent them the address to the King and the memorial to the British people. By these documents the administration would see that "it is not a little faction, but the whole of American freeholders from Nova Scotia to Georgia that now complain & apply for redress," Thomson wrote. The colonists would "resist rather than submit."[5] The Continental Congress had left no other option.

4. Worthington C. Ford *et al.* (eds.), *Journals of the Continental Congress, 1774–1789, Edited from the Original Records in the Library of Congress* (34 vols., Washington, D.C., 1904–1937), I, 104; Peter Force (ed.), *American Archives* (4th and 5th Ser., 9 Vols. Washington, D.C., 1837–1853), 4th Ser., I, 929; Letter to the agents, Oct. 26, 1774, in *ibid.*, 4th Ser., I, 932–933; and James C. Ballagh (ed.), *The Letters of Richard Henry Lee* (2 vols., New York, 1911–1914), I, 125–126. The address to the King is in Ford *et al.* (eds.), *Journals of the Continental Congress*, I, 115–121.

5. See "Memorandum Agents to whom the Address to the King is to be sent," Force (ed.), *American Archives*, 4th Ser., I, 938; Charles Thomson to Benjamin Franklin, Nov. 1, 1774, Benjamin Franklin Papers, Library of Congress, Ser. I, ii, f. 263.

By the time the documents arrived in London, Arthur Lee, after traveling night and day, had returned from Rome. Filled with fire and passion for the coming contest, he would not be content with a mere repeal of the "obnoxious" acts passed the previous session, but only with the "most solemn ratification of an American Bill of Rights." The "whole world would lament a pusillanimous submission," he warned Thomas Cushing. "Success is in the hand of God—our Cause is most just & we may with confidence appeal to him." Arthur Lee to [Thomas Cushing], Dec. 6, 1774, C.O. 5/118:187–189. See also Cushing to Lee, Feb. ?, 1775, Force (ed.), *American Archives*, 4th Ser., I, 1208.

Another American arrived in London that fall on a mysterious errand. At the "urgent solicitation of a number of warm friends," Josiah Quincy, Jr. had left his native Massachusetts for a hazardous journey to the mother country—indeed fatal, for he died on the return voyage. By his own account the "design" of his mission was "to be kept as long secret as possible. . . ." Rumor had it that he was the agent for the congress appointed and commissioned at the "Court of Great Britain" with credentials and instructions issued before his departure. It was not until he left for England, however, that Joseph Reed sent him the journals of the meeting at Philadelphia. Despite the secrecy of the mission General Thomas Gage, now Governor of Massachusetts, had forewarned the ministry—a development

Agents and Merchants

The tactics adopted by the delegates at Philadelphia were bankrupt inasmuch as they were based on faulty assumptions, and inasmuch as they left the agents no alternative in negotiating. Moreover, the channel they now used, the traditional agencies, was practically defunct. For some years now Rhode Island, the Delaware counties, Maryland, Virginia, and North Carolina had no agents, and many of the agents remaining showed themselves less than enthusiastic for the American cause that winter. On receiving instructions from the congress on December 19, Franklin sent a note to the other agents requesting that they meet the following noon at Waghorn's Coffee House in Westminster to consider the time and manner for presenting the petition to the King. The response of his colleagues was disheartening. Garth was out of town during the Christmas holiday, and it was doubtful if he would join the other agents. That winter he openly professed support for the administration's American program.[6] Burke, Paul Wentworth of New Hampshire, and Thomas Life all "declined being concerned" with the congressional petition, and "without consulting each other gave the same reason, viz., that they had no instructions

Quincy would have doubtless regretted, for he wrote John Dickinson shortly before his departure that should it transpire that he was going to England, "our public enemies here would be as indefatigable and perservering in my injury, as they have been in the cause in which I am engaged, heart and hand. . . ." Quincy to John Dickinson, Aug. 20, 1774, Josiah Quincy, *Memoir of the Life of Josiah Quincy, Junior, of Massachusetts Bay, 1744–1775* (Boston, 1825), p. 173; Quincy (Senior) to Quincy (Junior), Oct. [26], 1774, *ibid.*, pp. 182–184; and Reed to Quincy, Oct. 25, 1774, Reed, *Life and Correspondence of Joseph Reed*, I, 375. In London, Quincy soon contacted Benjamin Franklin and other Americans. See the entries for Nov. 18, Dec. 12, and Dec. 14, 1774, in Mark Anthony DeWolfe Howe (ed.), "Journal of Josiah Quincy, Jun., During His Voyage and Residence in England from September 28th, 1774 to March 3d, 1775," Massachusetts Historical Society *Proceedings*, L (1916–1917), 438, 439, 447, 448.

6. Later that winter, at the home of William Knox, Thomas Hutchinson observed that Garth, a fellow guest, had been in opposition "but speaks now in favour of the American measures" of the administration. Two weeks later Hutchinson dined at the home of Lord Chancellor Apsley, where Garth was also a guest. According to Hutchinson, Garth "condemned" the proceedings of the Americans and "thought it necessary, by an Act to declare the illegality of the Congress; and at least, to incapacitate all who should notwithstanding attend it, from all public offices, &c." Entries for Feb. 11, 26, 1775, Peter Orlando Hutchinson (ed.), *The Diary and Letters of Thomas Hutchinson* (2 vols., London, 1883–1886), I, 376, 396.

relating to it from their constituents." They did not recognize the congress. Wentworth, who had been nominated by John Sullivan and Daniel Folsom, the New Hampshire delegates at Philadelphia, advanced another reason. He declined participating in deference to Barlow Trecothick, who because of ill health had "withdrawn himself from all business" although he was nominally still agent for the colony.[7] But Wentworth, who was to be a British agent during the Revolutionary War, was even now playing a double game: he secretly gave John Pownall, Undersecretary of State for the American Department, full particulars on the activities of the other American agents. He had really declined acting with them, he informed Pownall, inasmuch as the congressional petition to the King was "an assertion of all their claims in a very high tone and with very offensive expressions."[8] The political issue had thus further reduced the ranks of the agents as Garth, Life, and Wentworth refused to become involved. There remained only Bollan, Franklin, and Arthur Lee, the hard core identified with the patriot movement in Massachusetts, to present the address of the congress.

The three agents unfortunately chose to operate through channels not best calculated to achieve success. Initially they decided to present the congressional petition to the Earl of Dartmouth, the Secretary of State, for by acting through this "regular official Method," they could expect an answer, as if this in itself would mean anything. A reply they received—albeit an unsatisfactory one. The monarch would not formally recognize the petition but would send the congressional address to Parliament after the

7. Franklin to Burke, Dec. 19, 1774, Burke Correspondence, Wentworth-Woodhouse Muniments, BK3/390; Franklin to Charles Thomson, Feb. 5, 1775, "The Papers of Charles Thomson," New York Historical Society *Collections* (New York, 1878), XI, 25–26; Garth to the South Carolina committee of correspondence, Jan. 20, 1775, Charles Garth–South Carolina committee of correspondence Letter Book, South Carolina Archives, Columbia, f. 185; and Wentworth to ?, Jan. 13, 1775, Nathaniel Bouton *et al.* (eds.), *Documents and Records Relating to the Province of New Hampshire* (40 vols., Concord, 1867–1943), XVIII, 658.

8. See the note dated Dec. 21, 1774, and endorsed, "Mr. Pownall," H.M.C., *Eleventh Report*, App., Pt. V (London, 1887), 372; also the entry for Dec. 21, 1774, Hutchinson (ed.), *Diary and Letters of Thomas Hutchinson*, I, 329, 330. As early as May, 1774, Wentworth had requested an audience with Dartmouth on private business. Wentworth to Dartmouth, May 8, 1774, Dartmouth Papers, II, 900.

recess.[9] Following this rebuff, the agents then turned to another channel. The next day, December 25, Arthur Lee visited the Earl of Chatham at his country seat to show him the petition. He reported the once great Commoner to be "in raptures with this, and the whole proceedings of the Congress. He will come forth with all his might for a full and solemn redress." The Rockingham faction would also join, and together the Whigs and the Chatham faction would form an "opposition, which supported by the popular voice" and the British merchants would be "irresistible."

Arthur Lee lived in a dream world. The following day he wrote his brother Richard Henry Lee that he had just "this moment" learned that the Court had resolved to repeal "all the Acts except the Declaratory & Admiralty Acts. . . ." There was to be an alteration in the ministry, with Dartmouth and North giving way to the Earls of Gower and Hillsborough, who would then begin their new administration with "these conciliatory measures."[10] Pure fantasy! There was no chance for an alteration of the ministry, much less one favorable to the colonists. Chatham and Rockingham were not strong enough to force any revision on George III, and Gower and Hillsborough certainly would not have been more conciliatory than North and Dartmouth. The three colonial agents were pursuing an unfruitful course in lobbying with the congressional remonstrances and unjustifiably raising the hopes of their correspondents with this "authentick" intelligence of the situation in Britain.

Neither did they work as closely with the British mercantile community as they had in the past. Apparently some English merchants offered to join the agents in presenting the address

9. See the note on the draft of Franklin, Lee, and Bollan to the speakers of the colonial assemblies, Dec. 24, 1774, Franklin Papers, Library of Congress, Ser. ii, Vol. II, f. 286; and the memorandum of 1774 by Arthur Lee, Arthur Lee Papers, Harvard College Library, Cambridge, Mass. The petition is in Benjamin Franklin Stevens (comp.), *Facsimiles of manuscripts in European Archives relating to America, 1773–1783* (25 vols., London, 1889–1898), IX, No. 850. See also Arthur Lee to Ralph Izard, Dec. 27, 1774, Anne Izard Dees (ed.), *Correspondence of Mr. Ralph Izard, of South Carolina, from the Year 1774 to 1804, with a Short Memoir* (2 vols., New York, 1844), I, 35.

10. Arthur Lee to Ralph Izard, Dec. 27, 1774, Dees (ed.), *Correspondence of Mr. Ralph Izard*, I, 36; Arthur Lee to Richard Henry Lee, Dec. 26, 1774, Arthur Lee Papers, American Philosophical Society Library, Philadelphia.

from the delegates at Philadelphia, but Franklin rejected their proposal. It might be appropriate for the merchants to join the agents if the document were a petition from American merchants concerning commerce, but since the remonstrance related to the political grievances of the colonists, the agent thought it best not to give the British merchants "the Trouble of accompanying it. . . ." In any case, Franklin suggested, they would probably present their own petition "on the mischievous Interruption their Commerce is likely to sustain by a continuance of their present Measures. . . ."[11]

Rebuffed by Franklin, the British merchants trading to North America were nonetheless stirring inasmuch as they feared the economic consequences of a rupture within the Empire. Through John Ellis, a Jamaica planter, they were able to bring in the West India interest, for an American embargo on exports to the West Indies would deprive the islands of provisions. In the absence of Barlow Trecothick, David Barclay, Jr. led the mercantile lobby and served as liaison with the agents. In December Barclay wrote Franklin that rather than advertising anonymously in the newspapers for support, the merchants had decided on a more "liberal Plan": an invitation for all merchants and "others interested in the Commerce of America" to meet on January 4. In the interval Franklin and Barclay conferred on several occasions to concert their activities.[12] Operating on the assumption that business would suffer from any Anglo-American crisis, the merchants went ahead with their campaign to secure some redress of the colonial grievances. Twice in January they met at the King's Arms Tavern under the chairmanship of Thomas Lane, discussed joint action, and agreed on a petition to Parliament. They repeated the tactics of 1766. According to the merchant Dennis DeBerdt, son of the former Massachusetts agent, the merchants would not base their petition on any "political principles, nor on any approval of the conduct of

11. Franklin to W. and R. Molleson, Dec. 21, 1774, Ford *et al.* (eds.), *Journals of the Continental Congress*, I, 123.

12. See the two notes from Barclay to Franklin, Dec. 22, 1774, Jan. 2, 1775, Franklin Papers, Library of Congress, Ser. ii, Vol. II, ff. 267, 272; Arthur Lee to Richard Henry Lee, Dec. 22, 1774, Arthur Lee Papers, Harvard College Library; and Arthur Lee to Ralph Izard, Dec. 27, 1774, Dees (ed.), *Correspondence of Mr. Ralph Izard*, I, 36.

the Americans, nor on a support of a redress of their injuries," but would confine their remonstrance to "commercial views." They would merely point out the "fatal consequences of an entire suspension of trade."

Evidently the traders had learned the proper technique from their experience in attempting to secure repeal of the Townshend duties in 1770. After London had taken the initiative, petitions from the other trading and manufacturing towns would follow. To DeBerdt this seemed the "only" probable way to bring about an accommodation. The petition of the merchants trading to America would be a face-saving device for the ministers. It would give them an "excuse" to repeal the Massachusetts Acts and an opportunity to censure the Americans, but at the same time allow them to "comply with their demands." Past experience indicated this to be the best procedure inasmuch as previous administrations in 1766 and 1770 had rejected any political argument and had seemingly acquiesced to those grounded on economic considerations.

Added support for the merchants trading to North America came from the traders dealing with the West Indies, who met on January 18 at the London Tavern with Beeston Long in the chair. The West Indian merchants and planters were concerned over the threat to the economy of the islands if the Americans cut off foodstuffs and supplies from the continental colonies. The Floridas and Canada could not supply sufficient staves and provisions. Consequently the island interest also agreed to petition the House of Commons to take measures calculated to quiet the Americans.[13]

13. DeBerdt to Joseph Reed, Jan. 6, 1775, Reed (ed.), *Life and Correspondence of Joseph Reed*, I, 101–102. For the meetings of the merchants on Jan. 4, 11, 18, 1775, see Force (ed.), *American Archives*, 4th Ser., I, 1086–1088, 1107–1110, 1147–1452. Despite these resolutions, William Lee, a member of the committee of London merchants responsible for drafting, presenting, and managing the petitions, was skeptical. "There is nothing very serious in this business," he warned his brother in Virginia, "therefore do not expect any good to come from it, for really nothing can arouse the good people here till they *feel*, which is not the case at present, but will be woefully so" in a year. The Americans must persevere in the plan adopted by the congress for an association against British commerce and "leave it work here. . . ." William Lee to Francis Lightfoot Lee, Jan. 13, 1775, Arthur Lee Papers, Harvard College Library. It seemed to Lee that effective economic pressure was all the more necessary since some British merchants were only lukewarm in support of the American cause; others were actually opposed and were taking the

Failure of a Lobby, 1774–1775

By mid-January the mercantile community of Bristol was already engaged with the political opponents of the ministry, but not without opposition from the supporters of the North administration. Burke's friends in the outport were particularly active.[14]

Yet two factors would limit the aid the merchants would give to the American cause. They would not suffer from as great an economic decline from the colonial boycott as many anticipated, since new markets were to take up the slack in the colonial trade and thus lessen the effects of the Continental Association. Even the previous summer Lord North was aware that the manufacturers of Manchester had found new markets in Spanish America.[15] Of more immediate importance, the administration would not now, as in the past, support the merchants in their efforts in behalf of the colonists.

III

The success of the merchants—and of the agents too—would depend, in large measure, on the attitude of the administration.

---

ministerial side. Those who appeared "foremost" in petitioning—"which they were permitted to do" by the administration, the Virginian claimed—hoped for "somebody to point out a path for them to get out of the scrape they were in"; they were much puzzled as to how to act, so as to "support their credit in America, and yet please their masters here." William Lee to Richard Henry Lee, Jan. 17, Feb. 25, 1775, Worthington C. Ford (ed.), *Letters of William Lee . . . 1766–1783* (3 vols., Brooklyn, 1891), I, 113–114, 130–131. Could Lee himself have been acting in bad faith in making these charges? He had written to a member of the Annapolis firm of Dick and Stewart: ". . . if you have any reasons to believe that the Americans will persevere in the plan adopted by the Congress . . . and will stop exports in September, or sooner, I would by all means advise you to purchase immediately 1000 or 1500 hhds. of your very best tobacco, and ship it off in ships of about 350 or 400 hhds., by which you may make a fortune. You will say perhaps, where, is the money to do this? I will tell you—draw on me at 60 or 90 days sight, when the ship sails, order insurance, and consign the tobacco to me. In this case the bills will be paid." William Lee to Anthony Stewart, Jan. 4, 1775, *ibid.*, I, 107–108.

14. Richard Champion to Willing and Morris, Jan. 17, 1775, George H. Guttridge (ed.), *The American Correspondence of a Bristol Merchant, 1766–1776, The Letters of Richard Champion* (Berkeley, 1934), p. 40.

15. See Thomas Hutchinson to ?, July 8, 1774, Hutchinson (ed.), *Diary and Letters of Thomas Hutchinson*, I, 182. Although subsequent developments proved North correct, at the time the manufacturers and merchants of Bristol were hard hit. See Richard Champion to Willing and Morris, Dec. 22, 1774, Guttridge (ed.), *American Correspondence of a Bristol Merchant*, p. 39.

In the past, pressure from the mercantile community had been successful only with the overt or implicit approval of previous ministries. But in the summer of 1774 Lord North had declared that notwithstanding the economic situation, past relations between the government and the merchants, and the previous temporizing policy, the current administration had at last "fixed and determined" on a firm course of action. Initially the American Department was certain of the correctness of the line the government had adopted and had even anticipated the reaction of the congress at Philadelphia. John Pownall, on the basis of the information he received from America, correctly predicted that the delegates would follow the advice of Franklin by drawing up a "state of their claims in the form of a petition, or rather bill of rights, and annex[ing] to it a resolution of non-importation untill those claims be yielded to. . . ." The ministry was, in fact, less concerned with the threat of the economic boycott than with the intercolonial congress as a center for organizing anti-British activities. The Earl of Dartmouth informed one colonial official that the "Propriety & Legality" of such a meeting "may be very much in doubt." If the object of the delegates was "humbly" to represent their grievances, their remonstrances would have more weight in London coming from the separate colonies than from any extralegal intercolonial gathering. The "measure has gone too far," Dartmouth feared, "to encourage any hope that it has been retracted."[16]

The complacency of the administration was severely shaken by two developments in the colonies: the actual decision by the congress to boycott British goods, and the inadequacy of the military force in Massachusetts in the face of resistance by the patriots of the Bay Colony. In the summer of 1774 the British merchants, perhaps misled by the failure of the American Whigs to hold the line on the non-importation agreement of 1768–1770, had apparently raised false hopes in the administration by implying that the congress would not

16. Hutchinson to ?, July 8, 1774, Hutchinson (ed.), *Diary and Letters of Thomas Hutchinson*, I, 182; Pownall to William Knox, Aug. 31, 1774, H.M.C., *Report on Manuscripts in Various Collections*, VI (London, 1919), 115; Dartmouth to Cadwallader Colden, Sept. 10, 1774, "The Letters and Papers of Cadwallader Colden," New York Historical Society *Collections* (11 vols., New York, 1877–1878, 1918–1924, 1935, 1937), LVI (1923), 248.

be able to take effective action. That fall news from America initially confirmed this prognostication. There seemed to be little unity among the colonies. Lieutenant Governor Cadwallader Colden predicted that New York would not join the association voted by the congress, for the farmers and merchants of the colony were "all disposed to remain quiet"; only the "lower" element in New York City were active in the anti-British movement. Further information apparently confirmed the lack of unity in America. William Knox, Undersecretary of State for the American Department, had obtained a copy of a letter from a delegate at Philadelphia who claimed that when the New Englanders had proposed a ban on both imports and exports, only the New England provinces, Virginia, and the Carolinas had favored nonimportation.

At this point, however, a ship had arrived in Philadelphia bearing letters from Franklin. The advice of the agent[17] in London had brought over the Pennsylvania delegation, and their vote in turn had carried the nonimportation agreement. With some justification then, the administration was to conclude that Franklin carried great weight with the delegates at Philadelphia. Disconcerted by the adoption of the colonial boycott and aware that pressure would now be exerted on the British merchants to stir them to petition for repeal of the Massachusetts Acts, the ministry now sought to organize a countermovement in the British mercantile community. When Lord North suggested that "a paper addressed to the [British] merchants will be of use," Knox, who had been a pamphleteer for the deceased George Grenville, was commissioned to draw it up.[18] The fear of the colonial boycott by the administration was short lived, however.

In October even more disturbing news came from General Thomas Gage, Governor of Massachusetts—information which forced the administration to reconsider its program with a view toward negotiating with the colonists, revising the imperial constitution, and granting a greater measure of home rule. Civil government under royal authority appeared nearly at an end in the Bay

17. Cf. Franklin's letter to Galloway of Sept. 7, 1774, Benjamin Franklin Papers, American Philosophical Society Library, Philadelphia, XLV, 92.

18. Knox to [Dartmouth], Nov. 15, 1774, Dartmouth Papers, II, 994; and also Knox's account "Secret of proceedings respecting America in the new Parliament," H.M.C., *Report on Manuscripts in Various Collections*, VI, 257–258.

Colony, and the populace seemed resolved to oppose by force the execution of the "intolerable" acts. Gage, who had been so confident earlier in the year that he could control the situation with four regiments of troops in the Bay Colony, now doubted that he could maintain order even with all the troops in North America, much less with those stationed in Boston. He now recommended that the home government suspend the objectionable legislation. Although the British ministers decided to reinforce the harassed commander-in-chief,[19] Gage's pessimistic reports forced them at least to reconsider their American program.

The concessions the British government were to offer the American agents in the winter of 1774-1775 went far beyond anything they had previously granted, and they were intended to apply even after the military crisis had passed. But any possible accommodation was limited by the attitude of the dominant personality in the imperial government, the King himself. Dismissing Gage's suggestion that the government suspend the Massachusetts Acts as "absurd," George III was adamant toward the colonists: "we must either master them or totally leave them to themselves and treat them as Aliens. . . ." Since the New Englanders were in a "State of Rebellion," force must be used to decide "whether they are subject to this Country or independent." The King was convinced that the Americans by their actions had "boldly thrown off the mask and avowed that nothing less than a total independence of the British Legislature will satisfy them. . . ." Temper, firmness, and a determination to stop all trade with those colonies which obeyed the mandate of the congress for nonconsumption of British goods was the only recourse left to the imperial government. Fortunately the King's ministers were more flexible than their master and were willing to negotiate. But the attitude of George III dashed the hopes of the agents that economic pressure would force a revision in the ministry and a repeal of the Massachusetts Acts. In a memorandum drawn up late in 1774 the King gave vent to his feelings

19. See Dartmouth to Sandwich, Oct. 4, 1774, Joseph Redington and Richard A. Roberts (eds.), *Calendar of Home Office Papers of the reign of George III, 1760–1775* (4 vols., London, 1878–1899), IV, 246; Sandwich to Dartmouth, Oct. 5, 1774, *ibid.*, IV, 247; Rochford to Dartmouth, Oct. 5, 1774, H.M.C., *Eleventh Report*, App., Pt. V, p. 364; Gower to Dartmouth, Oct. 6, 1774, *ibid.*, p. 364.

King George III

toward those English politicians who supported the colonists. This demonstrated how futile were the negotiations Franklin and Arthur Lee were conducting with Chatham, Shelburne, and Rockingham, how empty were their hopes that the King would replace the North ministry once Britain felt sufficient economic hardship. In reflecting on the political opposition politicians in England, "this motley tribe," George III complained bitterly that "Perhaps no one Period in our History can produce so strange a circumstance, as the Gentlemen who pretend to be Patriots . . . avowing the u[n]natural doctrine of encouraging the American Colonies in their disputes with the Mother Country. . . ."[20] The sentiments—or prejudices— of George III, the center of administration, were paramount. The Americans, their agents, and the British merchants would have to deal with the North ministry, not one formed by Rockingham or Chatham. The initial choice of ministers still lay with the monarch, for in the England of the eighteenth century, majorities in Parliament did not make ministries. Ministries generally made majorities.

The crucial decisions on America would be made by George III and the current cabinet: Lord Chancellor Apsley, North, Sandwich,

20. See the two letters from the King to Lord North, both dated Nov. 18, 1774, Sir John Fortescue (ed.), *The Correspondence of King George the Third, from 1760 to December 1783* . . . (6 vols., London, 1927), III, 153–154, and the undated memorandum, *ibid.*, III, 47–48. The editor ascribed this memorandum to the year 1773, but the reference to the nonimportation agreement adopted by the congress places it late in 1774. In an interview with Josiah Quincy, Lord North took about the same position. The Massachusetts patriot recorded in his London journal for Nov. 19, 1774: "His Lordship went largely and.repeatedly into an exculpation of the Ministry. He then said they were obliged to do what they did; that it was the most lenient measure that was proposed; that if Administration had not adopted it, they would have been called to account; that the nation were highly incensed, etc. . . . His Lordship more than thrice spoke of the powers of Gt. B., of the determination to exert to the utmost in order to effect the submission of the Colonies. He said repeatedly we must try what we can do to support the authority we have claimed over America, if we are defective in power we must set down contented and make the best terms we can, and nobody then can blame us after we have done our utmost; but till then we have tried what we can do, we can never be justified in receding; and we ought and shall be very careful not to judge a thing *impossible*, because it may be *difficult*, nay we ought to try what we *can* effect before we determine upon its impracticality." Howe (ed.), "Journal of Josiah Quincy, Jun.," p. 440.

and the three Secretaries of State, Dartmouth, Suffolk, and Rochford. During three meetings on December 1, 1774, and January 13, and January 21, 1775, they agreed on the course they would take and the concessions they would offer the colonists. From the estimates of the commander-in-chief in the colonies, a total military solution was not possible in the near future. Gage had asked for so many reinforcements that it would have taken a year to assemble the required troops and then only by placing the country on a wartime establishment. Since some concession was necessary, on January 13 the cabinet considered the advisability of appointing commissioners for America in order to bring "a nearer union with the Colonys for mutual Interest of both parts [of the] Empire. . . ." Dartmouth, then engaged in unofficial negotiations with Franklin and some merchants on a plan of union and accommodation, made this proposal to the cabinet evidently at the suggestion of his undersecretary, John Pownall. Both North and the King feared, however, that a policy only of negotiating might be interpreted as weakness and merely encourage the Whig leaders in the colonies to resist an accommodation. Consequently the cabinet decided to couple concessions with a show of limited force: reinforcements for Gage and economic sanctions by Parliament. The imperial legislature would temporarily prohibit those colonies joining the Continental Association from trading to any ports other than those in Great Britain, Ireland, and the British West Indies.[21] Not until January 21 did the cabinet finally decide on the terms of the public "olive branch." These conditions, in turn, may have been suggested to the Secretary of State by the negotiations emissaries of Dartmouth were then conducting with Franklin.

21. Minute of cabinet, Dec. 1, 1774, Dartmouth Papers, I, ii, 1084. North to Dartmouth [Dec. ?, 1774], Dartmouth Papers, II, 1073; minute of cabinet, Jan. 13, 1775, Dartmouth Papers, II, 1102. George III to Lord North, Dec. 15, 1774, Fortescue (ed.), *Correspondence of George III*, III, 156; George III to Dartmouth, Jan. 28, 1775 (2 letters), H.M.C., *Thirteenth Report*, App., Pt. IV (London, 1892), p. 501. For a different version of the plan for a commission, see the much later account of William Knox in H.M.C., *Report on Manuscripts in Various Collections*, VI, 257–258. The Undersecretary of State claimed that the failure of the commission lay with John Pownall in drafting a plan by which it would have been invested with too much authority to negotiate with an American "Parliament." At several points, however, this acount does not coincide with the King's contemporary letters. I have relied on the latter evidence.

Failure of a Lobby, 1774–1775

In arriving at terms for concessions to be made to the American colonies, the ministry was proceeding along two lines: negotiations carried on by spokesmen for Dartmouth with selected agents and merchants, and a public line to be taken in Parliament. On January 21, 1775, Apsley, Gower, Sandwich, Suffolk, Rochford, Dartmouth, and North formulated the "olive branch" to be publicly offered. The concession would implement a policy of more self-government under a formula recognizing the theory, not the exercise of Parliamentary authority over the internal affairs of America. If the provinces made sufficient and permanent provision for the support of civil government, the administration of justice, and defense, and in time of war raise extraordinary supplies in a reasonable proportion to those contributed by the mother country, Parliament would desist from the "exercise of the Power of taxation" except in matters of external commerce.[22] From a letter sent the King by Lord North later the next month, when this "olive branch" was before Parliament, it is clear that the ministers were sincere in this offer regardless of the military exigencies in the colonies. The proposed resolution relinquished "no right," and contained "precisely the plan *which ought to be adopted* by Great Britain; *even if all America were subdued.*"[23] By this concession the British government would desist from exercising, but would not repudiate or give up, the right to tax. Taken in conjunction with other terms offered Franklin by Dartmouth during private, informal negotiations, this approached home rule for the colonies.

While the cabinet was deciding on the program it was to place before Parliament during the coming session, another drama was being enacted behind the scenes. Through various intermediaries Dartmouth had been covertly sounding out Benjamin Franklin and certain merchants on possible grounds for accommodation and

22. Minute of cabinet, Jan. 21, 1775, Dartmouth Papers, I, ii, 1093.

23. North to George III [Feb. 19, 1775], Fortescue (ed.), *Correspondence of George III*, III, 176 (italics added). The concession to desist from taxing the colonies is a highly significant one, if it is really true as one writer has recently claimed (Jack P. Greene, *The Quest for Power. The Lower Houses of Assembly in the Southern Royal Colonies 1689–1776* [Chapel Hill, 1963], p. 364), that the realization by the provincial assemblies that "Parliamentary taxation was a direct challenge to their political power and might eventually even lead to the abolition of colonial law-making bodies forced them to resist."

union.[24] At the request of the Secretary of State, Brooke Watson
sent him his "Thoughts upon the Dispute between Great Britain
and her Colonies." The primary concern of the merchant was to
prevent the probable disruption of Anglo-American trade resulting
from a political crisis with the colonies. Britain must retain the
affection of her American provinces, he felt, inasmuch as one-third
of her commerce depended on the colonies. The loss of America
would ruin the mother country.

The solution Watson proposed to the current political dispute
lay in a revision of the imperial constitution by which the provinces
would not only retain their respective assemblies but also enjoy a
supra-colonial government consisting of a royally appointed Lord
Lieutenant, and two councilors selected from each of the colonies
as the upper house of an American Parliament. The provincial
assemblies were to choose the lower house.[25] Meeting annually, the
North American Parliament would have the power to vote taxes,
while the British Crown would enjoy a veto over its acts and the
British Parliament a legislative supremacy in all cases relating to
life, liberty, and property except in matters of taxation for general
aids or the immediate, internal support of the provincial governments.[26] There is nothing to indicate how Dartmouth reacted to
this proposal, but the plan was impractical if only because it fell
far short of the conditions posed by the Continental Congress.
Under Watson's plan, the powers enjoyed by the American Parliament were even less than those under the Galloway plan of union,
which the delegates at Philadelphia had already rejected.

Dartmouth did give some consideration, however, to the proposals

24. On his own initiative Franklin had been active in the cause of accommodation, but with the wrong people. He had shown Charles Pratt, Lord Camden,
and Chatham the plan of union proposed by Joseph Galloway in Philadelphia.
But there was little point to this approach. In the first place, Camden and Chatham
were not in the administration and had no chance in the foreseeable future of
coming to power. They were in no position to implement any plan of union or
accommodation between the colonies and the mother country. Furthermore, the
Continental Congress had already rejected the Galloway plan by the vote of one
colony and had expunged the record of the plan from the journal of the meeting.

25. Virginia and Massachusetts would have fifteen delegates; Pennsylvania, New
York, and Connecticut, twelve; South Carolina and New Jersey, eleven; North
Carolina, Maryland, New Hampshire, and Quebec, seven; West Florida, East
Florida, Georgia, Rhode Island, and Nova Scotia, five; and St. John's, three.

26. Watson to Dartmouth, Jan. 23, 1775, Dartmouth Papers, II, 1117.

Franklin made to the Secretary of State.[27] These articles for accommodation led to protracted, although indirect, discussions during the winter of 1774–1775. Obviously Franklin was the leader of the American agents in London acting for the Continental Congress, and as evidenced by the information the ministry had received, he appeared to be extremely influential with the delegates at Philadelphia. Moreover, the congress had seemingly followed the course Franklin had suggested earlier in 1774, when it adopted its remonstrance. The instructions to the agents entrusted with delivering the congressional case reached London on December 19 in the midst of these discussions and materially affected the line taken by Franklin during the negotiations. On December 2, David Barclay—now head of the committee of London merchants trading to America—called on the agent to discuss a proposed meeting with the merchants who were to petition Parliament and formulate the line the outports and manufacturing towns were to take. In their talks the two men broached the subject of a possible reconciliation between Britain and the colonies. Two days later Barclay brought Dr. John Fothergill and Thomas Villers, Baron Hyde, personal physician and close friend respectively of the Secretary of State for the American Department, into the negotiations. The merchant promised that if the agent set down his proposals on paper, he would show them to the more moderate ministers.

When Franklin on December 6 submitted his "Hints," consisting of seventeen items,[28] Barclay then transmitted the proposals to the Secretary of State. Among Dartmouth's papers there is a copy of Franklin's articles (containing sixteen proposals, for the sixteenth point was an alternative to the fifteenth) with comments or emendations probably discussed by Fothergill, Barclay, and the agent. In this collection there is another document in Dartmouth's hand

27. Franklin set down these proposals in a narrative of his negotiations written while en route to America in March, 1775. Copies of these proposals and Dartmouth's reactions are in the Dartmouth Papers. David Barclay's copies are in the Gurney and Barclay Family Papers, in the possession of Colonel Q. E. Gurney, Bawdeswell Hall, Norfolk, England. I am indebted to Colonel Gurney for photostatic reproductions. Franklin's account is printed in Albert H. Smyth (ed.), *The Writings of Benjamin Franklin with a Life and Introduction* (10 vols., New York, 1907), VI, 318–399.

28. See Franklin's "An Account of Negotiations . . .," Smyth (ed.), *Writings of Franklin*, VI, 326–327.

showing the reaction of the Secretary of State to each of these points.[29] Dartmouth may have prepared this document for presentation to the cabinet in case the negotiations with the agent proved fruitful. Franklin's articles for a durable union between Britain and the colonies fell into three groups: the first, eleventh, twelfth, and thirteenth articles dealt with Massachusetts and the "intolerable" acts (including the Quebec Act); the third, fourth, fifth, seventh, and fourteenth with the colonial economy and enforcement of the Acts of Trade and Navigation; the second, sixth, eighth, ninth, tenth, fifteenth, sixteenth, and seventeenth with taxation and the American civil and military establishment.

There was little agreement between the agent and the Secretary of State on the major points relating to the immediate crisis in Massachusetts. But they could agree on minor issues. Both men concurred that the Bostonians should pay for the tea destroyed in December, 1773. In reply to Franklin's request that Castle William —now occupied by the royal army—be restored to Massachusetts, Dartmouth suggested that the fort in Boston Harbor be put under the command of the colonial government with a garrison paid by the province. The two major points in this category were not as easily resolved. Franklin demanded that the ministry repeal the "intolerable" acts and grant a "free" government to Canada, or at least declare that the present form of government established by the Quebec Act did not extend beyond certain limits. Dartmouth would not compromise on these points. The older British colonies engaged in the current dispute with the mother country had nothing to do with the Quebec Act. When the people of the Bay Colony demonstrated any disadvantage or inconvenience arising from the recent legislation relating to Massachusetts, then the ministry would reconsider those statutes. The Secretary of State offered an alternative to Franklin's thirteenth point: a demand that Parliament formally disclaim the extension of the Treason Act of Henry VIII to the colonies. If the provinces should enact such laws

29. Franklin's "Hints for a Conversation upon the Subject of Terms that may probably produce a *Durable* Union between Great Britain and her colonies," with emendations, Dartmouth Papers, II, 1007; and "Hints & c.," Dartmouth Papers II, 1124. There are two copies of the latter document. One is a fair copy, and the other, a draft, is in Dartmouth's hand.

respecting treason in America as would give full security for an impartial trial for that offense—laws approved in England—then, Dartmouth suggested, there would be no need to extend the Tudor statute to the colonies.

The second group of five articles dealt with colonial commerce— an area where the British government could have offered real concessions since American trade was tied to Britain more by economic than by political connections. By the middle of the eighteenth century the Navigation Acts served at best a political, not an economic, purpose. In Franklin's written proposals, the agent called for the re-enactment by the colonial legislatures of all laws of trade and navigation; orally he had indicated an alternative: a compact between Britain and the provinces regarding those acts. Dartmouth categorically refused both, but agreed to Franklin's next point that a naval officer, appointed by the Crown, reside in each colony to see that the Acts of Trade and Navigation were enforced. He also acquiesced in the agent's request that the imperial government reconsider all laws restraining colonial industry. Franklin added an oral qualification that these statutes be reviewed with a view toward the accommodation of specific American grievances rather than total repeal. Since Franklin did not "tenaciously" support his request that collectors and customs house officials be appointed by the colonial governors and not be sent from England, Dartmouth rejected this article.

The final article in this group dealing with the enforcement procedures of the Acts of Trade and Navigation allowed Dartmouth to offer a real concession. Franklin asked that the powers of the vice-admiralty courts in America be reduced to those enjoyed by comparable courts in the mother country, and that the provincial legislatures re-enact the Parliamentary statutes relating to these courts. The Secretary of State pointed out that the prerogative courts were an ancient heritage, and all the laws relating to the plantation trade referred to them; but if exchequer courts—common-law courts having jurisdiction in cases involving the King's revenue and employing juries—were more agreeable to the Americans, there did not appear, "upon the general view, to be any ground of objection."

The eight remaining articles, concerning taxation and the colonial civil and military establishment, offered concrete grounds for accommodations and a greater degree of home rule. In assessing these points Dartmouth assumed that the colonists would accept the "olive branch" resolution by which the British Parliament would desist from taxing the Americans if the colonial assemblies, in the opinion of the imperial government, made adequate provision for their civil and defense establishments. Only on this condition would Parliament repeal or at least reconsider the tax on tea as Franklin asked. In a key concession the Secretary of State also agreed that all revenue from acts regulating the trade of the colonies be set aside for the public use of the respective provinces and paid into their treasuries. Franklin would grant to the mother country a monopoly of American commerce, and in return Britain would desist from levying requisitions on the colonies in time of peace. During wartime, requisitions on the provinces would be proportional to the amount contributed by the mother country. On this last point Dartmouth promised that requisitions would be made as heretofore. In effect he acquiesced in the agent's proposal, but he suggested further that the mainland colonies follow the precedent set by Jamaica and establish a permanent fund for military contingencies. No further requisitions would then be made except on extraordinary occasions. On one point concerning the military there was no compromise, however. To Dartmouth, Franklin's request that the imperial government not send or quarter troops in a colony without the consent of the provincial legislature was "utterly inadmissible." The ministry probably thought that until the Bay Colonists gave assurances by their actions, force would still be necessary to restore a balance in government and maintain the authority of Parliament.

The final articles, relating to the provincial civil establishment, naturally followed the question of taxation. The agent specified that judges in the royal colonies should be appointed for good behavior—not for the pleasure of the Crown—and be paid by ample and permanent salaries voted by the provincial legislatures who could obtain their removal by addressing the King in council or Parliament. If it was advisable, however, for the King to continue appointing judges during *his* pleasure, then the colonial assemblies would continue granting salaries during *their* pleasure. As was to be expected from the terms of the olive-branch concession, Dartmouth approved the first proposition: judges would be appointed for good behavior and thus be independent of the Crown if the colonial legislatures provided permanent, fixed salaries. But Franklin preferred the traditional system of paying the provincial governors as practiced in the northern and middle royal colonies—voluntary grants by the assemblies. Dartmouth preferred the olive-branch resolution. The salaries of the governors would be included in the general estimate voted for the civil establishment on a permanent basis by the assemblies.[30]

By the accommodations specified by Dartmouth in these negotiations with Franklin and the concessions made in the olive-branch resolution, the ministry indicated its willingness to negotiate on the imperial constitution and to allow a greater degree of home rule in America. If the provincial governments adequately provided for their own internal affairs Parliament would desist from exercising its authority. In reality the imperial legislature would merely regulate external trade. The colonial assemblies would enjoy complete power over finances and virtual control over internal affairs under a formula enunciated by Parliament and superintended by the Privy Council. The colonial assemblies, not Parliament, would legislate for treason, the courts enforcing imperial trade and revenue acts, and the civil and military establishments; the local legislatures, not Parliament, would tax and have exclusive control over all financial expenditures—even monies arising from the regulation of trade. This formula followed the procedures adopted earlier in suspending the Mutiny Acts in America and returning control of Indian affairs to the colonies.[31]

30. Cf. Franklin's "Hints for a Conversation . . ." and the draft of the "Hints & c.," in Dartmouth's hand, Dartmouth Papers, II, 1007, II, 1124.
31. In the half century preceding the pre-Revolutionary decade the lower houses of the provincial assemblies, at least in the royal colonies in the South, had won many powers. From a recent study (Greene, *The Quest for Power, passim*) it is clear that British acts after 1763 did not interfere with or threaten the power to frame money bills, audit accounts, disperse money, regulate fees, control the internal proceedings of the lower houses, or control public works or public printers or existing regulation of the militia. Salaries for governors and other points did not become important issues. Disputes on the appointment of colonial agents, regulation of Indian affairs, control of church patronage, and paper money were

The two sides were still far apart, however, on the immediate issue of the "intolerable" acts and the situation in Massachusetts. On December 22 David Barclay informed Franklin that *Lord Hyde* thought his propositions were "too Hard." Hyde was probably speaking for the Secretary of State.

The ministry now made a different approach through another emissary in its negotiations with Franklin. Five days later Richard, Lord Howe informed the Pennsylvanian that North and Dartmouth were ready for an accommodation. What did Franklin think of the ministry sending a commission to America to inquire into the grievances of the colonists, converse with the leading figures there, and attempt to reconcile existing differences? At this point the two sides grew further apart when Franklin shifted the basis of the argument by closely adhering to the instructions he had received from the congress on December 19. A day or two later he submitted his answer in the form of a paper of conditions based on the petition of the delegates at Philadelphia. Britain was to repeal all objectionable legislation, evacuate the troops from the colonies to Quebec and the Floridas, satisfy grievances over the payment of salaries to governors and judges, and disclaim the extension of the treason statute of Henry VIII to America. Moreover, further financial aids to Britain from the provinces should come from voluntary contributions rather than taxes imposed by Parliament. Finally, the imperial government must sanction some congress such as that held at Albany presided over by a person of weight and dignity appointed by the Crown.

It is difficult to see how Franklin expected the ministry to accept these terms, for they were much more stringent than the articles in his "Hints" which the administration had already rejected as "too hard." Furthermore in the previous decade various ministries had consistently refused to sanction intercolonial action through any type of "congress." But the congressional instructions had left Franklin with little alternative in negotiating. As might be expected, Howe informed the agent that his latest proposals were not likely to produce good results. Still the emissary returned to the quest.

---

resolved before 1774 on terms generally favorable to the assemblies. The critical issue after 1773 was Parliamentary taxation.

Courtesy of Clements Library

The Earl of Dartmouth

During the second week in January, Howe through his sister asked the agent if he would engage for the colonists to pay for the tea destroyed at Boston as a preliminary to a settlement of general issues. Would the Bay Colonists rely on a promised redress of grievance by the ministry to future petitions from the Massachusetts assembly? Did Franklin still promise financial aids from the colonists to the mother country as he had proposed the previous month in his "Hints"?

The agent repudiated his previous commitment by pointing out that the Americans were convinced that Parliament had no right to tax them—consequently all the money illegally "extorted" from them by the Revenue Acts *preceding* the destruction of the tea was a great injury. This must be remedied first. Furthermore it was unjust to ask the Bostonians to reimburse the East India Company now that the British government had inflicted much more damage on the Bostonians by closing the port and seizing Castle William. Such reasoning did little to settle matters. After Parliament reconvened on January 19, Howe plainly told Franklin that the ministers would not accept the latter's propositions. They thought the agent had instructions from the congress to make concessions. Disabusing Howe of this notion, the agent maintained he could only act on what was presented in the petition to the King. However, he was willing to listen to counteroffers from the ministry.[32]

It was some days before Franklin heard anything further on the matter, for the ministry took its case to Parliament. But in the interval Franklin worked with Barclay in preparing the petition from the London merchants to the House of Commons and in soliciting the aid of the Earl of Chatham for some accommodation. Both these efforts were pointless, for any successful plan needed the approval of the ministry, the politicians in office.

Early in February the emissaries for Dartmouth again contacted the agent. On February 4 Barclay and Fothergill told him that the ministers were well disposed, considered several of his "Hints" reasonable, and might admit others with "small Amendments." Apparently the immediate obstacles to accommodation were the

32. Franklin's "An Account of Negotiations . . .," Smyth (ed.), *Writings of Franklin*, VI, 352–359.

"intolerable" acts.[33] After a general discussion Franklin protested that as long as Parliament claimed and exercised the power of "altering our Constitutions [i.e., charters] at pleasure, there could be no Agreement; for we were render'd unsafe in every Privilege we had a Right to, and were secure in nothing." Significantly, Franklin had shifted his argument. He no longer posed particular points, as he had done in his "Hints" of December 6, but the basic issue of sovereignty and the right of the subject.

More than a week passed before Barclay again resumed discussions. He had spoken with Lord Hyde, who wanted another meeting with Franklin and Fothergill. On February 16,[34] Barclay presented to the agent a plan of union for Britain and the colonies. Basically a slight modification of Franklin's "Hints," it generally repeated his main points. Discussion initially centered on the first article, calling for compensation for the Boston Tea Party. After an agent for the colonists had engaged to pay for the tea, a royal commissioner would be authorized by Parliament to suspend the Boston Port Act. Although Franklin submitted written comments on Barclay's proposals—comments delivered to the Secretary of State—the plan was doomed if only because it was predicated on the appointment of a commission, a procedure ruled out that winter by the King. Neither did Barclay's propositions satisfy the conditions

33. Someone may have been misrepresenting the situation here. In a letter of February 6, 1775, Fothergill made it clear that Dartmouth faced much opposition in the cabinet. The obstacles to accommodation, as Fothergill saw it, were the Massachusetts Acts. Fothergill to ?, Feb. 6, 1775, Dartmouth Papers, II, 1133. In his account of the negotiations Franklin listed the ministerial reactions to his "Hints" of December 6, 1774, as purportedly told him by Barclay and Fothergill (Smyth (ed.), *Writings of Franklin*, VI, 371–372), but in several instances these do not agree with the objections listed in the document by Dartmouth, "Hints & c.," (Dartmouth Papers, II, 1124). A case in point is the Quebec Act (eleventh article in the Franklin list, the twelfth article in the Dartmouth list). Franklin related that Barclay and Fothergill told him that the ministry was willing to amend the Quebec Act by reducing the boundaries of the colony to its ancient limits, but the document among the Dartmouth papers reads: "As to the Quebec Act, this article rejected." That is, no concessions were to be made on this statute.

34. In the meantime Hyde was scheduled to confer with Dartmouth on February 10. Hyde to Howe, Feb. 10, 1775, Dartmouth Papers, II, 1143.

of the ministry on the Massachusetts charter, enforcement of the Acts of Trade and Navigation, and the provisions for the colonial civil and ministry establishments incorporated into the olive-branch resolution.[35]

The private negotiations in the winter of 1774-1775 broke down for a variety of reasons. Significantly Franklin had shifted his position after receiving instructions from the Continental Congress. In rejecting the proposal of Galloway that the delegates empower commissioners to deal with the royal government on accommodation and union, the congress had given Franklin no latitude in his negotiations. A valuable opportunity to save the cause of Anglo-American union was lost. Both sides were unwilling to retreat on the issue of sovereignty. Although the administration was willing to negotiate basic concessions tending toward home rule, it would not alter its program to meet the immediate revolutionary crisis in Massachusetts unless the Bay Colonists demonstrated some willingness to accept the imperial authority. Unable to reach an agreement with the agent in private negotiations, the North ministry would commit itself publicly only to the olive-branch resolution. It would give up the exercise, but not the authority, of Parliamentary power to tax. Operating on the assumption that they could not bring the Americans to negotiate as long as the Whig leaders in the colonies interpreted concession as weakness, the ministers coupled the olive-branch resolution with force—military and economic sanctions authorized by Parliament.

On January 19 Lord North had introduced the initial elements of the administration's program into the House of Commons. At that time he presented one hundred and forty documents relating to the situation in Massachusetts in particular, and America in general. All were intended to prove that a rebellion actually existed in the colonies. The last two papers—not distinguished from the others—were the extracts of the votes and proceedings of the delegates at Philadelphia, and their petition to the King presented the

35. Franklin's "Account of Negotiations . . .," Smyth (ed.), *Writings of Franklin*, VI, 372-375. Barclay's proposals and Franklin's comments are printed in *ibid.*, VI, 375-382 (manuscript copy in Dartmouth Papers, II, 1149).

preceding December by the agents Franklin, Lee, and Bollan. The last was merely labeled a petition from sundry persons on behalf of themselves and the inhabitants of the colonies.[36] The imperial government would not recognize the Continental Congress.

In Parliament the opposition to the ministerial program centered about the efforts of the colonial agents associated with the patriots, the Rockingham faction, and the British mercantile community to petition for the colonists. In the ensuing debates some deserted the American cause as the basic issue became clear. "Governor" Thomas Pownall[37] and Charles Garth were conspicuous defectors. But another agent stood firm. Burke contended that the "Americans do not attack the sovereignty [of Parliament] itself, but a certain exercise and use of that sovereignty." The agent's attitude was pointless, except in terms of partisan opposition, for his doctrine did not differ from that of the ministry as expressed in the olive-branch resolution. In rebuttal North pointed out that he "did not mean to tax America"; he only wanted a formal acknowledgment by the colonies; "if they would submit, and leave to us the constitutional right of supremacy, the quarrel would be at an end."[38]

Dissatisfied with the government's proposal to desist taxing the colonies if they passed adequate tax laws for their own establishments, Burke termed the olive-branch resolution a "method of ransom by auction. . . ." Unless the colonies universally accepted the concession there would be great difficulty, he warned. Misinterpreting the proposal, Burke assumed that the colonial agents would have some role in settling the amount of money each province would contribute. From this he erroneously deduced that the agents would have general powers of taxing the colonies at their own discretion. After offering further ill-founded objections, Burke submitted his own plan of conciliation, a return to the situation before

36. Great Britain, Parliament, *Journals of the House of Commons* (London, 1547—), XXXV, 66.

37. During the general election of 1774 North had written to Henry Fownes Luttrell recommending Pownall as a candidate for Luttrell's borough of Minehead. Ian R. Christie, *The End of North's Ministry 1780–1782* (London, 1958), p. 60.

38. William Cobbett (ed.), *The Parliamentary History of England from the Earliest Period to the Year 1803* (36 vols., London, 1813), XVIII, 262, 264–265; *Commons Journal*, XXXV, 99, 112, 129, 144, 152, 182, 220, 225.

1763.[39] In so doing, however, Burke sought to ignore the crucial question of the right of Parliament—a point he himself as a proponent of the Declaratory Act was committed to defend, and a point challenged by the Americans themselves. Once raised, this contention that Parliament had no right made "a return to the old system as impossible as a return to childhood."[40] Throughout the preceding decade this had been the basic issue on which all attempts at reconciliation had faltered. And the declaration of immunity from Parliamentary authority was now contained in the petition to the King. Lee and Franklin had urged the colonists to stress it when holding out for a firm declaration of American rights. The contention became the argument of the American lobby in 1775.

In the early weeks of 1775 a small band of colonial agents attempted unsuccessfully to get the British government to take official notice of the petition submitted by the Continental Congress. The congress had named those agents still in London to present their case. All but Lee, Franklin, and Bollan declined to act for the extralegal assembly. It remained for the three Massachusetts agents to carry on. They sought to draw attention to the remonstrance by another petition presented by Sir George Savile, but on January 25 the House of Commons by a vote of 218 to 68 rejected their plea. Burke, agent for New York, evidently did not speak on their behalf during the debate, when the ministry argued against hearing from an illegal body.[41] Moreover, the petitioners, Franklin, Lee, and Bollan, were not "Agents of the Congress nor in any State of Responsibility for that Meeting"; they were agents only of the Bay Colony. Being "only Carriers and Deliverers," they had discharged their duty once

---

39. Cobbett (ed.), *Parliamentary History*, XVIII, 319, 330, 335, 482, 530; [John Almon,] *The Parliamentary Register; or History of the Proceedings and Debates of the House of Commons 1774–1780* (17 vols., London, 1775–1780), I, 199.

40. Charles R. Ritcheson, *British Politics and the American Revolution* (Norman, Okla., 1954), pp. 189–190.

41. Franklin to Charles Thomson, Feb. 5, 1775, Smyth (ed.), *Writings of Franklin*, VI, 304; Force (ed.), *American Archives*, 4th Ser., I, 1532; Cobbett (ed.), *Parliamentary History*, XVIII, 182–183; [Almon,] *Parliamentary Register*, I, 115, 124; North to George III, Jan. 26, 1775, Fortescue (ed.), *Correspondence of George III*, III, 169. North enclosed a list of speakers on the question. Burke was not among them.

they had presented the address to the King.[42] Thus the House of Commons dismissed the messengers.

The British mercantile community fared little better when it sought to remonstrate in favor of the Americans. That same day the House of Commons rejected a petition from the London merchants presented by Alderman Hayley. It was one of several from the trading and manufacturing towns of Bristol, Liverpool, and Glasgow.[43] But if the friends of America were marshaling the British merchants, the ministry was also organizing sentiment to oppose the colonists. On February 1 the House of Commons received two petitions from Leeds, one for the Americans, another against them. Later that month Nottingham presented a petition for maintaining order and the supremacy of Parliament in the provinces.[44] When the Birmingham merchants advertised for a public meeting, the prominent manufacturer Matthew Bolton spoke out against the colonies. He had attended the gathering, he wrote the Secretary of State, to prevent if possible, "some of my neighbors from running into unwise measures, by the intrigues of American & minority

42. Charles Garth to the South Carolina committee of correspondence, Jan. 27, 1775, Charles Garth–South Carolina committee of correspondence Letter Book, f. 187. Arthur Lee took this opportunity to reopen the controversy on the Massachusetts agency and particularly Wedderburn's attack on Franklin at the Cockpit the previous year. See Arthur Lee, *A Speech intended to have been delivered in the House of Commons, in support of the Petition from the general Congress at Philadelphia: by the author of An Appeal to the Justice and Interests of Great Britain* (London, 1775), pp. 19–21.

43. *Commons Journal*, XXXV, 71, 74–75, 80, 81; Force (ed.), *American Archives*, 4th Ser., I, 1513–1515; Garth to the South Carolina committee of correspondence, Jan. 24, 1775, Charles Garth–South Carolina committee of correspondence Letter Book, f. 184; [Almon,] *Parliamentary Register*, I, 116; Cobbett (ed.), *Parliamentary History*, XVIII, 168–171. Suspicious as usual, William Lee cast some doubt on the sincerity of the Glasgow merchants. Lee to Thomas Adams, March 10, 1775, "Letters to Thomas Adams," *Virginia Magazine of History and Biography*, VI (1898–1899), 30. According to Lee, the Glasgow merchants gave Lord North "to understand by their member, J. F. Campbell, that they did not mean any opposition [to the ministry], but to gain credit in America, & thereby more easily collect their debts. This is currently reported here but I cannot vouch it for fact, therefore only mention it as a report." Garritt P. Judd, IV, *Members of Parliament, 1734–1832* (New Haven, 1955), p. 141, does not list a J. F. Campbell, but a Frederick Campbell as member for the Glasgow Burghs.

44. *Commons Journal*, XXXV, 89, 90, 141.

agents," who, he had reason to believe, had been in Birmingham and most of the other manufacturing towns.

In attempting to dissuade the Birmingham group from supporting the colonists, both Bolton and Dr. John Roebuck, a ministerial agent, argued that there was no reason to be concerned over the assumed economic distress from the "pretended" nonimportation agreement adopted by the Continental Congress. On the contrary, trade was remarkably "good at present."[45] Bolton and Roebuck may have been responsible for a counterpetition from Birmingham. The appearance of this remonstrance supporting the ministry led Burke and Arthur Lee to charge that it was not the work of merchants at all. According to Lee, Dr. Roebuck "could, if he chose it, inform the public; *how* and *from whom*" the petition was obtained. But for that matter William Lee might have supplied the same information on the circumstances behind the petition of the London merchants supporting the Americans. In the House of Commons, Burke maintained that the Birmingham petition against the colonists was drawn up by Roebuck and "clandestinely, without the least notice," carried from house to house to be signed. But his motion for an investigation failed by a vote of 85 to 37.[46]

How far the administration was involved in these attempts is not known, but through the Undersecretary of State for the American Department, William Knox, the ministry did attempt to influence mercantile opinion. In a pamphlet inspired by Lord North, Knox argued that the ministerial program for America would best meet the interests of the merchants. The "avowed and main object" of the colonists, he warned, was to set aside the authority of Parliament.

45. Bolton to Dartmouth, Jan. 12, 17, 30, 1775, Dartmouth Papers, II, 1099, 1105, 1120.
46. Arthur Lee, *A Second Appeal to the justice and interests of the people on the measures respecting America By the author of the first* (London, 1775), p. 12; [Almon,] *Parliamentary Register*, I, 125-126; *Commons Journal*, XXXV, 87. After conferring with Grey Cooper at the Treasury in an effort to have the bill restraining the trade of the New England colonies modified, Thomas Hutchinson charged that "the whole affair of the [London] merchants' Petition against it was managed by [William] Lee, the late sheriff [William] Baker, and one or two more, and was calculated merely to serve Opposition against the Ministry, and not to serve the Colonies." Entry for March 4, 1775, Hutchinson (ed.), *Diary and Letters of Thomas Hutchinson*, I, 402.

Agents and Merchants

Once admit that Parliament had no authority to pass laws binding on the colonies, then all of "its Acts instantly become waste-paper" and the British merchants could no longer apply to the imperial legislature to correct the unjust proceedings of an American assembly. Continuance of trade with the colonies "clearly and entirely" depended on the laws of Great Britain having force there. These laws secured the property of the trader. Support and maintain the authority of Parliament, and the trade of the colonies would remain with the mother country; but "Give up the authority of Parliament," Knox warned, and "there is an end to your trade, and a total loss of your property."[47]

Subsequent events proved Knox wrong, for after a period of adjustment following the Revolution, Anglo-American trade was resumed on a scale greater than ever. A political connection was not necessary for the economic nexus. How many British merchants realized this in 1775 cannot be determined, but in all probability most were immediately concerned with the present economic threat posed by the colonial boycott. But as Richard Champion, a merchant of Bristol, pointed out, some manufacturing towns such as Manchester and Norwich had not felt the pinch. In any case, the British mercantile community in 1775 generally supported the American position.

Early in February the planters and merchants of the West India trade joined with the London merchants trading to North America in petitioning the House of Commons. At the suggestion of William Baker they also decided to petition the House of Lords. The West Indians would have preferred that the Earl of Dartmouth present their petition to the peers had he been agreeable, but it was the Marquis of Rockingham who read their supplication.[48] The grand show came during late February and March, when representatives

47. William Knox, *The Interests of the Merchants and Manufacturers of Great Britain, In the Present Contest with the Colonies, Stated and Considered* (London, 1774), pp. 40–43, 49–50.

48. Richard Champion to Willing and Morris, March 13, 1775, Guttridge (ed.), *American Correspondence of a Bristol Merchant*, p. 51; *Commons Journal*, XXXV, 91; Cobbett (ed.), *Parliamentary History*, XVIII, 210–221; [Almon,] *Parliamentary Register*, I, 131–132; Force (ed.), *American Archives*, 4th Ser., I, 1219–1221, 1571; Stephen Fuller to Dartmouth, Feb. 7, 1775, Dartmouth Papers, II, 1135.

of the Atlantic trading community testified before both houses of Parliament against the bills for restraining American commerce. Among those who appeared were Stephen Higginson and John Lane of New England; Benjamin Lister and George Davis, merchants in the Newfoundland fishery; Molyneux Shuldham and Sir Hugh Pallister, former governors of Newfoundland; George Walker and John Ellis of the West India interest; and Seth Jenkins and Brooke Watson. Managing the whole affair and summing up the testimony was David Barclay.[49] Had Franklin and Barlow Trecothick been there it might have seemed as if the events of 1766 were being repeated. But there was a further difference: the merchants were unsuccessful, for the ministry was not behind their effort. The North administration did not support the merchants as the Rockingham ministry had nine years before.[50] The lobby failed.

IV

What more could the American agents in London do? Josiah Quincy, Jr., rumored to be a secret emissary of the Massachusetts patriots, and Arthur Lee were possibly considering at this early date an appeal to some foreign power, but Benjamin Franklin dissuaded Quincy from such a drastic move. Franklin still professed the hope that within a year economic pressure would bring the ministers to their senses. In a letter to Charles Thomson, secretary to the Continental Congress, he recommended continued economic sanctions. The administration, already staggering, Franklin confided, would have fallen but for reports from America that the colonists themselves were unsteady in their devotion to the patriot cause. Franklin's advice to Thomson was well calculated to nullify the olive-branch resolution, for he warned that once the colonists had submitted, "possibly they may obtain a Quebec Constitution." The only

49. Cobbett (ed.), *Parliamentary History*, XVIII, 380–383, 421–478; [Almon,] *Parliamentary Register*, I, 256–279, 327–360; Force (ed.), *American Archives*, 4th Ser., I, 1637–1670, 1721–1743.

50. On March 30, 1775, Apsley, Suffolk, Sandwich, Rochford, North, and Dartmouth agreed to recommend to the King that a commission be given to the Governor of Massachusetts to issue a proclamation requiring all persons having committed acts of treason and rebellion to surrender to the civil authority. Minute of cabinet, March 30, 1775, Dartmouth Papers, II, 1197.

salvation was union in an economic boycott.[51] Such was the "authentick" intelligence of the most influential agent. Franklin's views were to be all the more important when he departed for America on March 20, 1775; he would now advise the congress personally. Before leaving England, however, he turned over to Arthur Lee the affairs of the Massachusetts agency.

Thus the ranks of the agents were further reduced. Only Lee, Life, Burke, and Paul Wentworth remained. The latter was no agent but in reality a tool of the administration who tried to persuade Lee to cease pamphleteering and travel abroad. He even offered the Virginian a "loan" of £300. In addition, the agent might have the "Ministry's countenance, or at least their connivance," for a place in the City to succeed Sergeant John Glynn as Recorder when he died.[52] Lee was impervious to these blandishments. But the other agents were of little consequence. Thomas Life confined his activities to an expression of regret that both sides had not agreed on conciliatory measures. Since each had taken "so very decided a part it does not seem possible to end amicably for some time at least."[53] Burke was to do little more, for he was more a member of an opposition political faction than an agent. When he did deliver a memorial from the legislature of New York to the House of Commons it was rejected, for it implied sentiments contrary to the Declaratory Act. That Burke—the defender of this statute—should have delivered the memorial is ironic.[54] Henry

51. Entries for March 1, 3, 1775, Howe (ed.), "Journal of Josiah Quincy, Jun.," pp. 468, 469; Franklin to Thomson, March 13, 1773, Smyth (ed.), *Writings of Franklin*, VI, 315–316.

52. Entry for April 27, 1775, Hutchinson (ed.), *Diary and Letters of Thomas Hutchinson*, I, 434–435. There seems to be no corroborating evidence for the story Wentworth related to Hutchinson, but Dartmouth did write Lee on April 13 asking him to call on the following Sunday. Arthur Lee Papers, Alderman Library, University of Virginia, Charlottesville.

53. Life to Jonathan Trumbull, July 5, 1775, Connecticut Archives, War, 1675–1775, Colonial, Vol. X, Pt. 2, 1751–1775, Connecticut State Library, Hartford, Doc. 4352.

54. *Commons Journal*, XXXV, 376. There is further irony in a note Burke sent Dartmouth on May 9, 1775. "Mr. Burke presents his best Compliments to Lord Dartmouth. He received the honour of his Lordship's Message on his return home this Evening. He is much afraid that he may not be able to find a Peer whom he can prevail upon to deliver the New York Memorial to the house of Lords

Cruger, son of the speaker of the New York assembly and now a member for Bristol, had little faith in the agent. "Today, he shall be the *first* great *Promoter* of a *Declaratory* Bill. Tomorrow, he shall *insinuate* the Parliament have not a right to bind the Americans in all cases—and yet, *put him in power*, and the third day you shall find him asserting the supremacy of this country with a vengeance."[55] Cruger's thesis could not be tested, for Burke's party did not come to power at this time. Out of office he could do nothing. Neither could the other agents in London. To Arthur Lee it seemed that "Everything depends on the wisdom, firmness and unanimity" of the congress at Philadelphia, where Benjamin Franklin, who had already sailed for America, would assist "with every profession and every incentive to do right."[56]

V

Franklin arrived in Philadelphia on May 5; and the next day the Pennsylvania assembly appointed him a delegate to the Second Congress. This definitely marked the turning point for the former agent. In June he wrote Thomas Life that on leaving London he had proposed returning that fall, but due to the situation in America, "I now think it not likely I shall ever again see England. . . ."[57] By this time actual hostilities had begun. In July, 1775 the congress adopted the course that Franklin had suggested to Quincy and Charles Thomson and repeated the tactics of the previous year. The colonial agents were asked to join with Richard Penn in presenting a petition to the King stating the rights of the Americans. They were then to transmit to the congress and the respective

---

Tomorrow, as his Particular Friends in that House are not in Town. He will certainly do his best for that day but cannot answer for his success. . . ." (Dartmouth Papers, II, 1264). The Rockingham peers were not assiduous in business.

55. Henry Cruger to Peter Van Schaack, May 3, 1775, Henry C. Van Schaack, *Henry Cruger: The Colleague of Edmund Burke in the British Parliament* (New York, 1859), pp. 19–20.

56. Lee to Ralph Izard, April 23, 1775, Dees (ed.), *Correspondence of Mr. Ralph Izard*, I, 69–70.

57. Votes of the assembly, Samuel Hazard *et al.* (eds.), *Pennsylvania Archives* (9 series, Philadelphia and Harrisburg, 1852–1935), 8th Ser., VIII, 7231; Franklin to Life (extract), June 5, 1775, Dartmouth Papers, II, 1291.

legislatures the earliest information on matters of importance relating to America.[58]

But the lobby of agents had ceased to exist. On August 22, in reply to a letter from Arthur Lee, Burke refused to join him in presenting the petition to Dartmouth. He should be happy to do so, he argued, if "in the slightest degree" authorized by the colony he represented. However, the assembly of New York had refused to send delegates to the congress; and consequently he could not act contrary to the authority of his constituents. William Bollan also declined to act, informing Lee and Penn that he was "unfit for that service." Alone, Lee and Penn presented the petition to Dartmouth on September 1, but on requesting an answer they were informed that since the King did not receive the document while "on the throne," none would be forthcoming. The petition was published and read before the House of Lords on November 7, however, and three days later Penn testified on behalf of the congress.[59] But it was useless.

The agencies were no more; that same month a committee of the congress appointed Arthur Lee its secret representative for negotiations in Europe.[60]

The petitions by the agents failed, but what of the economic sanctions that Franklin, Lee, and others had so confidently expected would produce economic chaos in Britain, a change in administration, and a redress of American grievances? Some centers trading to the colonies—Bristol, for example—were severely affected, but these were exceptions. North of the Tweed, where Scottish merchants

58. Ford *et al.* (eds.), *Journals of the Continental Congress, 1774–1789*, II, 162, 170–171. The petition dated July 8, 1775, is in Stevens (comp.), *Facsimiles of manuscripts in European archives relating to America, 1773–1783*, V, No. 454.

59. Burke to Arthur Lee, Aug. 22, 1775, Arthur Lee Papers, Alderman Library; Bollan to Lee and Penn, n.d., *ibid.*, Dartmouth to Lee and Penn, Aug. 24, 1775, *ibid.*; Lee and Penn to the President of the Continental Congress, Sept. 2, 1775, *ibid.* (copy in Arthur Lee Papers, Harvard College Library); and Cobbett (ed.), *Parliamentary History*, XVIII, 896–900, 910–916. Lee enclosed a copy of the petition to the Marquis of Rockingham, claiming that the ministry "refused" an answer. Lee to Rockingham, Sept. 2, 1775, Wentworth-Woodhouse Muniments, R150–157.

60. Resolution of Nov. 29, 1775, Secret Journals of the Congress, Francis Wharton (ed.), *The Revolutionary Diplomatic Correspondence of the United States* (6 vols., Washington, D.C., 1888–1889), II, 61–62; committee of correspondence to Lee, Dec. 2, 1775, *ibid.*, II, 63–64.

had dominated the trade with the tobacco colonies, it became evident as "the first shock wore off" that the disappearance of American markets "was not occasioning the commercial and industrial distress which might have been expected." New markets were found.[61]

Generally the same situation prevailed in England. In London, a South Carolinian observed that notwithstanding the crisis with America the merchants, "dreadfully alarmed as they are, sit perfectly satisfied and contented. . . ." The stock market, always regarded as "the political barometer," had risen as if "no storm was to be apprehended." From Manchester, a Virginian reported that the manufacturers claimed they felt no "*great* loss *yet*" because of the American Association, for the decline in the colonial demand had coincided with an increase in the European market. Their trade had "only shifted to another channel."[62]

The congressional strategy of economic coercion based on the advice of Franklin and Lee had proved bankrupt. Having already committed themselves on the assumption that this policy would achieve their ends short of war or an open break with the mother country, the patriots in America found themselves with little alternative but to continue on a course destined to lead to separation within a year. Yet even if the congressional policy had succeeded, to the extent of making the British merchants conscious of the economic loss, the resulting pressure which they might have exerted on Parliament and the ministry would not have been sufficient to override one important factor. By this time war was a reality and George III—the key political figure—was adamant that there be no further compromise. On receiving the news of Lexington and Concord, the King, a man not "apt to be over sanguine," was convinced that with firmness and perseverance America will be brought to "submission. . . ." It must be a colony of Britain, he declared, or treated as an enemy. A distant possession standing on

61. Walter E. Minchinton (ed.), *The Trade of Bristol in the Eighteenth Century* (Bristol Records Society, *Publications*, Vol. XX [Bristol, 1957]), x–xi, p. 48n1; M. L. Robertson, "Scottish Commerce and the American War of Independence," *Economic History Review*, IX (1956), 124.

62. Ralph Izard to George Dempster, May 31, 1775, Dees (ed.), *Correspondence of Mr. Ralph Izard*, I, 79; George Mercer to Izard, Aug. 18, 1775, *ibid.*, I, 116–117.

equal footing with the "superior State is more ruinous than being deprived of such connections."[63]

Doubtless most Members of Parliament and the administration may not have been as extreme or outspoken, but they believed then, and had believed for the past decade, that the basic issue between Great Britain and the American colonies—an issue which could not be compromised—was the sovereignty of the mother country. Since the colonies apparently had not accepted conciliation and a greater measure of home rule when tentatively offered, force was now needed to assert this supremacy. This determination defeated the efforts of the agents and merchants.

63. George III to Dartmouth, June 10, 1775, H.M.C., *Thirteenth Report*, App., Pt. IV, 501.

CHAPTER IX

Conclusion

THE failure of the colonial agents and British merchants in the months preceding the outbreak of the American Revolution overshadowed their positive achievements during the previous decade and minimized the fact that they had played a significant part in the flexible, often pragmatic, administration of the First British Empire. Given any practical issue not posed in terms of a challenge to the authority of the mother country, they had either won concessions or obtained significant modifications of particular measures. Although the members of the lobby—colonists and Britons, lawyers, merchants, and members of Parliament—had infrequently disagreed on procedures, in general they had worked in concert, not at cross purposes. On one issue only, paper currency, and then for only a brief time, had some merchants disagreed in 1764 on a substantive matter with the agents.

The aims of the two groups had been the same. Who could say whether Dennys DeBerdt, the Thomlinsons, or Barlow Trecothick served the colonies because they were merchants or agents? They saw their roles as complementary, not conflicting. Although some merchants in aiding the provinces may have followed primarily their own economic interests as they saw them, they considered that the prosperity of Britain depended on the well-being of the American colonies. Years of friendship, blood relationship, marriage, and common ideals also tied the British merchants to the English-speaking communities across the Atlantic.

227

Agents and Merchants

Despite its ultimate failure the combination of agents and merchants enjoyed marked successes, particularly in the years following the French war. Since many of the measures of the imperial government relating to the colonies were initially practical attempts to resolve specific problems, various ministries accepted the advice of the agents and merchants, and the alternatives the lobbyists suggested in the offices of Whitehall. The experienced "men of business" serving on the Grenville administrative boards consulted the agents and merchants, familiar with conditions in America, on almost all of the measures relating to the colonies. The lobbyists, by a process of "give and take," were able to secure modifications of the Molasses and Currency Acts in 1764. Through the agents Grenville initially sought an alternative to the stamp bill, and when the measure was enacted because of political considerations he allowed the agents and merchants to nominate the stamp distributors so as to facilitate the implementation of the revenue measure in the colonies. The lobby was most effective during the Rockingham Ministry early in 1766, for the inexperienced Whigs relied heavily on the agents and merchants to supply the rationalization and much of the organization for the ministerial program relating to the colonies. The result of their efforts was the repeal of the Stamp Act, a reduction of many of the duties on American commerce, and an amelioration of the restrictions on colonial trade. And in later years the agents and merchants secured repeal of the Townshend duties as well as practical accommodations on the Currency and Mutiny Acts.

But several factors operated against the lobby and, in the end, nullified its efforts. The influence of the British merchants was effective on political issues only when supported by the various ministries. Other conditions—political apathy and factionalism within the colonial governments—also curtailed the agencies. Disputes among and within the various branches of the provincial governments for the right to nominate the agents, when posed in terms of the authority of the governors and representative assemblies, were crucial. Consequently the agent in time was often identified with a patriot party in the lower houses, especially in the Bay Colony. Those provinces which retained agents tended to appoint men sympathetic to the patriot cause; one such agent, Benjamin

228

Conclusion

Franklin, who in later years acted for four colonies, represented a group in Massachusetts which, in the minds of various British ministers, challenged the authority of the mother country by enunciating a doctrine that the British Parliament had no legislative authority over the colonies.

This revolutionary challenge to the authority of the imperial government, narrowly confined in 1765 to the question of taxation and gradually extended to exclude the authority of Parliament completely, proved the decisive issue and defeated the lobby in the last crisis. Had it not been for the issue of Parliamentary authority, the agents and merchants might have been able to bring about a resolution of any dispute on practical terms. But in many instances the Whigs in the colonies insisted on basing their demands for repeal of objectionable legislation on a challenge to the right of the imperial government to enact those statutes. Some agents such as DeBerdt, Richard Jackson, and Charles Garth—agents who conscientiously served their constituents—often remonstrated that this colonial challenge made any practical accommodation all the more difficult, indeed impossible. Other agents such as Franklin and Arthur Lee made it the central issue. And it was Franklin who formulated the theory, publicly enunciated by 1773 and later incorporated into the Declaration of Independence, that Parliament had no right to legislate for the separate, distinct American states. That Parliament had this right was the single point to which all British ministries adhered. If the Americans were upholding a principle, British officials were also, and this principle of Parliamentary jurisdiction was a common theme from the Stamp Act to the olive-branch resolution by which the imperial legislature waived the exercise of its right for a recognition by the colonies of its legal authority.

Why did both sides so tenaciously support these legal abstractions? The motivation of the Whig leaders in America may be rooted in what has been termed an area of permanent conflict created by the divergence between political and social leadership at the topmost level of society in America. Political factions may have branded various British measures as a threat to home rule and used this rationalization to achieve status and power. And entrenched groups with their position threatened by the dissentent factions had to prove themselves no less devoted to the cause of local liberty.[1]

But what motivated the British ministers? Why did they think themselves called upon to introduce measures simply to enforce a legal abstraction? Were they guilty of a plot against colonial self-government, as recent patriot historians have charged? Or was their gravest fault a "lofty ignorance," as one English scholar has indicated, of the inappropriateness of their policy to the situation of the American colonies by the middle of the eighteenth century?[2] In some instances British measures—those instituted by the Grenville ministry, for example—arose not out of a desire to subvert local government but out of practical considerations in administration and were based on first-hand information supplied by colonists, the agents in London, and the British merchants. Neither were the so-called "coercive" Acts of the North ministry intended as a plot against representative government in North America, but rather as measures to restore a balanced government and by legal means to control an incipient revolutionary movement. In the final analysis—and this was by no means evident at the time—the estimates of the British ministers of the military requirements to enforce the policy were faulty. But in view of the evidence presented in this study on the activities of the agents and merchants, and the processes of imperial administration, were North, Hillsborough, Grenville, and Dartmouth really so ignorant of conditions in the colonies, and were their measures, limited in nature and scope, really so inappropriate? It has often been said that Grenville lost the colonies because he read the dispatches from America as preceding ministers during the

1. Bernard Bailyn's provocative essay "Politics and Social Structure in Virginia," in James Morton Smith (ed.), *Seventeenth-Century America: Essays in Colonial History* (Chapel Hill, 1959), p. 90–115, is also relevant for the eighteenth century. Somewhat the same conclusion may be drawn from the presentation of the issues in later Virginia. See Carl Bridenbaugh, *Seat of Empire·The Political Role of Eighteenth-Century Williamsburg* (new edn., Williamsburg, 1958). For a more extended analysis of this thesis as applied to the American Revolution see also Don R. Gerlach, *Philip Schuyler and the American Revolution in New York, 1733–1777* (Lincoln, Nebr., 1964).

2. See the review by Richard Pares of Robert E. Brown's *Middle-Class Democracy and the Revolution in Massachusetts, 1691–1780*, in *English Historical Review*, LXXII (1957), 125.

period of "salutary neglect" had not done. Grenville and most other ministers following him were informed, but as the late Professor Lewis Namier pointed out some years ago, long before them the Duke of Newcastle as Secretary of State and head of the Treasury "applied himself with much zeal even to the detail of colonial government and business," as did the Earl of Halifax at the Board of Trade.[3] Following the Great War for the Empire, the critical factor in imperial relations was not the fresh attention to American affairs, as some have claimed, or the "lofty ignorance" of British officials, as others have contended, but the colonial challenge to the authority of the mother country.

Was the attempt to secure recognition of the authority of Parliament in the face of the colonial challenge the meaningless pursuit of an empty legal abstraction? The dilemma is best appreciated, perhaps, by men who are responsible for the exercise of governmental authority. No doubt many felt as did the Duke of Newcastle, when in the debate on the repeal of the Stamp Act he expressed the wish that the question of the authority of Parliament had never come up. But, he declared, "it was the fault of [the] Americans who by their Resolutions and their opposition to Law first made the Question."[4] Once challenged, any government, representative or not, must either act or abdicate if it is to rule responsibly. Britain acted when it asserted the authority of Parliament; but the North administration also recognized the legitimate desire for home rule. As have many governments in modern times, it had to answer difficult questions. When is revolution justified? How far in turn may government compromise? When is government justified in resisting a challenge to its authority?

The basic problem in 1775 was not home rule, for this might have been possible if the colonial leaders had recognized the authority of the home government and given the colonial agents latitude to negotiate. Nor was the basic problem a form of imperial federalism,

3. Lewis B. Namier, "Anthony Bacon, M.P., An Eighteenth-Century Merchant," *Journal of Economic and Business History*, II (1928), 28.

4. From the Earl of Hardwicke's notes of the debates in the House of Lords, March 11, 1766, Add. MSS., British Museum, 35912, ff. 76 *et seq.* edited by J. Franklin Jameson and H. W. V. Temperly, "Debates on the Declaratory Act and the Repeal of the Stamp Act, 1766," *American Historical Review*, XVII (1912), 578.

assigning various jurisdictions or powers to particular legislatures, colonial and imperial, but rather who, in case of dispute, would make the final decision. Where would ultimate authority reside? In the final analysis, the colonists claimed these powers for their assemblies while the British nominally claimed them for Parliament. The locus of ultimate authority can rest in only one government, as the Americans themselves were to realize in the course of the following century. While the American union after 1787 was an attempt at divided sovereignty, a division of powers, the subsequent course of American history demonstrated that the final decision over the respective powers and authority of the state and federal governments lay with the central body. So Jefferson told the New England Federalists, so Jackson told the Nullifiers, and so Lincoln told the Secessionists. So Grenville and Mansfield argued in 1766, and so North, Dartmouth, and George III argued in 1775.

The ministers at Whitehall were themselves guilty of blunders, not the least of which was allowing the American leaders to think that economic pressure had indeed forced the imperial government to retreat. Perhaps the greatest blunder was in not making it clear in America what the home government sought to do and what the conditions were for home rule in the colonies. In the vacuum thus created by their disdain for directly and emphatically communicating their position, by default they allowed men such as Franklin, Burke, and Lee to win the propaganda battle when these agents informed colonial leaders that a plot existed against representative government and individual liberties. By 1774 effective communication between America and England had broken down. Emotionalism and partisan politics colored the judgment of Franklin and Lee, whose advice played a major role in shaping the policy of the delegates at Philadelphia and their assessment of the British offer for greater self-government. Operating on the fallacious assumption that economic coercion would achieve the desired goal, the delegates to the Continental Congress found themselves in a position they had not anticipated and which many had not wanted. There was then no alternative open to them except submission or resistance.

The failure of the American colonists to accept proffered concessions, and the galling defeats in the war that followed, embittered many British politicians and confirmed their belief that a lenient colonial policy had merely encouraged rebellion. Rather than forcing the imperial government to retreat, colonial resistance brought to power such inflexible ministers as Lord George Germain, who replaced the Earl of Dartmouth as Secretary of State for the American Department.[5] Ironically the rejection of negotiation and the ensuing war postponed[6] until the nineteenth century, rather than hastened, a liberal revision of the imperial constitution. But Canadians, Australians, and New Zealanders later were to prove themselves no less devoted to liberty than Americans. This was no accident of history or the result of any frontier process, for these English-speaking peoples shared a common heritage. British imperialism transplanted to the distant corners of the world the political institutions and values of the mother country: the rule of law and representative government limited by guarantees of individual rights. The Commonwealths and Dominions emerging as a result of the decentralization of the Second Empire—a process still continuing in our day—demonstrated many of the basic characteristics of the American Republic whose founding sundered the first British Empire.

5. On the stiffening of colonial policy under Germain, see Gerald Saxon Brown, *The American Secretary The Colonial Policy of Lord George Germain, 1775–1778* (Ann Arbor, 1963).

6. In 1780 the Privy Council approved the establishment of a new colony for the American loyalists, "New Ireland," to be established between Nova Scotia and Massachusetts Bay. In the plan for this government the ministry deliberately attempted to establish the "ground for an Aristocratic Power," by leasing lands in large tracts. It had been impressed with the fact that New York, the only colony with a large tenantry, was the least inclined to rebellion. See the proposal for the new colony in the Shelburne Papers, Clements Library, Ann Arbor, 66:513–528.

Select Bibliography

A definitive bibliography on British policy and the development of the American Revolution would be unmanageable; consequently the following list is confined to those items of particular interest and those cited in this study. It does not include many other materials consulted in the course of research.

MANUSCRIPTS AND ARCHIVAL SOURCES

James Abercromby Letter Book, 1746–1773, Virginia State Library, Richmond.
Additional Manuscripts, British Museum.
Jeffrey Amherst Papers (transcripts), Public Archives of Canada, Ottawa.
Belknap Papers, Force Transcripts, Library of Congress, Washington, D.C.
Bernard Papers, Harvard College Library, Cambridge, Mass.
Chatham Papers, Public Record Office, London.
Connecticut Archives, War, 1675–1775, Colonial, Vol. X, Pt. 2, 1751—1775, Connecticut State Library, Hartford.
George Croghan Papers, John Cadwallader Collection, Historical Society of Pennsylvania, Philadelphia.
William Legge, Earl of Dartmouth Papers, William Salt Library, Stafford, England.
Charles Wyndham, Earl of Egremont Papers, Public Record Office, London.
Benjamin Franklin and Joseph Galloway Letters, William L. Clements Library, Ann Arbor.
Benjamin Franklin Papers, American Philosophical Society Library, Philadelphia.
Benjamin Franklin Papers, Library of Congress, Washington, D.C.
General Thomas Gage Papers, William L. Clements Library, Ann Arbor.
Charles Garth–South Carolina committee of correspondence Letter Book, South Carolina Archives, Columbia.
George Grenville Letter Book, Stowe Collection, Huntington Library, San Marino, Calif.
George Grenville Papers, in the posssession of Sir John Murray, 50 Albemarle St., London, W.1.
Georgia Miscellaneous Manuscripts, 1732–1796, Force Transcripts, Library of Congress, Washington, D.C.

Agents and Merchants

Gurney and Barclay Family Papers, in the possession of Colonel Q. E. Gurney, Bawdeswell Hall, Norfolk, England.
Philip Yorke, Earl of Hardwicke Papers, British Museum, London.
Charles Jenkinson Papers (Liverpool Papers), British Museum, London.
William Samuel Johnson Journals and Papers, Connecticut Historical Society, Hartford.
William Knox Manuscripts, William L. Clements Library, Ann Arbor.
Arthur Lee Papers, Alderman Library, University of Virginia, Charlottesville.
Arthur Lee Papers, American Philosophical Society Library, Philadelphia.
Arthur Lee Papers, Harvard College Library, Cambridge, Mass.
Henry E. McCulloch-Edmund Fanning Papers, Southern Historical Collections, University of North Carolina, Chapel Hill.
Henry Marchant, "Journal of Voyage from Newport in the Colony of Rhode Island to London, Travels thro' many Parts of England & Scotland began July 8th 1771 . . . ," microfilm copy, Rhode Island Historical Society, Providence.
Massachusetts Archives, Vol. XXII, State House, Boston.
Miscellaneous Papers, Colonial Series, North Carolina Department of Archives and History, Raleigh.
Thomas Pelham-Holles, Duke of Newcastle Papers, British Museum, London.
Petworth House Archives, Vol. 163, Petworth House, Sussex, England.
Public Record Office, London
   Colonial Office, Class 5, 28, 42, 137, 152, 323, 324, 325, 326, 388, 389, 390.
   State Papers, Class 30, 37, 41.
   Treasury, Class 1, 11, 27, 28, 29.
Rhode Island Agents, Official Letters, Brown University Library, Providence.
William Petty, Earl of Shelburne Papers, William L. Clements Library, Ann Arbor.
Joseph Sherwood Letters, New Jersey Historical Society Library, Newark.
Joseph Sherwood Papers, Brown University Library, Providence, R.I.
John Temple Correspondence, Stowe Collection, Stowe Americana, Huntington Library, San Marino, Calif.
Trumbull Papers, Connecticut Archives, Connecticut State Library, Hartford.
Wentworth-Woodhouse Muniments (Rockingham papers), Sheffield City Library, Sheffield, England.

OTHER UNPUBLISHED SOURCES

Johnson, Allen S., "The Political Career of George Grenville." Ph.D. dissertation, Duke University, 1955.
Thomas, Leslie Joseph. "Partisan Politics in Massachusetts During Governor Bernard's Administration, 1760–1770." Ph.D. dissertation, University of Wisconsin, 1960.
Vering, Alice. "James Otis." Ph.D. dissertation, University of Nebraska, 1954.

Zimmerman, John Joseph. "Benjamin Franklin: A Study of Pennsylvania Politics and the Colonial Agency, 1755–1775." Ph.D. dissertation, University of Michigan, 1956.

PRINTED LETTER COLLECTIONS, DIARIES, AND PAPERS

Adams, Charles Francis (ed.). *The Works of John Adams.* 10 vols. Boston, 1850–1856.

[Adams, Richard.] "Letters of Richard Adams to Thomas Adams," *Virginia Magazine of History and Biography*, XXII (1914), 379–395.

[Almon, John.] *A Collection of Interesting, Authentic Papers, Relative to the Dispute between Great Britain and America; Shewing the causes and Progress of the Misunderstanding, from 1764 to 1775.* London, 1777.

Anson, Sir William R. (ed.). *The Autobiography and political correspondence of Augustus Henry, third Duke of Grafton, K.G. from hitherto unpublished documents in the possession of his family.* London, 1898.

"The Aspinwall Papers," 2 vols. of Massachusetts Historical Society *Collections*, 4th Ser., Vols. IX–X (Boston, 1871).

Ballagh, James C. (ed.). *The Letters of Richard Henry Lee.* 2 vols. New York, 1911–1914.

"The Belknap Papers," Massachusetts Historical Society *Collections*, 6th Ser., Vol. IV (Boston, 1891).

[Bland, Richard.] "Virginia in 1771," *Virginia Magazine of History and Biography*, VI (1898–1899), 127–134.

"The Bowdoin and Temple Papers," Massachusetts Historical Society *Collections*, 6th Ser., Vol. IX (Boston, 1897).

Bradford, Alden (ed.). *Memoirs of the Life and Writings of Jonathan Mayhew, D.D. Pastor of the West Church and Society in Boston, . . . 1747, . . . 1766.* Boston, 1838.

———— (ed.). *Speeches of the Governors of Massachusetts from 1765 to 1775; and the Answers of the House of Representatives To the Same; with their resolutions and addresses for that period and other Public Papers, relating to the Dispute between this country and Great Britain, which led to the Independence of the United States.* Boston, 1818.

The Burd Papers: Extracts from Chief Justice William Allen's Letter Book Selected and Arranged by Lewis Burd Walker Together with an Appendix Containing Pamphlets in the Controversy with Franklin. Pottsville, Pa., 1897.

Burnett, Edmund C. (ed.). *Letters of the Members of the Continental Congress.* 8 vols. Washington, D.C., 1921–1938.

Butterfield, L. H. (ed.). *The Letters of Benjamin Rush.* 2 vols. Philadelphia, 1951.

Campbell, Charles (ed.). *The Bland Papers: Being a Selection from the Manuscripts of Colonel Theodorick Bland, Jr.* 2 vols. Petersburg, Va., 1840–1843.

Carter, Clarence E. (ed.). *The Correspondence of General Thomas Gage.* 2 vols. New Haven, 1931–1933.

Channing, Edward, and Coolidge, Archibald Cary (eds.). *The Barrington-Bernard Correspondence and Illustrative Matter 1760–1770 Drawn from the "Papers of Sir Francis Bernard" (Sometime Governor of Massachusetts-Bay).* Cambridge, Mass., 1912.

Agents and Merchants

"The Commissions of Georgia to Benjamin Franklin to act as Colonial Agent at the Court of St. James," *Georgia Historical Quarterly*, II (1918), 150–162.

Copeland, Thomas W. (ed.). *The Correspondence of Edmund Burke Volume I April 1744–June 1768*. Cambridge and Chicago, 1958.

"Correspondence between William Strahan and David Hall, 1763–1777," *Pennsylvania Magazine of History and Biography*, X (1886), 86–99, 217–232, 322–333, 461–473.

"Correspondence of Charles Garth," *South Carolina Historical and Genealogical Magazine*, XXVI (1925), XXVIII (1927), XXIX (1928), XXX (1929), XXXI (1930), XXXIII (1932).

Crane, Verner W. (ed.). *Benjamin Franklin's Letters to the Press, 1758–1775*. Chapel Hill, 1950.

Cunningham, Anne Rowe (ed.). *Letters and Diary of John Rowe*. Boston, 1903.

"The [Silas] Deane Papers," New York Historical Society *Collections*, Vol. XIX (New York, 1886).

[Debrett, John.] *A Collection of Scarce and Interesting Tracts*. 4 vols. London, 1788.

Dees, Anne Izard (ed.). *Correspondence of Mr. Ralph Izard, of South Carolina, from the Year 1774 to 1804* [1777], *with a Short Memoir*. 2 vols. New York, 1844.

Dexter, Franklin B. (ed.). "A Selection from the Correspondence and miscellaneous papers of Jared Ingersoll," New Haven Colony Historical Society *Papers*, Vol. IX (New Haven, 1918).

Dobrée, Bonamy (ed.). *Letters of William Stanhope, Earl of Chesterfield*. 6 vols. London, 1932.

"The Fitch Papers. Correspondence and Documents During Thomas Fitch's Governorship of the Colony of Connecticut 1754–1766," 2 vols. of Connecticut Historical Society *Collections*, Vols. XVII–XVIII (Hartford, 1918–1920).

Ford, Paul L. (ed.). *The Writings of John Dickinson. Vol. 1 Political Writings, 1764–1774*. Philadelphia, 1895.

Ford, Worthington C. (ed.). "Letters of Governor Shirley and William Bollan to the Lords of Trade, respecting the disregard in New England of the Navigation Laws, 1743," Publications of the Colonial Society of Massachusetts *Transactions*, VI (1899–1900), 297–304.

——— (ed.). *Letters of William Lee, sheriff and alderman of London; commercial agent of the Continental Congress in France; and minister to the courts of Vienna and Berlin, 1766–1783*. 3 vols. Brooklyn, N.Y., 1891.

Fortescue, Sir John (ed.). *The correspondence of King George the Third, from 1760 to December 1783, Printed from the Original Papers in the Royal Archives at Windsor Castle*. 6 vols. London, 1927.

[Garth, Charles.] "Stamp Act Papers," *Maryland Historical Magazine*, VI (1911), 282–305.

Gibbs, Robert Wilson (ed.). *Documentary history of the American Revolution: consisting of letters and papers relating to the contest for liberty, chiefly in South Carolina*. 3 vols. New York, 1853–1857.

Greig, John Y. (ed.). *The Letters of David Hume*. 2 vols. Oxford, 1932.

Guttridge, George H. (ed.). *The American correspondence of a Bristol Merchant, 1766–1776, The Letters of Richard Champion.* Berkeley, 1934.

Hawes, Lila M. (ed.). "Letters to the Georgia Colonial Agent, July 1762, to January, 1771," *Georgia Historical Quarterly,* XXXVI (1952), 250–286.

Hoffman, Ross J. S. (ed.). *Edmund Burke, New York Agent, with his letters to the New York Assembly and intimate correspondence with Charles O'Hara 1761–1776.* Philadelphia, 1956.

Howard, Robert Mowbray (ed.). *Records and Letters of the Family of the Longs of Longville, Jamaica, and Hampton Lodge, Surrey.* 2 vols. London, 1925.

Howe, Mark Anthony DeWolfe (ed.). "Journal of Josiah Quincy, Jun., During his Voyage and Residence in England from September 28th, 1774 to March 3d, 1775," Massachusetts Historical Society *Proceedings,* L (1916–1917), 433–471.

Hutchinson, Peter Orlando (ed.). *The Diary and Letters of Thomas Hutchinson.* 2 vols., London, 1883–1886.

Jucker, Ninetta S. (ed.). *The Jenkinson Papers, 1760–1766.* London, 1949.

Keppell, George Thomas, sixth Earl of Albemarle. *Memoirs of the Marquis of Rockingham and his contemporaries. With original Letters and Documents now first published.* 2 vols. London, 1852.

Kimball, Gertrude S. (ed.). *The Correspondence of the Colonial Governors of Rhode Island, 1723–1775.* 2 vols. Boston and New York, 1902.

Knollenberg, Bernhard (ed.). "Thomas Hollis and Jonathan Mayhew: Their Correspondence," Massachusetts Historical Society *Proceedings,* LXIX (1947–1950), 102–193.

Knox, William. *Extra Official State Papers, Addressed to the Right Hon. Lord Rawdon and the other Members of the Two Houses of Parliament, Associated for the Preservation of the Constitution and Promoting the Prosperity of the British Empire. By a Late Under Secretary of State.* London edn., 1789.

Labaree, Leonard W. (ed.). *Royal Instructions to British Colonial Governors, 1670–1776.* 2 vols. New York, 1935.

"The [Charles] Lee Papers," 4 vols. of New York Historical Society *Collections,* Vols. IV–VII (New York, 1871–1874).

Lee, Richard H. *Life of Arthur Lee . . . with his political and literary correspondence and his papers on the diplomatic and political subjects and the affairs of the United States.* 2 vols. Boston, 1829.

"Letter Book of John Watts, Merchant and Councillor of New York . . . ," New York Historical Society *Collections.* LXI (New York, 1928).

"Letters of Bowdoin and Pownall," Massachusetts Historical Society *Proceedings,* V (1860–1862), 237–248.

"Letters of [Benjamin] Franklin to the committee of correspondence of the Assembly of Pennsylvania," *Pennsylvania Magazine of History and Biography,* V (1881), 353–355.

"The Letters of Hon. James Habersham, 1756–1775," Georgia Historical Society *Collections,* Vol. VI (1904).

"Letters of John Hancock, 1760, 1761," Massachusetts Historical Society *Proceedings,* XLIII (1909–1910), 193–200.

Agents and Merchants

"Letters of Joseph Sherwood, Agent for the Province of New Jersey in Great Britain, 1761–1766," New Jersey Historical Society *Proceedings*, 1st Ser., V (1850–1851), 133–153.

"The Letters and Papers of Cadwallader Colden," New York Historical Society *Collections*, 11 vols. (New York, 1877–1878, 1918–1924, 1935, 1937).

"Letters of Samuel Cooper to Thomas Pownall, 1769–1777," *American Historical Review*, VIII (1901), 301–330.

"Letters to Thomas Adams," *Virginia Magazine of History and Biography*, VI (1898–1899), 30–32.

"Letters of Thomas Cushing from 1767 to 1775," Massachusetts Historical Society *Collections*, 4th Ser., IV (Boston, 1858), 347–366.

Lincoln, Charles (ed.). *Messages From The Governors [of New York]*. 11 vols. Albany, 1909.

Mathews, Albert (ed.). "Letters of Dennys DeBerdt, 1757–1770," Publications of the Colonial Society of Massachusetts *Transactions*, XIII (1910–1911), 293–461.

Mulkearn, Lois (ed.). *George Mercer Papers relating to the Ohio Company of Virginia*. Pittsburgh, 1954.

Mure, William (ed.). *Caldwell Family Papers, Selections from the family papers preserved at Caldwell*. (Maitland Club *Publications*. 2 vols. in 3 pts.) Glasgow, 1854.

Norton, J. E. (ed.). *The Letters of Edward Gibbon*. 3 vols. London, 1956.

"The Papers of Charles Thomson," New York Historical Society *Collections*, XI (New York, 1878).

"The Papers of Lewis Morris, Governor of the Province of New Jersey, from 1738 to 1746," New Jersey Historical Society *Collections*, IV (1852).

"Papers of Oxenbridge Thacher," Massachusetts Historical Society *Proceedings*, XX (1882–1883), 46–56.

Papers Relating to Public Events in Massachusetts Preceding the American Revolution. Printed for the Seventy-Six Society. Philadelphia, 1856.

"The Pitkin Papers Correspondence and Documents During William Pitkin's Governorship of the Colony of Connecticut 1766–1769," Connecticut Historical Society *Collections*, Vol. XIX (Hartford, 1921).

Preston, R. A. (ed.). "Sir William Keith's Justification of a Stamp Duty in the Colonies, 1739–1742," *Canadian Historical Review*, XXIX (1948), 168–182.

"Proceedings of the Virginia Committee of Correspondence," *Virginia Magazine of History and Biography*, IX (1902), 355–360; X (1903), 337–356; XI (1903–1904), 1–25, 131–143, 346–357; XII (1904–1905), 1–14, 157–169, 225–240, 353–364.

Quincy, Josiah. *Memoir of the Life of Josiah Quincy, Junior, of Massachusetts Bay, 1744–1775*. Boston, 1825.

Redington, Joseph, and Roberts, Richard A. (eds.). *Calendar of Home Office Papers of the reign of George III, 1760–1775*. 4 vols. London, 1878–1899.

Reed, William B. *Life and Correspondence of Joseph Reed*. 2 vols. Philadelphia, 1847.

Reed, William B. *Life of Esther Reed*. Philadelphia, 1853.

Sabine, William H. W. (ed.). *Historical Memoirs From 16 March to 9 July 1776 of William Smith Historian Of The Province of New York Member of the Governor's Council And Last Chief Justice of That Province Under the Crown Chief Justice of Quebec From the previously unpublished Manuscript in the New York Public Library.* New York, 1956.

Schneider, Herbert W., and Carol S. (eds.). *Samuel Johnson, His Career and Writings.* 4 vols. New York, 1929.

Sedgwick, Romney (ed.). *Letters from George III to Lord Bute, 1756–1766.* London, 1939.

"Selections from the Letterbook of Thomas Wharton, of Philadelphia, 1773–1783," *Pennsylvania Magazine of History and Biography*, XXXIII (1909), 319–339, 432–453.

Shaw, William A. (ed.). *Miscellaneous representations relative to our concerns in America, submitted [in 1761] to the Earl of Bute by Henry McCulloch.* London, 1905.

Smith, William J. (ed.). *The Grenville Papers, being the Correspondence of Richard Grenville Earl Temple, K.G., and the Right Hon. George Grenville, their Friends and Contemporaries.* 4 vols. London, 1852–1853.

Smyth, Albert H. (ed.). *The Writings of Benjamin Franklin with a Life and Introduction.* 10 vols. New York, 1907.

Sullivan, James, *et al.* (eds.). *The Papers of Sir William Johnson.* 12 vols. Albany and New York, 1921–1957.

Sutherland, Lucy S. (ed.). *The Correspondence of Edmund Burke Volume II July 1768– June 1774.* Cambridge and Chicago, 1960.

Taylor, W. S., and Pringle, J. H. (eds.). *Correspondence of William Pitt, Earl of Chatham.* 4 vols. London, 1838–1840.

"The Trumbull Papers," 4 vols. of Massachusetts Historical Society *Collections*, 5th Ser., Vols. IX–X, 7th Ser., Vols. II–III (Boston, 1885–1902).

Tyler, J. E. (ed.). "Colonel George Mercer's Papers," *Virginia Magazine of History and Biography*, LX (1952), 414–420.

Van Doren, Carl (ed.). *Benjamin Franklin's Autobiographical Writings*. New York, 1945.

—— (ed.). *Letters and Papers of Benjamin Franklin and Richard Jackson, 1753–1785.* Philadelphia, 1947.

Walpole, Horace. *Memoirs of the reign of King George the Second*, ed. Lord Holland. (2nd revised edn.). 3 vols. London, 1847.

——. *Memoirs of the reign of King George the Third*, ed. G. F. Russell Barker. 4 vols. London, 1894.

Wharton, Francis (ed.). *The Revolutionary Diplomatic Correspondence of the United States.* 6 vols. Washington, D.C., 1888–1889.

Wolkins, George G. (ed.). "Letters of Charles Paxton," Massachusetts Historical Society *Proceedings*, LVI (1922–1923), 343–352.

MISCELLANEOUS PRINTED SOURCES

[Almon, John.] *The Parliamentary Register; or History of the Proceedings and Debates of the House of Commons* [House of Lords] *1774–1780.* 17 vols. London, 1775–1780.

Bartlett, John Russell (ed.). *Records of the Colony of Rhode Island and Providence Plantations, in New England.* 10 vols. Providence, 1856–1865.

Bouton, Nathaniel, *et al.* (eds.). *Documents and Records Relating to the Province of New Hampshire.* 40 vols. Concord, 1867–1943.

Browne, William H., *et al.* (eds.). *Archives of Maryland.* 66 vols. Baltimore, 1883—.

Candler, Allen P. (ed.). *The Colonial Records of the State of Georgia.* 26 vols. Atlanta, 1904–1916.

Cobbett, William (ed.). *The Parliamentary History of England from the Earliest Period to the Year 1803.* 36 vols. London, 1813.

[Cooper, William.] "Minutes of the Tea Meeting, 1773," Massachusetts Historical Society *Proceedings,* XX (1882–1883), 10–17.

Cushing, Henry A. (ed.). *Writings of Samuel Adams.* 4 vols. New York, 1904–1908.

[Debrett, John.] *The History, debates, and proceedings of both houses of Parliament . . . 1743 to 1774.* 7 vols. London, 1792.

Delaware (Colony). *Votes and Proceedings of the House of Representatives of the Government of the Counties of New-Castle, Kent and Sussex Upon Delaware . . . [1762].* Reprinted Wilmington, 1930.

Delaware (Colony). *Votes and Proceedings of the House of Representatives of the Government of the Counties of New-castle, Kent and Sussex Upon Delaware . . . [1765–1770].* Wilmington, 1770 (reprinted Wilmington, 1931).

Doughty, Arthur S., and Shortt, Adam (eds.). *Documents relating to the constitutional history of Canada, 1759–1791.* Ottawa, 1907.

Drinker, Henry. "Effects of the 'Non-Importation Agreement' in Philadelphia, 1769–1770," *Pennsylvania Magazine of History and Biography,* XIV (1890), 41–45.

Elsey, George M. (ed.). "John Wilkes and William Palfrey," Publications of the Colonial Society of Massachusetts *Transactions,* XXXIV (1937–1942), 411–428.

Force, Peter (ed.). *American Archives.* 4th and 5th Ser. 9 vols. Washington, D.C., 1837–1853.

Ford, Worthington C., *et al.* (eds.). *Journals of the Continental Congress, 1774–1789, Edited from the Original Records in the Library of Congress.* 34 vols. Washington, D.C., 1904–1937.

Foulke, Samuel. "An Account of the Proceedings of the General Assembly of Pennsylvania Commenc'd Oct. 14, 1761 with some remarks on Such Occurrences as were most worthy of notice, Written For my Own satisfaction & Retrospection hereafter," *Pennsylvania Magazine of History and Biography,* VIII (1884), 407–413.

Great Britain, Board of Trade. *Journals of the Lords Commissioners of Trade and Plantations.* 14 vols. London, 1920–1938.

Great Britain, Parliament. *Journals of the House of Commons.* London, 1547—.

———. *Journals of the House of Lords.* London, 1558—.

Griffin, Frederick (ed.). *Junius Discovered.* Boston, 1854.

Hazard, Samuel, *et al.* (eds.). *Pennsylvania Archives.* 9 series. Philadelphia and Harrisburg, 1852–1935.

Hutchinson, Thomas. *The History of the Colony and Province of Massachusetts Bay,* ed. Lawrence Shaw Mayo. 3 vols. Cambridge, Mass., 1936.

Jameson, J. Franklin, and Temperly, H. W. V. (eds.). "Debates on the Declaratory Act and the Repeal of the Stamp Act, 1766," *American Historical Review*, XVII (1912), 563–586.

Jasper Mauduit Agent in London for the Province of the Massachusetts Bay 1762–1765. (Massachusetts Historical Society *Collections*, Vol. LXXIV.) Boston, 1918.

London *Gentleman's Magazine: and historical Chronicle.*

McIlwaine, Henry R., and Kennedy, John P. (eds.). *Journals of the House of Burgesses of Virginia.* 13 vols. Richmond, 1905–1913.

Massachusetts Historical Society *Collections.* 1st Ser. Vols. III, VI. Boston, 1794, 1800.

Massachusetts Historical Society *Proceedings.* Vol. XX (1882–1883), Vol. LVIII (Boston, 1924–1925).

Minchinton, Walter E. (ed.). *The Trade of Bristol in the Eighteenth Century.* (Bristol Records Society *Publications*, Vol. XX.) Bristol, England, 1957.

Minutes of the Provincial Council of Pennsylvania, 1693–1776. 10 vols. Harrisburg, 1851–1852.

Munroe, James (ed.). *Acts of the Privy Council, Colonial Series.* 6 vols. Edinburgh, 1908–1912.

New York (Colony). *Journal of the Legislative Council of the Colony of New York, 1691–1775.* 2 vols. Albany, 1861.

Niles, Hazekiah (ed.). *Principles and Acts of the Revolution in America.* Baltimore, 1822 (reprinted New York, 1876).

O'Callaghan, Edmund B., and Fernow, Berthold (eds.). *Documents Relative to the Colonial History of the State of New York.* 15 vols. Albany and New York, 1856–1887.

Ricord, Frederick W., and Nelson, William (eds.). *Archives of the State of New Jersey.* 36 vols. Newark, 1881–1941.

Royal Historical Manuscripts Commission. *Tenth Report.* App., Pt. I, London, 1885.

———. *Eleventh Report.* App., Pt. IV. London, 1887.

———. *Eleventh Report.* App., Pt. V. London, 1887.

———. *Thirteenth Report.* App., Pt. IV. London, 1892.

———. *Report on Manuscripts in Various Collections.* Vol. VI. London, 1919.

———. *Report on the Manuscripts of the Earl of Denbigh Preserved at Newnham Paddox, Warwickshire.* App., Pt. V. London, 1911.

———. *Report on the Manuscripts of the Marquess of Lothian preserved at Blickling Hall, Norfolk.* London, 1905.

———. *Report on the Manuscripts of Mrs. Stopford-Sackville, of Drayton House, Northamptonshire.* 2 vols. London, 1904.

Saunders, William L. (ed.). *Colonial Records of North Carolina.* 10 vols. Raleigh, 1888–1890.

"State of the Trade, 1763," Publications of the Colonial Society of Massachusetts *Transactions*, XIX (1916–1917), 379–390.

Stevens, Benjamin Franklin (comp.). *Facsimiles of manuscripts in European Archives relating to America, 1773–1783.* 25 vols. London, 1889–1898.

Trumbull, J. H., and Hoadley, C. J. (eds.). *Public Records of the Colony of Connecticut (1636–1776)*. 15 vols. Hartford, 1850–1890.

Virginia Gazette (Purdie and Dixon).

The Works of the Right Honorable Edmund Burke (4th edn.). 12 vols. Boston, 1871.

Wright, John (ed.). *Sir Henry Cavendish's debates of the House of Commons, during the thirteenth Parliament . . . 1768–1774*. 2 vols. London, 1841–1843.

PAMPHLETS

Bollan, William. *The Petition of Mr. Bollan, Agent for the Council of the Province of Massachusetts Bay, lately presented to the two Houses of Parliament; with a brief introduction . . . to which is subjoined the Council's defense against the charge of certain misdemeanors.* London, 1774.

————. *The Petition of Mr. Bollan, Agent for the Council of the Province of Massachusetts Bay, to the King in Council, dated January 26, 1774.* London, 1774.

Knox, William. *The Claim of the Colonies to an Exemption from Internal Taxes Imposed by Authority of Parliament, Examined.* London, 1765.

————. *The Controversy Between Great Britain and her Colonies Reviewed.* London, 1769.

————. *The Interests of the Merchants and Manufacturers of Great Britain, In the Present Contest with the Colonies, Stated and Considered.* London, 1774.

Lee, Arthur. *A Speech intended to have been delivered in the House of Commons, in support of the Petition from the general Congress at Philadelphia: by the author of An Appeal to the Justice and Interests of Great Britain.* London, 1775.

————. *A Second Appeal to the justice and interests of the people on the measures respecting America By the author of the first.* London, 1775.

Lloyd, Charles. *The Conduct of the Late Administration Examined.* London, 1767.

Massachusetts Colony, Council. *Letters to the Right Honourable The Earl of Hillsborough from Gov. Bernard, Gen. Gage, &c The Honourable His Majesty's Council for Massachusetts Bay.* Boston and London, 1769.

Mauduit, Israel. *The Letters of Governor Hutchinson, and Lieut. Governor Oliver, & C., Printed at Boston, and Remarks Thereon With the Assembly's Addresses, and the Proceedings of the Lords Committee of Council. Together with the Substance of Mr. Wedderburn's Speech relating to those Letters and the Report of the Lords Committee to his Majesty in Council.* (2nd edn.) London, 1774.

————. *A Short View of the History of the New England Colonies, with Respect to their Charters and Constitution.* (4th edn.) London, 1776.

Pownall, Thomas. *The Administration of the Colonies.* (4th edn.) London, 1768.

Whately, Thomas. *Considerations on the Trade and Finances of this Kingdom, and on the Measures of Administration, with respect to those great National Objects since the conclusion of the Peace.* (3rd edn.) London, 1769.

[Whately, Thomas, and/or Knox, William.] *The Present State of the Nation Particularly with Respect to its Trade, Finances, &c. &c.* London, 1768.

Whately, Thomas. *The Regulations lately Made concerning the Colonies and the Taxes Imposed upon Them, Considered.* London, 1765.

Select Bibliography

BOOKS

Alden, John Richard. *The South in the American Revolution, 1763–1789*. Baton Rouge, La., 1957.

Andrews, Charles McLean. *The Colonial Period of American History*. 4 vols. New Haven, 1934–1938.

Armytage, Francis. *The Free Port System in the British West Indies. A Study in Commercial Policy 1766–1882*. London, 1953.

Auger, Helen. *The Secret War of Independence*. New York, 1955.

Beaven, Alfred B. *The Aldermen of the City of London*. 2 vols. London, 1908–1913.

Bezanson, Anne, Gray, R. D., and Hussey, Miriam. *Prices in Colonial Pennsylvania*. Philadelphia, 1935.

Bridenbaugh, Carl. *Seat of Empire The Political Role of Eighteenth Century Williamsburg*. (new edn.) Williamsburg, 1958.

Brown, Gerald Saxon. *The American Secretary The Colonial Policy of Lord George Germain, 1775–1778*. Ann Arbor, 1963.

Brown, Robert E. *Middle-Class Democracy and the Revolution in Massachusetts, 1691–1780*. Ithaca, New York, 1955.

Burns, James J. *The Colonial Agents of New England*. Washington, D.C., 1935.

Christie, Ian R. *The End of North's Ministry 1780–1782*. London, 1958.

Clark, Dora Mae. *British Opinion and the American Revolution*. New Haven, 1930.

Clark, Sir George N. *War and Society in the Seventeenth Century*. Cambridge, England, 1958.

Cole, Arthur H. *Wholesale Commodity Prices in the United States 1700–1861 Statistical Supplement*. Cambridge, Mass., 1938.

Coleman, Kenneth. *The American Revolution in Georgia 1763–1789*. Athens, Ga., 1958.

Cone, Carl B. *Burke and the Nature of Politics. The Age of the American Revolution*. Lexington, Ky., 1957.

Crane, Verner W. *Benjamin Franklin and a Rising People*. Boston, 1954.

Davidson, Philip. *Propaganda and the American Revolution, 1763–1783*. Chapel Hill, 1941.

Dickerson, Oliver M. *The Navigation Acts and the American Revolution*. Philadelphia, 1951.

Donoughue, Bernard. *British Politics And The American Revolution. The Path to War, 1773–1775*. London, 1964.

East, Robert A. *Business Enterprise in the American Revolution*. New York, 1938.

Gerlach, Don R. *Philip Schuyler and the American Revolution in New York 1733–1777*. Lincoln, Nebr., 1964.

Gipson, Lawrence Henry. *The British Empire Before the American Revolution*. 10 vols. to date. Caldwell, Idaho and New York, 1936—.

——. *Jared Ingersoll: A Study of American loyalism in relation to British colonial government*. New Haven, 1920.

Greene, Jack P. *The Quest for Power. The Lower Houses of Assembly in the Southern Royal Colonies 1689–1776*. Chapel Hill, 1963.

Groce, George C. *William Samuel Johnson*. New York, 1937.

Harlow, Vincent T. *The Founding of the Second British Empire, 1763–1793.* London and New York, 1952.

Harrington, Virginia D. *The New York Merchants on the Eve of the Revolution.* New York, 1952.

Holdsworth, Sir William. *A History of English Law.* 12 vols. London, 1938.

Judd, Gerrit P. IV. *Members of Parliament, 1734–1832.* New Haven, 1955.

Keith, Arthur B. *Constitutional History of the First British Empire.* Oxford, 1930.

Lilly, Edward P. *The Colonial Agents of New York and New Jersey.* Washington, D.C., 1936.

Lonn, Ella. *The Colonial Agents of the Southern Colonies.* Chapel Hill, 1945.

McIlwain, Charles. *The American Revolution: a constitutional interpretation.* New York, 1923.

Miller, John C. *Origins of the American Revolution.* Boston, 1943.

Mims, Steward L. *Colbert's West Indian Policy.* New Haven, 1912.

Morgan, Edmund S. and Helen M. *The Stamp Act Crisis. Prologue to Revolution.* Chapel Hill, 1953.

Namier, Lewis B. *Additions and Corrections to Sir John Fortescue's Edition of the Correspondence of King George the Third (Vol. I).* Manchester, England, 1937.

———. *Charles Townshend His Character and Career, The Leslie Stephen Lecture, 1959.* Cambridge, England, 1959.

———. *England in the Age of the American Revolution.* London, 1930.

———. *The Structure of Politics at the Accession of George III.* 2 vols. London, 1929.

Namier, Sir Lewis, and John Brooke. *The History of Parliament: The House of Commons 1754–1790.* 3 vols. New York, 1964.

Nettels, Curtis P. *The Money Supply of the American Colonies Before 1720. (University of Wisconsin Studies in the Social Sciences and History.* No. 20.) Madison, Wisc., 1934.

Pares, Richard. *Yankees and Creoles: The Trade between North America and the West Indies before the American Revolution.* Cambridge, Mass., 1956.

Penson, Lillian M. *The Colonial Agents of the British West Indies: a study in colonial administration mainly in the eighteenth century.* London, 1924.

Porter, Kenneth Wiggins. *The Jacksons and the Lees. Two Generations of Massachusetts Merchants, 1765–1844.* 2 vols. Cambridge, Mass., 1937.

Pownall, Charles A. W. *Thomas Pownall, Governor of the Colony of Massachusetts Bay; author of the Letters of Junius, etc.* London, 1908.

Ritcheson, Charles R. *British Politics and the American Revolution.* Norman, Okla., 1954.

Sachse, William L. *The Colonial American in Britain.* Madison, Wisc., 1956.

Schlesinger, Arthur M. *Prelude to Independence; the newspaper war on Britain, 1764–1776.* New York, 1958.

Schutz, John A. *Thomas Pownall, British Defender of American Liberty; a study of Anglo-American Relations in the Eighteenth Century.* Glendale, Calif., 1951.

Schuyler, Robert Livingston. *Parliament and the British Empire; some constitutional considerations concerning jurisdiction.* New York, 1929.

Shipton, Clifford K. *Biographical Sketches of Those Who Attended Harvard College in the Classes 1736–1740 with Biographical and Other Notes; Sibley's Harvard Graduates.* Vol. X. Boston, 1958.

Smith, James Morton (ed.). *Seventeenth-Century America: Essays in Colonial History.* Chapel Hill, 1959.

Sosin, J. M. *Whitehall and the Wilderness: The Middle West in British Colonial Policy, 1760–1775.* Lincoln, Nebr., 1961.

Taylor, A. J. P. *Englishmen and Others.* London, 1956.

Tolles, Frederick B. *Meeting House and Counting House: The Quaker Merchants of Colonial Philadelphia, 1682–1763.* Chapel Hill, 1948.

Tudor, William. *The Life of James Otis.* Boston, 1823.

Ubbelohde, Carl. *The Vice-Admiralty Courts and the American Revolution.* Chapel Hill, 1960.

Unwin, George. *Studies in Economic History: the Collected Papers of George Unwin,* ed. R. H. Tawney. London, 1927.

Van Schaack, Henry C. *Henry Cruger: The Colleague of Edmund Burke in the British Parliament.* New York, 1859.

Van Tyne, Claude H. *England & America. Rivals in the American Revolution.* Cambridge and New York, 1927.

Ward, A. W., Prothero, G. W., and Leathes, Stanley (eds.). *The Cambridge Modern History.* 13 vols. London, 1902–1912.

Wolff, Mabel Pauline. *The Colonial Agency of Pennsylvania 1712–1757.* Philadelphia, 1933.

ARTICLES

Aldridge, Alfred Owen. "Benjamin Franklin as Georgia Agent," *Georgia Review,* VI (1952), 161–173.

Andrews, Charles McLean. "Boston Merchants and the Non-Importation Movement," Publications of the Colonial Society of Massachusetts *Transactions,* XIX (1916–1917), 159–259.

Appleton, Marguerite. "The Agents of the New England Colonies in the Revolutionary Period," *New England Quarterly,* VI (1933), 371–387.

Bailyn, Bernard. "Politics and Social Structure in Virginia." In James Morton Smith (ed.), *Seventeenth-Century America: Essays in Colonial History* (Chapel Hill, 1959), pp. 90–115.

Barnwell, James W. "Hon. Charles Garth, M.P., The Last Colonial Agent of South Carolina in England, and Some of his Work," *South Carolina Historical and Genealogical Magazine,* XXVI (1925), 67–92.

Bellot, H. Hale. "The Literature of the Last Half-Century on the Constitutional History of the United States," Royal Historical Society *Transactions,* 5th Ser., VII (1957), 159–182.

———. "Thomas Jefferson in American Historiography," Royal Historical Society *Transactions,* 5th Ser., IV (1954), 135–155.

Bond, Beverley W., Jr. "The Colonial Agent as a Popular Representative," *Political Science Quarterly,* XXXV (1920), 372–392.

Clark, Dora Mae. "George Grenville as First Lord of the Treasury and Chancellor of the Exchequer, 1763–1765," *Huntington Library Quarterly*, XIII(1950), 383–397.

Courtney, W. P. "Barlow Trecothick," *Notes and Queries*, 11th Ser., III (1903), 330–332.

Crandall, Ruth. "Wholesale Commodity Prices in Boston during the Eighteenth Century," *Review of Economic Statistics*, XVI (1934), 117–128, 178–183.

Crane, Verner W. "Benjamin Franklin and the Stamp Act," Publications of the Colonial Society of Massachusetts *Transactions*, XXXII (1937), 56–77.

———. "Certain Writings of Benjamin Franklin on the British Empire and the American Colonies," Bibliographical Society of America *Papers*, XXVIII (1934), 1–27.

Doyle, John A. "The Quarrel with Great Britain, 1761–1776." In A. W. Ward, G. W. Prothero, and Stanley Leathes (eds.), *The Cambridge Modern History* (13 vols., London, 1902–1912). Vol. VII.

East, Robert A. "The Business Entrepreneur in a Changing Economy, 1763–1795," *The Journal of Economic History, Supplement*, VI (1946), 16–27.

Ericson, Fred J. "Contemporary British Opposition to the Stamp Act, 1764–1765," Michigan Academy of Science, Art, and Letters, *Papers*, XXIX (1943), 489–505.

Ervin, Samuel James, Jr. "The Provincial Agents of North Carolina." In *The James Sprunt Studies in History and Political Science*, XVI, No. ii, 63–77.

Ferguson, E. James, "Currency Finance: An Interpretation of Colonial Monetary Practice," *William and Mary Quarterly*, 3rd Ser., X (1953), 153–180.

Freiberg, Malcolm. "How To Become A Colonial Governor: Thomas Hutchinson of Massachusetts," *Review of Politics*, XXI (1959), 646–656.

———. "Missing: One Hutchinson Autograph Letter," *Manuscripts*, VIII (1956), 179–184.

———. "William Bollan, Agent of Massachusetts," *More Books: The Bulletin of the Boston Public Library*, 6th Ser., XXXIII (1948), 43–53, 90–100, 135–145, 168–182, 212–220.

Harper, Lawrence A. "Mercantilism and the American Revolution." In "The American Revolution: A Symposium," *Canadian Historical Review*, XXIII (1942), 1–15.

High, James. "Henry McCulloch: Progenitor of the Stamp Act," *North Carolina Historical Review*, XXIX (1952), 24–38. But cf. the letter by Charles G. Sellers, Jr., in *ibid.*, pp. 460–462.

Jellison, Richard M. "Antecedents of the South Carolina Currency Acts of 1736 and 1746," *William and Mary Quarterly*, 3rd Ser., XVI (1959), 556–567.

Jensen, Merrill. "Democracy and the American Revolution," *Huntington Library Quarterly*, XX (August 1957), 321–342.

Jervey, Theodore D. "Barlow Trecothick," *South Carolina Historical Genealogical Magazine*, XXXII (1931), 157–169.

Johnson, Allen S. "British Politics and the Repeal of the Stamp Act," *South Atlantic Quarterly*, LXII (1963), 169–188.

———. "The Passage of the Sugar Act," *William and Mary Quarterly*, 3rd Ser., XVI (1959), 507–514.

Levy, Leonard W. "Did the Zenger Case Really Matter? Freedom of the Press in Colonial New York," *William and Mary Quarterly*, 3rd Ser., XVII (1960), 35–50.

Lokken, Roy N. "The Concept of Democracy in Colonial Political Thought," *William and Mary Quarterly*, 3rd Ser., XVI (1959), 568–580.

Minchinton, Walter E. "The Merchants in England in the Eighteenth Century." *Explorations in Entrepreneurial History*, X (1957), 62–71.

Morgan, Edmund S. "Colonial Ideas of Parliamentary Power, 1764–1766," *William and Mary Quarterly*, 3rd Ser., V (1948), 311–341.

———. "The Postponement of the Stamp Act," *William and Mary Quarterly*, 3rd Ser., VII (1950), 353–392.

Mullett, Charles F. "James Abercromby and French Encroachments in America," *Canadian Historical Review*, XXVI (1945), 48–59.

Namier, Lewis B. "Anthony Bacon, M.P., An Eighteenth-Century Merchant," *Journal of Economic and Business History*, II (1928), 20–70.

———. "Charles Garth, Agent for South Carolina," *English Historical Review*, LIV (1939), 632–652.

Ostrander, Gilman M. "The Colonial Molasses Trade," *Agricultural History*, XXX (1956), 77–84.

Pares, Richard. Review of Robert E. Brown, *Middle-Class Democracy and the Revolution in Massachusetts, 1691–1780* (Ithaca, N.Y., 1956). In *English Historical Review*, LXXXII (1957), 122–125.

Penson, Lillian M. "The London West India Interest in the Eighteenth Century," *English Historical Review*, XXXVI (1921), 373–392.

Plum, Jack H. "The Mercantile Interest: the Rise of the British Merchant after 1689," *History Today*, V (1955), 762–767.

Pole, J. P. "Historians and the Problem of Early American Democracy," *American Historical Review*, LXVII (April 1962), 626–646.

Price, Jacob M. "The Rise of Glasgow in the Chesapeake Tobacco Trade, 1707–1775," *William and Mary Quarterly*, 3rd Ser., XI (1954), 179–199.

Robertson, M. L. "Scottish Commerce and the American War of Independence," *Economic History Review*, IX (1956), 123–131.

Root, Winfred T. "The American Revolution Considered." In "The American Revolution: A Symposium," *Canadian Historical Review*, XXIII (1942), 16–28.

Sachs, William S. "Interurban Correspondence and the Development of a National Economy Before the Revolution: New York as a Case Study," *New York History*, XXXVI (1955), 320–335.

Schutz, John A. "Succession Politics in Massachusetts, 1730–1741," *William and Mary Quarterly*, 3rd Ser., XV (1958), 508–520.

Sheridan, Richard B. "The Molasses Act and the Market Strategy of the British Sugar Planters," *The Journal of Economic History*, XVII (1957), 62–83.

Smith, James Morton. "Communications and Trade: The Atlantic in the Seventeenth Century," *Journal of Economic History*, XIII (1953), 378–397.

Soltow, James H. "The Role of Williamsburg in the Virginia Economy, 1750–1775," *William and Mary Quarterly*, 3rd Ser., XV (1958), 467–482.

Soltow, James H. "Scottish Traders in Virginia, 1750–1775," *Economic History Review*, 2nd Ser., XII (1959), 83–98.

Sosin, J. M. "Imperial Regulation of Colonial Paper Money, 1764–1773," *Pennsylvania Magazine of History and Biography*, LXXXVIII (1964), 174–198.

———. "The Massachusetts Acts of 1774: Coercive or Preventive?" *Huntington Library Quarterly*, XXVI (1963), 235–252.

———. "A Postscript to the Stamp Act. George Grenville's Revenue Measures: A Drain on Colonial Specie?" *American Historical Review*, LXIII (1958), 918–923.

———. "The Proposal in the Pre-Revolutionary Decade for Establishing Anglican Bishops in the Colonies," *The Journal of Ecclesiastical History*, XIII (1962), 76–84.

Stebbin, Calvin. "Edmund Burke, His Services as Agent to the Province of New York," American Antiquarian Society *Proceedings*, New Ser., IX (1893), 89–101.

Sutherland, Lucy S. "The City of London in Eighteenth Century Politics." In Richard Pares and A. J. P. Taylor (eds.), *Essays Presented to Sir Lewis Namier* (London, 1956), pp. 49–74.

Tanner, Edwin P. "Colonial Agencies in England during the Eighteenth Century," *Political Science Quarterly*, XVI (1901), 24–49.

Thayer, Theodore. "The Land-Bank System in the American Colonies," *Journal of Economic History*, XIII (1953), 145–159.

Varga, Nicholas. "The New York Restraining Act: Its Passage and Some Effects, 1766–1768," *New York History*, XXXVII (1956), 233–258.

Walett, Frances G. "The Massachusetts Council, 1766–1774: The Transformation of a Conservative Institution," *William and Mary Quarterly*, 3rd Ser., VI (1949), 605–627.

Wheeler, Harvey. "Calvin's Case (1608) and the McIlwain–Schuyler Debate," *American Historical Review*, LXI (1956), 587–597.

Whitson, Agnes M. "The Outlook of the Continental American Colonies on the British West Indies, 1760–1775," *Political Science Quarterly*, XL (1930), 56–86.

Wilkinson, Norman B. "The Colonial Voice in London," *The Historian*, II (1940), 22–36.

Wolkins, George G. "The Seizure of John Hancock's Sloop 'Liberty,'" Massachusetts Historical Society *Proceedings*, LV (1921–1922), 239–284.

Zimmermann, John J. "Benjamin Franklin and the Pennsylvania Chronicle," *Pennsylvania Magazine of History and Biography*, LXXXI (1957), 351–364.

Acknowledgments

MANY individuals have greatly aided the research of the author. Consequently he wishes to acknowledge his indebtedness and appreciation to the librarians and archivists of the Virginia State Library (Richmond); the Dominion Archives of Canada (Ottawa); the Library of Congress; the Public Record Office (London); the Connecticut State Library (Hartford); The Historical Society of Pennsylvania (Philadelphia); The William L. Clements Library (Ann Arbor); the American Philosophical Society Library (Philadelphia); the William Salt Library (Stafford, England); The South Carolina Archives (Columbia); The Henry E. Huntington Library and Art Gallery (San Marino, California); the British Museum; the Connecticut Historical Society (Hartford); Harvard College Library; The Alderman Library, University of Virginia; the Rhode Island Historical Society (Providence); University of North Carolina Library; North Carolina Department of Archives and History (Raleigh); New Jersey Historical Society; Brown University Library (Providence, R.I.); and the Sheffield (England) City Library.

Sir John Murray graciously allowed me to examine his collection of George Grenville papers. For access to documents from Petworth House I am indebted to Lord Leconsfield.

Certain portions of this book relating to paper money and the Massachusetts Acts of 1774 appeared in modified versions in the *Pennsylvania Magazine of History and Biography* and the *Huntington Library Quarterly* respectively and are used here with permission.

Research for this book, in part was made possible by a grant from the University of Nebraska Research Council.

Index

Abercromby, James, 15; and North Carolina agency, 16; on revenue, 15 n.; and Virginia agency, 15, 15 n.

Adams, John, on Boston Tea Party, 168

Adams, Samuel, 71, 122, 144, 149; and Boston Tea Party, 167–169; and Hutchinson letters, 158; and Massachusetts agency, 70

Adams, Thomas, as merchant, 4

Admiralty Board, and Townshend laws, 102

Agency, 33; Board of Trade on, 11, 142–145, 147–148; Burke on, 148; for Connecticut, 8, 142; for Delaware counties, 13; disputes over, 16–17, 148–149, 181–182; and Franklin, 148–149, 155, 160, 229; George III on, 180; for Georgia, 143; Hillsborough on, 152; history of, 7; and imperial administration, 15–16; for Maryland, 13, 144; for Massachusetts, 17, 18, 143–145, 149–150, 153 n.; for New Hampshire, 142, 146, 146 n., 194–195; for New Jersey, 11, 143, 144, 145, 149, 149 n.; for New York, 12, 142, 144, 147 n., 147–148; for North Carolina, 15, 16–17, 144, 145; for Pennsylvania, 142, 143; and politics, 11–13, 15–19, 68 n., 69–70, 111, 143, 149–150; Privy Council on, 152; and revolutionary movement, 143 ff.; for Rhode Island, 8, 142; rules for, 145; and Stamp Act, 67 ff.; state of, 176, 194–195, 222, 224

Agents, 100, 103, 104, 114, 118, 124, 125, 128, 140–141, 142, 161, 190–191, 194, 203, 216; appointments of, 7–8,

253